D0335060

FEMININE POWER

Feminine
POWER

Conversations with Some of the World's Most Influential

Women in the Fields of Politics, Business and Entertainment

Mona Bauwens &
Peter Thompson

MAINSTREAM
PUBLISHING

EDINBURGH AND LONDON

First published in Great Britain in 1998 by
MAINSTREAM PUBLISHING COMPANY (EDINBURGH) LTD
7 Albany Street
Edinburgh EH1 3UG

ISBN 1 84018 092 7

A catalogue record for this book is available from the British Library

Typeset in Bembo
Printed and bound in Great Britain by Butler and Tanner Ltd

Contents:

Part Two:

SOCIETY, STARDOM & STYLE

Acknowledgements

WE would like to thank Bill Campbell of Mainstream for his advice and encouragement from the outset and the many other people whose expertise proved invaluable either in opening doors or helping us in our fact-finding missions.

In Washington, Elias Aburderne made important introductions and gave us free range of his facilities. His secretary, Anila Pahwa, was intrepid in dealing with the White House and government departments. Mary King and her husband Dr Peter Bourne gave up their precious time to guide us and their first-hand experience gave us valuable insight into the American political scene.

In New York, Dr Oudeh Aburderne's persistence and faith in this project gained us access to the political and diplomatic élite of New York. No one knows New York better than Herbert Kasper, who was unfailingly kind in opening his address book to us.

In Los Angeles, Nabila Khashoggi proved herself a true friend.

In Cairo, childhood friends Zein Baring and Fatima El Guindi and their mother, Mimi Touliemat, helped in securing interviews and in our understanding the subtleties of Egypt.

In Israel, Simha Stern made us feel welcome in her home and gave us the benefit of her vast knowledge of the region.

In Jerusalem, Sari Nusibeh not only provided transport but arranged our interviews.

In Paris, Sonia Fares tried to make us understand the complexities of French fashion.

In London, Lyn Rothman's and Ira Kettner's patience coped with our many, many requests. Baker Oweidh was an unfailing source of information and encouragement.

Our sincere thanks also go to Sheik Mubarak Al Sabah, Victoria Schofield, Anthony Harris, David Morgan, John Thayil, Janet Millar, William Morris, Zaki Nusibeh and Nayala Moussali. They know why!

Thanks are also due to our long-suffering families, particularly Khalida and Jawid Al Ghussein. Tawfik. Jocelyn and Helen. Arnold who was with us in spirit, and finally but not least, our mascot, Soraya.

Preface by *Mona Bauwens*

DAWN had just exploded like fire over the Judean hills when British Airways Flight No. 163 to Tel Aviv swooped in over the crystalline surface of the Mediterranean for the final approach into Ben-Gurion airport. I had already travelled many thousands of miles in search of feminine power, but this was a far cry from a night in Annabel's with Ivana Trump, or meeting Dewi Sukarno in her Park Avenue apartment, or taking tea with Benazir Bhutto in Knightsbridge. This was the flip side of the celebrity coin and the next location was a war zone.

Over the intercom, a voice warned us that taking photographs through the 737's windows was strictly prohibited and the nervousness I had felt ever since we took off from Heathrow five hours earlier became acute. I had no intention of taking aerial pictures of Israel's military installations, but the mere thought of spending time in prison, far-fetched though that might have been, frightened the hell out of me. The years of regarding the Israelis as 'the enemy' were not easy to shrug off and my camera remained in the overhead locker, but I did risk a peep out of the window. Viewed from a few thousand feet up, the curving shoreline gave way to a city of whitewashed, concrete buildings, half of them still shadowy in the encroaching dawn light, with ribbons of road threading through orange groves and neat, palm-fringed settlements towards a jagged rim of ochre-coloured hills. Somewhere on the horizon was the holy city of Jerusalem, where my Aunt Nusha still lived.

As they fastened their seatbelts prior to landing, many of the other passengers chattered excitedly among themselves. They were on their way to the biggest birthday party in the world: lavish celebrations to mark the founding of the State of Israel 50 years ago. For the Jewish people, David Ben-Gurion's proclamation of independence at 4 p.m. on 14 May 1948, had been the most momentous political event in their history. For 3.5 million dispossessed Palestinians like me, however, it was nothing of the sort: in Arabic, we called it *al Nakabe* – the Catastrophe. I was about to set foot in occupied enemy territory, where the quest for peace had turned, once again, to violence and mistrust.

The irony was not lost on me. I had come here to interview Leah Rabin, widow of Yitzhak Rabin, the Israeli Prime Minister whose Herculean efforts to make peace in the Middle East had cost him his life. It was Yitzhak Rabin who had shaken hands with Yasser Arafat in Washington and, braving threats from his own people, pursued our claims for the return of at least part of our homeland and for a measure of self-rule. Leah Rabin had accompanied her husband to Washington for that historic handshake and she had been only a few steps behind him two years later when he was fatally wounded after a peace rally in Tel Aviv on 4 November 1995. Her husband had been killed by a Jewish fanatic, but how would she receive me, a Palestinian, one of the old enemy?

My travels to research the roles that women had played in Middle Eastern political affairs had already taken me to Cairo to meet Jehan Sadat, who had seen her husband, President Anwar Sadat, murdered by Muslim extremists in an earlier attempt to sabotage the peace process. Jehan, half-English, half-Egyptian, described to me her husband's mission that had led him from the battlefield to the Knesset and, eventually, to Camp David, the US President's summer residence in Maryland. This was where President Jimmy Carter had arranged the summit meeting between Sadat and the Israeli Prime Minister, Menachem Begin, that had first set the wheels of the peace process in motion.

In Atlanta, Georgia, President Carter's wife, Rosalynn, disclosed the vision and political manoeuvring that had enabled her husband to broker the original Camp David accord, despite the scepticism of a disbelieving world. Leah Rabin, Jehan Sadat and Rosalynn Carter formed three sides of a triangle which had determined the shape of Middle Eastern politics for the nineties. I was also due to meet Umm Jihad, the Palestinian Minister of Social Welfare, who had been dubbed 'Fatah's Secret Weapon' because of her active involvement with the most powerful section of the PLO. Like Jehan Sadat and Leah Rabin, she had also seen her husband gunned down in front of her eyes. I wanted to hear their sides of the story and, more importantly, to find out what sort of women they were.

After landing at Ben-Gurion airport, my passport was checked by an immigration official under the grim-eyed scrutiny of armed Israeli soldiers. I was searched for explosives by a white-gloved security guard and escorted to my transport, a beaten-up van that had been provided by my cousin Sari, Dean of Al Quds University, and driven up the winding highway that carves through the hills to my aunt's home in Jerusalem.

The following morning, I set off down that same highway to meet Leah Rabin at her office in Ramat Gan on the outskirts of Tel Aviv. We got lost on the way and arrived half an hour late for our appointment. The first thing Mrs Rabin said was that she didn't like the questions I had faxed in advance from London, so we put the questions to one side and talked for the next two hours. With great dignity, she told me how she had dealt with the grief of her husband's murder and how she was now tackling the backlash against the peace process that had inevitably followed Israel's election of a right-wing government.

Every piece in her office, from sculptures to paintings to books, had some kind of symbolism relating to her husband's work and hearing her story from her own lips in these intimate surroundings was a heart-rending experience, made all the more poignant because I was an Arab woman whose own family had originally come from Palestine. When she spoke about her husband's assassination, I was moved to tears. Leah Rabin, widow, mother, grandmother and political activist, was defending her husband's legacy with every fibre of her being.

It was a draining and exhilarating experience and I could feel the tension inside me when I left her office. My limited time in the Holy Land meant that I had to drive to Ramallah immediately to interview Umm Jihad. She, too, had suffered the pain of losing her husband, the PLO leader Abu Jihad, aka Khalil Al Wazir, in an assassination. How would I feel talking to her? Despite my natural compassion as a Palestinian, I did not think it would be possible to be more moved than I had been by Mrs Rabin.

I recalled Abu Jihad's assassination in Tunisia in April 1989, an act of sheer nerve on the part of the Israeli high command. Headlines the world over screamed about a 'terrorist execution' and any protests that this was an act of aggression towards a neutral country had been shrugged away.

In Ramallah, Umm Jihad greeted me cordially and described to me in quiet, unemotional tones how her husband's body had been riddled with machine-gun bullets by Israeli commandos in front of her eyes and how she had believed that she and two of her children were about to be murdered as well. Her daughter, Hanan, had been a 16-year-old schoolgirl when the assassins burst in and murdered her father. When I asked her what she felt towards the Israelis, however, she showed not one sign of bitterness, but replied that peace must be achieved through the democratic process and that she would be letting her father down if she felt or believed anything to the contrary.

'It still haunts us now,' she said. 'His main aim was to give Palestinians back their land and I still believe in his vision. I still believe that we should fight to reach a Palestinian state, but we can fight them in a different way. We do not all have to carry arms to fight. Fighting was a period and we all believed in armed struggle then. Now we are facing a new period when we have to fight in other ways.'

These interviews, remarkable for their fearless honesty, enabled me to keep a balanced view when it came to writing the chapters on the Middle East. I had started writing at an early age for magazines specialising in Middle Eastern affairs, focusing on the political and economic dilemmas at the heart of the Israeli-Palestinian conflict. As I had been educated at private English schools, I knew many people in the Establishment, which was a great asset in my efforts to promote a dialogue between the West and the Arabs who, in the circumstances of the time, found it very difficult to make their voice heard.

Accordingly, I was invited to sit on several committees and think-tanks, and to give talks and lectures at a number of universities in the United States and Britain on the Arab-Israeli conflict and on the role of Arab Muslim women in modern society.

After the Oslo agreements, which heralded a ceasefire between the Palestinians and the Israelis, I deliberately stepped aside from any involvement in the peace process. I gave up my talks and relinquished my position on various committees. The reality, though, was that I, like many Palestinians, was involved in politics whether I wanted to be or not. It was a part of our lives that we could not escape, no matter where we chose to live or what kind of lives we were leading. My emotions, which had lain dormant for so long, were awakened by my meetings with Leah Rabin and Umm Jihad and her daughter Hanan, three women from different generations whose lives had been inextricably entwined by history.

I realised I could neither escape the heritage of my birth, nor, indeed, did I want to. The great truth for me was that the ordeals of these women, who came from conflicting cultures on opposite sides of the political divide, transcended politics. Their stories forcefully brought home the manner in which this conflict has ripped apart the lives of millions of women and their families. No one could fail to be moved by their courage, their honesty and their humanity.

Through our research, I came across many women in politics, society, entertainment and fashion who had what I describe as feminine power, however dissimilar their lives might be. Our choice of subjects was based on the concept that while some women had achieved status through the men in their lives and others through their own abilities and talents, all shared an unshakeable commitment to their own beliefs.

Benazir Bhutto had boldly stepped into politics after the judicial murder of her father and had twice been elected Prime Minister of Pakistan. Mona Abdel Nasser, on the other hand, had played no active political role, but her proximity to her father, President Nasser of Egypt, had given her an invaluable insight into a vital period of history. Her decision to stay out of politics enabled her to preserve her father's legacy, unclouded by her own ambition, and that, for me, reflected power behind the scenes.

Jehan Sadat used her influence as Egypt's first lady to improve the lot of women and bring a touch of Western modernity to the role, which enabled her successor, Suzanne Mubarak, to tackle social issues with greater acceptability. Similarly, in Washington, when Rosalynn Carter became the first President's wife to attend Cabinet meetings, she was setting a precedent that enabled Hillary Clinton to go a step further by introducing proposals for legislation, notably her ill-fated health care reforms.

All of these women are vivid in my memory and I am grateful to them and many, many others for sharing their experiences. That some had succeeded more than others only highlights the need to examine the problems facing women in today's world.

THIS book is about the potency of feminine power and how it is used to influence events in modern life. Feminine power is the hallmark of women who have rejected the subservient roles of wife or lover and broken through the glass ceiling of male domination to emerge with voices of their own, while still retaining their femininity.

In an age of political correctness, few feminists will publicly admit that the platforms they occupy today have been provided by the men in their lives, be they husbands, fathers or lovers, and neither will they accept that women are often at their most effective when working in partnership with men. Yet many of the women interviewed for *Feminine Power* argued that rather than fearing men or trying to emasculate them, they had achieved far greater independence when they joined forces with the opposite sex in achieving goals that were mutually advantageous.

It is my belief that the empowered woman of the New Millennium has won undreamed-of status in most modern societies, irrespective of the gloomy predictions of some leading *feministas* (on the Left) and *feminazis* (on the Right). I unhesitatingly accept, however, that she is a beneficiary of the revolution led by courageous women who refused to accept inequality as their God-given place in society. As Sandra M. Gilbert and Susan Gubar wrote in *Sexchanges* (Yale University Press, 1989): 'To many late nineteenth and early twentieth century men, women seemed to be agents of an alien world that evoked anger and anguish, while to women in those years men appeared as aggrieved defenders of an indefensible order.'

Just as the term *fin de siécle* had come into vogue in the 1880s to describe particular kinds of cultural decline, so the word 'feminism' was coined by men a few years later to denote a disturbing trend among women. Feminism rapidly came to mean a new breed of middle-class females, educated, independent and mainly American, who were epitomised by the phrase 'New Woman'. By the turn of the century, many men regarded 'the insidious power of New Women' as a direct challenge to traditional family values and female emancipation was seen as a threat to the very fabric of society.

The 'agents of an alien world', however, have since emerged from the vaporous mists to reveal themselves in this generation as nothing more frightening than Julie Burchill, Gloria Steinem ('In my own mind, I am still that fat brunette from Toledo and I always will be'), Germaine Greer and Camille Paglia, while the 'indefensible order' of male domination is under attack on all fronts.

Nowadays, feminine power threatens even the most chauvinist of societies, even if it comes via a satellite dish in the shape of Oprah Winfrey. Oprah's global audience of 100 million viewers arguably makes her the most powerful woman in the world and she isn't coy about attributing her rise to stardom to a man. 'My father turned my life around by insisting I be more than I was and by believing I could be more,' she said. 'His love of learning showed me the right way.'

Feminine power beamed in from outer space, or simply introduced through more orthodox social exchange, has shifted previously immovable objects and the walls of the last male bastions are finally shaking. In 1998, London's Carlton Club, exclusive male preserve of the Tory establishment, voted in principle to admit women for the first time. The only woman who had previously been allowed to join was Margaret Thatcher, whom many regarded, mistakenly in my view, as an honorary man.

Any male member of Thatcher's Cabinet will swear that her personal brand of feminine power was clinically lethal, although she was not above fluttering her eyelashes at Ronald Reagan when she wanted a political favour. Most men, however, feel threatened by powerful women and Margaret Thatcher exploited that fear to the utmost. 'One of the things politics has taught me,' she said pointedly, 'is that men are not a reasoned or reasonable sex.'

Germaine Greer may have had someone like Mrs Thatcher in mind when she wrote in her 1970 bestselling feminist polemic, *The Female Eunuch*: 'If women understand by emancipation the adoption of the masculine role, then we are lost indeed.'

Despite the last 30 years of female emancipation in the Western world, many women were still powerless over the demands of a male-dominated society and the glass ceiling, although higher, was still manifestly intact. Some feminists were concerned that the initiative had been lost and that the true focus of the women's movement had become blurred. They urged their sisters to concentrate on the real issues of gender politics instead of discussing the relative merits of enhanced femininity, such as wearing make-up or having cosmetic surgery. These arguments, however, were really part of a whole that not only brought politics into women's lives, but also offered them greater freedom of choice.

Far more opportunities were now visible to women, especially to young women, and the focus had shifted accordingly. The empowered woman of today may have a young sportsman on her arm and a Cartier Pasha watch on her wrist as the latest status symbols, but she may also have enormous prestige in the highest decision-making circles of the corporate and political worlds. And even though she may appear merely decorative, she can be feisty, sassy, intelligent and very astute in making vast commercial fortunes in the manner of Madonna and Ivana Trump, or even the much-ridiculed Spice Girls.

Empowered women like these have pushed aside the barriers of gender, race, class and nationality to challenge many of the feminist stereotypes. Scilla Elworthy, founder and Director of the Oxford Research Group, wrote in *Power & Sex* (Element Books, England, 1996): 'The hardest thing for a feminist to learn about is her femininity. Yet therein lies her route to any real power. This is because real power comes from the interaction of, and the eventual union of, male and female within a person. Feminists develop their masculine sides and qualities – they need them to escape from being oppressed – but in order to be whole and powerful, they need their feminine side as well.'

Dewi Sukarno summed it up for me when she said: 'When a woman loses her femininity, she is not a woman any more. You are just another human being – neutral; you become a neutral human.' Nicole Petschek, a forthright American, took that a step further when she explained: 'Empowerment is *only* about empowering yourself. Nobody else can give you personal power, just as no one can give you self-confidence. You give it to yourself: you take it, you make it, you bake it and you lay it out.'

Benazir Bhutto, who joined the women's movement in America in the early 1970s and went on to become the first female leader of a Muslim country, put the issue into perspective when she told me: 'I was never a feminist in the way that some of my friends were – I was more of a feminist in today's definition of a feminist. My friends didn't believe, for instance, that one should wear lipstick, or perfume, or dress in anything other than baggy T-shirts, but I felt that being a feminist did not mean not being a woman. They used to think I was a soppy feminist; I had not really entered the real world of feminism yet.'

The truth remains that countless women have been catapulted to their positions of power by male influence. That these women have subsequently gone on to achieve great feats in their own right is not in question; the point is that their rise to prominence owed much to men.

Who could forget the provocative Versace pin dress that Elizabeth Hurley, erstwhile lover of rising star Hugh Grant, wore to a film premiere? With front-page pictures all over the world, it would have been justifiable to dismiss her as just another beautiful starlet who, in time, would fade into obscurity. Yet she has become a prime example of a woman who used that publicity not only to secure a lucrative contract with Estee Lauder for a reported $3 million, but to become a respected film producer and an actress of some acclaim. She might well have achieved success without Hugh Grant, but it is an irrefutable fact that she used the opportunity afforded to her as his lover to launch her own talents.

Similarly, Ladies Who Lunch are often dismissed as idle, rich women whose contribution to society extends no further than lending their names – and their chequebooks – to worthy causes. However, to categorise all of them in that genre would be to seriously underestimate the roles that many of these women play behind the scenes in building their husbands' careers. Moreover, it would ignore the discipline required in their own lives and the unfailing devotion they show towards their menfolk. Lucky Roosevelt, former Washington hostess and Chief of Protocol in the White House, put the issue succinctly when she said: 'It would be impossible for me to look upon men as the enemy. I think being a woman is simply wonderful and I adore it.'

One of the most surprising things for me was to discover that behind the carefully maintained public image of confidence, glamour and power, many successful women shared the same fears, insecurities and vulnerabilities as anyone else. Fame and wealth did not shield them from pain and hurt. As Shirley Bassey put it so movingly: 'There has to be vulnerability. It *has* to be there.'

Feminine Power is a highly personalised exploration of the roles of contemporary women who have taken empowerment as their watchword for a new form of female liberation. The women quoted in this book celebrate their womanhood and enjoy their feminine power. They know what they want and how to go after it; they also know what is important. And they are unafraid. Their stories prove that the female of the species has come a long way since Jacqueline Kennedy Onassis opined: 'There are two kinds of women: those who want power in the world, and those who want power in bed.'

As our interviews disclose, there is now a third kind of woman to consider and, at the threshold of the New Millennium, her star is very much on the rise . . .

PART ONE

POLITICS, POWER & PEACE

1

Hillary and Cherie

SIPPING a glass of white wine and carefully picking over a selection of *hors d'oeuvres*, Hillary Clinton, First Lady of the United States of Amèrica, stood alone beside the buffet table at an intimate little cocktail party in Cleveland Heights, Washington. It was 7.30 p.m. on a frosty evening in March 1998, the third month of the Zippergate scandal, but if people expected Hillary Clinton to be devastated by the sexual allegations swirling around her husband's presidency they were to be disappointed. Hillary Clinton was a tough lady; she had to be.

The party was taking place in the sedately furnished living-room of one of the President's political allies to celebrate the publication of the second volume of the definitive biography of Martin Luther King. Bill and Hillary Clinton had been friends with the author, Taylor Branch, ever since they had worked together in Texas on George McGovern's unsuccessful presidential campaign back in 1972. No one except Branch and his hosts had known that the Clintons would be attending the party and not more than 20 people had bothered to turn up. This select few were provided with a rare opportunity to observe America's First Couple at the most severely testing time of their married life.

In the living-room, Dr Peter Bourne, one of Jimmy Carter's former aides, was talking to Jack Nelson, Washington bureau chief of the *Los Angeles Times*, when Bill and Hillary walked in. The President strolled over to them to say hello and Bourne, who had known him since 1980, immediately raised the question of American sanctions against Cuba. The President discussed the issue with Bourne at some length, made a short speech about Taylor Branch, then departed with David Kendall, the lawyer advising him in the Monica Lewinsky case.

Hillary, however, elected to stay at the party and when Bourne noticed her standing alone beside the buffet table, he went over to chat to her. The Clintons had just returned to Washington from a highly publicised trip to Africa and, as Bourne was off to Ghana shortly, he wanted to hear about it from Hillary herself.

Bourne said to her: 'I gather you had a great time in Ghana. I'm going there next week and I'll be seeing Gerry Rawlings [the Ghanaian President].'

Hillary replied: 'Well, tell him that you had a private conversation with me and convey to him how extraordinarily grateful Bill and I are for the magnificent hospitality he laid on for us. He really mobilised the entire country for the reception we received.'

There was no Southern cadence in Hillary's flat, Middle Western accent despite all her years in Arkansas. She was stylishly, though modestly, dressed in a suit, with her dyed blonde hair expertly sculpted into her trademark frosted bob. Nor was there any sign of the depression that had afflicted her for months after the collapse of her health care initiative when she had unwisely considered herself America's 'co-president'. She had learned some harsh lessons during that first term on Capitol Hill and her reborn political persona was very much that of a woman who was now quietly and confidently at ease with her feminine power.

Bourne said to her: 'It's clear you have an interest in Africa.'

'Yes I do,' replied the First Lady, then quietly asked: 'Now tell me: what are we going to do about Sami Abacha in Nigeria?'

It was a good question and not one that Bourne had been expecting. The Clintons had deliberately excluded Nigeria from their African tour because Sami Abacha, then head of the ruling military junta, had been widely condemned for human rights abuses ever since he had seized control of the oil-rich country.

Bourne said: 'I was just telling the President that embargoes serve no useful purpose because they hurt the people and don't affect those in power.'

'Well, basically I agree with you,' said Hillary, sipping her white wine, 'but what do you do with a guy like this who won't listen to anybody? Don't you think if the oil companies were willing to terminate buying oil from Nigeria that would really put the squeeze on the regime?'

'That's a very good point,' said Bourne, 'but I'm not sure it would change things that much. Sanctions have failed in Burma and the US has done nothing particularly useful to solve the situation there.'

'Yes,' said Hillary, 'I agree with you.'

Forget Zippergate. Peering through the contact lenses covering her blue eyes, Hillary Clinton was clearly focused on what she considered to be the important political issues of the day. Peter Bourne told us: 'We talked about a number of other African leaders and I was very, very impressed at how savvy she was in terms of these issues. She's not at all hesitant to get into that kind of conversation because she feels her opinions are as valid as anybody elses. I can't remember a first lady before, maybe Jackie Kennedy to some extent, who really had such exposure to the international arena that they were able to formulate opinions.

'Rosalynn Carter was quite like that, but she had no background in foreign affairs and she was in the process of learning, and neither Barbara Bush nor Nancy Reagan nor Betty Ford would ever have ventured an opinion like that. Hillary knows this stuff, so she doesn't feel at all insecure.'

According to Hillary, the alternative to speaking out as first lady was 'to totally withdraw and perhaps put a bag over your head, or somehow make it clear that you have no opinions about anything and never express them, publicly or privately'. There were many people on the right of American politics who wished she would do precisely that, but the chances were nil while her husband was still President.

Hillary knew that she was stronger than Bill; that she had a clearer set of political priorities; that she was more unbending and more uncompromising than him. She was also much less vulnerable to the blandishments of some passing White House intern, no matter how beguiling, because the consequences were so predictable that she would never consider taking such a risk. 'She's really quite a formidable figure as far as her convictions and the consistency of her work go,' said a Washington political analyst. 'This is something a lot of people don't understand and the news media has a lot of trouble presenting a woman who has that kind of background.'

Even their political antagonists grudgingly agreed, however, that Bill and Hillary Clinton were extraordinary people. One political observer said: 'I can't imagine enduring the stress they've been under and functioning as normally as they do. Oh yes, she has been hurt. It's appallingly hurtful and embarrassing to her, but she's dealt with it because she's strong. She's very much self-contained.' The real question, however, is: was there ever anything more to this marriage than just incredible opportunism on both sides?

HILLARY RODHAM CLINTON has always been an enigma, not least because her professional detachment led to a widely held belief that she is an emotionally cold woman. 'Sister Frigidaire' was the nickname she had earned at high school in Chicago and many of her critics felt that she had never outgrown it. The only time she showed any sign of emotion during the Lewinsky affair was when she learned that one of the gifts her husband had bestowed upon his fleshy young lover was *Leaves of Grass*, a book of poems by Walt Whitman. She looked shaken and said: 'He gave me the same book after our second date.'

There were also wild rumours about her sexuality, which somehow excused or explained Bill Clinton's zipper problem. Gennifer Flowers, the nightclub singer who had a 12-year affair with him, claimed in a book that he believed Hillary had lesbian tendencies. True, there are no fluttering eyelashes or flirtatious asides, but Hillary's female friends, such as the political consultant Betsey Wright, Hillary's White House chief-of-staff, Melanne Verveer, and a dozen other women, regard her as a warm, open person who simply feels protective towards her husband. 'She fell in love with him and she just loves him,' said one long-term acquaintance. 'He's a very easy person to live with, except for his occasional peccadilloes. She views that as falling within the category of addiction, like someone who is a compulsive gambler, or someone who goes out and gets drunk every two months. But she doesn't think that those relationships are imbued or invested with any content, or that they have any meaning whatsoever.'

No one disputes that Hillary is a good mother who has always been extremely devoted and attentive to her 18-year-old daughter, Chelsea, a medical student at Stanford University, and even men with political views opposed to her own concede that she has a 'rigorous' sense of humour. 'She doesn't take things too seriously and you can joke around with her without her taking offence,' said one male acquaintance. 'She's sometimes a little bit difficult to talk to because she tends to be very knowledgeable about everything and in a conversation she has a bit of a tendency to want to have the last word. You will say something and she will one-up you.'

Mary King, an international political scientist who first met Hillary in Little Rock in 1979, said: 'This is not someone who sort of fell into things. She marks a difference with other first ladies in that she was trained as a professional and prepared herself for a life of public engagement with a series of issue. She is a person of substance, she's serious and she has a consistent political agenda. The issues she was concerned about when I met her are exactly the same issues she's working on now 20 years later: legal aid for the poor, education for all and health care.'

Benazir Bhutto, the former Prime Minister of Pakistan who visited

Hillary in the White House in April, 1998, told us: 'She is a remarkable lady – absolutely remarkable. She is unflappable in the midst of all these allegations and counter-allegations. I've never seen her looking better: slim, trim, smart, calm, cool, all together. She should run for president.'

Leah Rabin, Israel's former first lady, was equally unstinting in her praise. 'I have great admiration for Hillary Clinton,' she told us. 'She's a super woman, a fighter, and I admire her for that and for the way she meets the challenges that she has had to meet, unfortunately, in recent times. She is brilliant, so brilliant, and I think – and I don't know who to give the credit to, maybe both – but I think they have done a remarkable job with Chelsea. Raising a child in the White House is not an easy task and they have managed to raise a lovely, lovely young girl. She seems to be so normal and so easy with people. They have managed to help her overcome all the barriers and bring her into life as a very well-adjusted and wonderful young woman.'

Dewi Sukarno, widow of President Sukarno of Indonesia, praised Hillary's determination and her ability to take 'powerful action' and added: 'If she had been a man, she would have made a very good president. I like her very much. I think she's great and her mind is very clear. People said she supported the President because she didn't want to lose her position and I would say, "Why not?" She fought for this ever since she was married. They are a partnership, so why should they lose everything because of this scandal? I'd have fought for him. Loyalty to the man, loyalty to the husband, loyalty to the President, comes first and I would be very disappointed if people didn't understand that.'

Everything in Bill Clinton's life had been meticulously calculated in terms of a political career and, like his hero John F. Kennedy, his choice of a wife was crucial. 'He could have married some cute chick from Arkansas, but he wasn't about to do that: he wanted to have affairs with them,' said a Washington insider. 'He wanted somebody as a wife who would be a real complement to him in his political career, so he married Hillary, who was then extraordinarily unattractive, with dull brown hair and thick eyeglasses with lenses like the bottom of a Coke bottle. People were astonished that attractive Bill Clinton could marry this drab law student he'd met in the Yale Law School library, but he'd intellectualised it and seen what a complement she would be to him.'

For her part, Hillary Rodham had been raised as a doctor's daughter in an affluent section of Chicago. Her parents were Republican voters and she was a staunch conservative until she worked as a volunteer in inner-city slums. She attended Wellesley College, Massachusetts, where she buried her middle-class guilt and became a feminist with strong liberal leanings. After graduating from Yale, she worked in Washington for the House Judiciary Committee, preparing for the impeachment of Richard Nixon. She had access to all sorts of handsome, intellectual men on Capitol Hill, yet she chose to abandon a glittering legal career and marry a penniless young man from one of the most backward states in America. 'I fell in love with him,' she said, 'because he wasn't afraid of me.'

Apart from his fearlessness, Hillary had also seen that William Jefferson Clinton had strong political ambitions and she wanted to ride along with him because she was also very politically motivated. She had arrived in politics on the cusp between the time when a woman could have strong aspirations in her own right and the earlier period when her political ambitions were sublimated into attaching herself to an ambitious man. Bill and Hillary used each other for political advantage and it worked for both of them. As Camille Paglia put it: 'She chose to gain power through her husband. She's like Evita or Imelda Marcos.'

'DO you have any advice for me?' Hillary asked Rosalynn Carter at Bill Clinton's presidential inauguration in January 1993. Rosalynn replied: 'Make up your mind what you want to do and just do it because they're going to criticise you anyway.'

During the 1992 campaign, the Clintons had made some serious strategic blunders. Hillary had worn her hair schoolgirl style, with a black velvet Alice band pulling the hair back severely, and they had talked about forming a co-presidency: that you get two for the price of one. Clinton's campaign slogan was: 'Vote for me and you'll get Hillary free.' 'The feedback was dreadful,' said the Washington analyst. 'The American public did not like it. They were in danger of losing the campaign.'

Hillary was pushed to the forefront after Gennifer Flowers alleged she had had an affair with Bill when he was Governor of Arkansas. Declaring on television that she was no little woman standing by her man like Tammy Wynette, Hillary added: 'I'm sitting here because I love him and I respect him and I honour what he has been through and what we have been through together.' Hillary's very presence at Bill's side enabled him to admit there was a problem. Shame-faced and apparently contrite, he said: 'I caused pain in my marriage.' The voters accepted this guarded *mea culpa* and the Comeback Kid, as he had dubbed himself, was elected to the highest office in the world. The black Alice band instantly disappeared.

After 11 years in the Governor's Mansion in Little Rock, the Clintons moved into 1600 Pennsylvania Avenue, Washington, with high hopes built on Hillary's tenacity and Bill's photogenic appeal. But with the spectre of Whitewater and lurid tales of Bill's connections with key figures in the Dixie Mafia trailing behind them, it was inevitably going to end in scandal.

Hillary's first mistake was to behave like a co-president when she was appointed head of a task force to reform the nation's health care system. She failed to understand that, as the wife of the head of state, she had an emblematic and symbolic role, but as the wife of the head of government she had no role whatsoever 'except trotting out for a photograph on the odd occasion'. Nevertheless, she veered into the executive branch of government and, once again, the American public howled with disapproval. 'She did not have checks done on her by the FBI as any other political appointee has to have,' said the Washington analyst. 'She had not been vetted, she had not gone through the Senate confirmation hearings. She was first lady and she had moved into the intricacies of governing, which was considered inappropriate.'

It was only after the abject failure of the health care initiative in 1994 that Hillary ceased acting as co-president. She had tried to do things that, in the United States, are restricted to elected officials and that antagonised many people, including those who were well disposed to her in other ways. It was quite a serious setback and, personally, she was discouraged because it closed the door on a whole array of other things she had wanted to do and it forced her to re-examine her whole role as first lady.

She was depressed for a long time and it had a very detrimental effect on her energies. She was actually not sure what she was going to do because she had failed at something in which she had invested so much time and effort. 'She did not do a very good job in that role,' said the Washington analyst. 'I was surprised at the lack of *savoir faire* with which she went about it because it was virtually a secret process and she did not do the kind of outreach which is really obligatory. In that situation, you had to bring with you the professionals, you had to bring with you the various camps within the health care communities and that meant very aggressive consultation, so that stakeholders had a chance to speak and to put their points of view to her. She didn't do that at all.'

Hillary had run a secret process because she was poorly advised and was still adjusting to the enormity of her office. In the second term, she moved to being clearly the wife of the head of state and using that position as an advocacy role very effectively. 'She would have been far better off if she had adopted an advocacy role on behalf of those denied health care,' said the Washington analyst, 'but once she seemed to be taking hold of the reins of government people got upset and she failed to understand that distinction from the beginning.' Mary King said: 'There's no way that you can be in the vortex of the American presidency and not change. It's impossible.'

WHEN Zippergate burst upon America in January 1998, Hillary went on the *Today* TV programme as her husband's first defender. Looking cool and unflustered in an elegant black jacket over trousers, with a heavy pearl choker and a brooch in the shape of an American eagle, she said: 'I do believe this is a battle. It is this vast right-wing conspiracy that has been conspiring against my husband since the day he announced he was running for president.'

Hillary's remarks were aimed not at her husband's Republican opponents in Congress, but at the Christian right, to whom, symbolically, her every utterance was affront. 'It took courage for her to articulate that, although I'm not sure it was a shrewd thing for her to do politically,' said a Washington feminist. 'But it took courage for her to say that and there's a great deal of truth in what she said. They detest her and there's a great deal of literature being circulated which is close to hate literature about the Clintons.

'There is a political phenomenon of people who feel threatened by the advances that women have made and that is very real. You can go out and see stadiums filled with angry white men holding rallies about it. There's a great deal of racism in it and there's a great desire to prevent women from making any more advances. Hillary knows about it.'

There is no question that the United States has a large, well-funded Christian right political formation. Some are called Promise Keepers, men who make vows to return as the true head of the family. They have television channels and they can be influential in certain state elections. Hillary is despised by these people because she represents the emergence of well-educated women who have professional aspirations that are just as important to them as any aspirations that their husbands might have. She personifies what they consider to be a challenge to their perception of the proper Christian home. They are fundamentalists in the sense that they make literal translations of passages in the Bible, such as Paul's directive, 'Wives, be subservient to your husbands'. Hillary, as a Methodist, believes in the egalitarian approach that each person must take responsibility for himself or herself. Her political priorities are antithetical to them and that is why they loathe her.

After a prayer session in the White House on the eve of the President's admission to the grand jury in August 1998 that he did, in fact, have an inappropriate relationship with Monica Lewinsky, the Rev. Jesse Jackson said of the Clintons: 'They're in love and their marriage will survive this.' But no matter how it might be dressed up for the public, the union had long since turned into a marriage of convenience, with Hillary clearly figuring it was better to tough it out with Slick Willie than going it alone. 'There is nothing in it for Hillary to be on the road outside the White House with two suitcases hailing a cab,' said the Washington analyst. 'Whatever perceived humiliation there might be in having your husband publicly ridiculed for having affairs, it is less than she would have lost by walking out.

'If she'd walked out, she would have had absolutely nothing. She would have helped to destroy him, probably, so being the separated wife of a President who was thrown out of office was not as attractive as staying the course with him despite all the bad stuff.'

Only Hillary knows, however, if she'll still be standing by her man after he leaves office on 20 January 2001, and heads for the Hollywood Hills with movie buddies like Steven Spielberg and David Geffen.

THE chief beneficiary of Hillary Clinton's errors of judgment in the White House was Cherie Booth Blair. An articulate woman with firmly held socialist beliefs, Cherie remained mute during the election campaign in April 1997 after promising her husband: 'I'm going to be with you, not in any political sense, but as your wife.' Labour's spin doctors, who had dreaded comparisons being made between Cherie and a talkative, abrasive, Left-wing feminist like Hillary, sighed with relief.

Cherie kept her promise and, when Tony Blair swept into 10 Downing Street on a wave of popular support for New Labour, she moved house with a minimum of fuss and then quietly resumed her career in the law courts as a Queen's Counsel and assistant recorder, the most junior kind of judge. As Sally Quinn, the Washington hostess and author, observed: 'Mrs Blair has already done so well. She's gone about her life, gone back to work and not tried to run the country. She's learnt by observation, by watching Mrs Clinton's immolation from afar.'

But the Americanisation of British politics which had enabled Blair to recast the old Labour Party into an electable entity in much the same way as Clinton had restyled the Democratic Party also led to Cherie being hailed as Britain's 'First Lady'. It was not a title that she found appropriate. Unlike Hillary Clinton, she had never sought or wanted a co-premiership with her husband and there was no quasi-official role for her to assume, although she was expected to turn up with him at official receptions, lunches and dinners.

Lady Archer, wife of Baron Archer of Weston-super-Mare, told us: 'She isn't First Lady, clearly, the Queen is the first lady. But I admire Cherie Blair. I really admire the way she went back into court the week after

Tony Blair got into Number 10. I met her before Tony Blair became Prime Minister at a very nice dinner given by Michael Beloff, her head of chambers. She was pleasant, fairly contained, a fairly private person, I would have said.'

The 'First Lady' tag, however, followed Cherie everywhere and she must have squirmed when, at one point, she was described as 'the People's First Lady' and the *Sunday Times* solemnly announced that 'the nation increasingly expects her to fulfil the role of an American-style First Lady'. After nearly a year in Downing Street, Cherie was still as unaffected as ever, and had even managed to pacify the style gurus by paying more attention to her appearance. 'Her great triumph is that, very quietly, she has done something revolutionary,' media consultant Scarlett McGwire told the *Independent*. 'Very quietly she has said, "This is me," and everybody just accepted it. She is a modern, professional nineties woman and she shows that it can be done.'

Leah Rabin met the Blairs when they visited Israel in April 1998 and paid their respects at the tomb of Yitzhak Rabin on a hilltop overlooking Jerusalem. 'I was most impressed with Tony Blair's very wonderful, warm, informal attitude,' Leah told us. 'I enjoyed even the few moments we were together with him and his wife. He's absolutely wonderful – he's competition to Clinton's charm and warmth and I'm not surprised they get on so well.

'I only met Mrs Blair that day and she made an excellent, excellent [impression]. They were travelling in separate limousines and we were standing there waiting for them. First the Prime Minister came out, and then she got out of the car and came running and said, "This is the story of my life. I have to run after my husband." I said, "Tell me about it! They put you in the second or third car and when they arrive you have to run to catch up." She looked great. She looked like a well-adjusted and content and happy person. They left me with a wonderful impression of both of them.'

Cherie Booth, of course, was far too independent to run after her husband, or any other man for that matter, and the real story of her life was that she had been brought up in humble circumstances after her father, the actor Tony Booth of *Till Death Us Do Part* fame, had abandoned his wife, Gale, when Cherie was seven and her sister, Lyndsey, five. Gale had taken the children to Liverpool, where they were raised in the tiny terraced house of her parents-in-law. She worked in a fish and chip shop to support them.

'I had a fairly uneventful childhood until my parents split up,' said Cherie, writing in a book to mark the 25th anniversary of the Dyslexia Institute. 'This was fairly unusual in those days. I started not paying attention to my schoolwork.' But with the help of her teachers at Seaforth Convent Grammar School Cherie excelled academically and went on to top her year in law at the London School of Economics and also finish first in her Bar finals.

Far more so than Hillary Clinton, Cherie was a natural Left-winger and feminist, although her Catholicism may have modified some of her radicalism. She had always felt passionately about social injustice and inequality, though, and had joined the Labour Party at the age of 16. She met Tony Blair in 1976 when they were both trainee lawyers in the chambers of Alexander 'Derry' Irvine, now Lord Irvine of Lairg, the Lord Chancellor.

Cherie said: 'I was with someone else at the time, but at the end of the pupillage I'd finished with him and started going out with Tony.' She invited him to a friend's Christmas party and they played a parlour game which involved passing a balloon between their knees. Tony saw the extroverted side of his seriously brilliant colleague for the first time and pursued her until she agreed to marry him two years later. 'Once you've succumbed to Tony's charm,' she said, 'you never really get over it.'

Cherie and Tony were married in 1980 in the chapel of St John's College, Oxford, and, in quick succession, had three children, Euan, Nicky and Kathryn. Cherie's ambition to become a Labour MP was abandoned only when her husband was elected to the safe Labour seat of Sedgefield in 1983. She became a tremendous constituency wife and was very popular with the people of Sedgefield, but she was concerned about the effect on her children when her husband rose through the ranks to the Shadow Cabinet.

'I'm quite a private person and want to protect our children,' she said. 'When Tony takes them to school the other kids are always saying, "We saw you on the telly last night." I don't want my children growing up thinking they're special, just because of what their daddy does.' It was not something that Hillary Clinton had ever said about Chelsea, but then the Blairs' marriage was not ultimately a political exercise.

When John Smith, the Labour leader, died suddenly of a heart attack in May 1994, Tony, then Shadow Home Secretary, was confronted with the prospect of succeeding him. He agonised over the decision until Cherie told him: 'You didn't ask for this, you didn't plan it, but it's here and you've got to do it. You'll never be happy again if you don't do it.' Despite her reservations about fame, she had gauged the likely detrimental effect it would have on her husband if he stepped aside and left the field open to Gordon Brown. Tony was elected leader and Cherie became his political consort in the mould of her predecessors, Elizabeth Smith and Glenys Kinnock.

She told Tony: 'I can either hide away, in which case people will say I'm not being supportive, or I accept that I'm going to be in the spotlight. I can make sure that, at least, I look like a credit to you.' She lost two stones in weight and experimented with different fashion styles, including Indian saris. Tony later told Lynda Lee-Potter of the *Daily Mail*: 'I'm very proud of the way she's done it because it did not come naturally to her. She really worked at it. She wanted to be a credit to me and to the country, really.'

THE Clintons fêted the Blairs at a White House reception in February 1998 and such was the solidarity between Bill and Tony that Elton John, one of the performers that night, remarked: 'It's a bit like playing a wedding reception.' Unlike the bravura, buddy-buddy performance of their husbands, however, there was no similar rapport between the two women.

'There was none of the easy familiarity between them that bonds their husbands,' wrote Nick Hopkins in the *Daily Mail*. 'Part of the reason is that Mrs Clinton isn't anything like as affable and easy-going as the President. But also, the First Lady is ruthless about her politics and in the grand scheme of things Mrs Blair can offer her nothing.'

In Washington, Cherie Blair might be a mere decoration on her husband's arm, whereas Hillary Clinton still sees herself as the queen of Capitol Hill. But in London, Cherie Booth, the quiet careerist who retains her maiden name in her profession while supporting her Prime Ministerial husband and raising three children in Downing Street, has struck a far more valiant blow for women than Hillary Rodham has ever succeeded in doing.

2

Battling Benazir

BENAZIR BHUTTO arrived at the old Hyde Park Hotel, Knightsbridge, from the Palace of Westminster in an ordinary black London cab. As one of the world's leading exemplars of feminine power, her choice of transport would have seemed a trifle understated had it not been for the fact that she had just become the world's most famous fugitive. Her arrival in a stretch limousine would have attracted attention and that was the last thing this tall, graceful, tenacious woman wanted. The former Prime Minister of Pakistan was travelling incognito and she knew that nothing was more inconspicuous during the great British rush hour than an ordinary black London cab.

For street cred, Benazir Bhutto had few equals among politicians anywhere in the world; but then, few politicians, and certainly no woman politician since Indira Gandhi, had faced such dire perils. Benazir had once called Mrs Gandhi 'this silk and steel woman', but she was well aware of the violent fate that had befallen Mrs Gandhi and, today, it was Benazir Bhutto who had to live with the risk, the uncertainty and the fear.

As the eldest of Nusrat and Zulfikar Ali Bhutto's four children, Benazir had been imprisoned, abused and threatened by her father's political enemies for so many years that she had grown accustomed to being a marked woman. Even as a student at Oxford University in the seventies, she had received terrorist death threats and a Scotland Yard detective had been assigned to teach her some elementary survival techniques which she had never forgotten. Ever since the current Pakistani regime had expressed a desire to destroy her, she had been using those same survival techniques to keep one step ahead of the enemy.

The fugitive, however, was far from unrecognisable. When she stepped out of the taxi, head uncovered and very much unbowed, she was smartly saluted by the hotel's top-hatted doorman. With a Gucci handbag swinging on her right forearm, she walked quickly across the pavement and up the marble steps into the hotel, which had just been renamed the Mandarin Oriental.

Since her father's judicial murder at the hands of the dictator General Zia in 1979, Benazir had twice been elected as Prime Minister of Pakistan, only to be dismissed from office on both occasions. She was sacked for the second time in 1996 amid a welter of allegations of corruption. Since then, she had been on the receiving end of the kind of rough justice that Pakistan reserves for the people it fears most. None of the scandal, or the opprobrium, however, seemed to have rubbed off on her.

She was elegantly dressed in a neatly embroidered lemon-and-tan *shalwar khameez*, with white cotton trousers and flat, black pumps. A few weeks short of her 45th birthday, no lines were to be seen on her face and nothing sagged. Her long black hair had been brushed to a glowing sheen, then pulled back to expose a finely etched profile. Her alabaster face had been expertly made up and she wore several pieces of expensive jewellery. Talking animatedly to us, she walked into the hotel's almost deserted dining-room, sat down at a table facing Hyde Park and ordered a glass of Coca-Cola.

Benazir Bhutto's political downfall had begun in 1995 when agents of the Pakistan Muslim League, then the country's opposition party, had met a team of private investigators in another London hotel room which, ironically, also overlooked the leafy green of Hyde Park. On offer to Benazir's political enemies on that occasion was a collection of documents which had allegedly been stolen from the Geneva office of a Bhutto family lawyer, Jens Schlegelmilch, and which later changed hands for a reputed $1 million. It was these documents – all forgeries, Benazir claimed – which were now the source of her current legal problems.

This very afternoon she had visited 'influential friends' at the House of Commons as part of a globe-trotting campaign to enlist support at the highest levels for herself and her husband, Asif Ali Zardari, who was languishing in a Karachi jail. Three days earlier, she had returned from a trip to the United States, where she had sought, and apparently received, a similar pledge of support from Hillary Clinton. 'She was very kind,' said Benazir. 'I asked to see her and she very kindly received me in the White House.'

The most visible clue to Benazir Bhutto's brand of feminine power was to be found in the direct gaze of her liquid, brown eyes which locked on to your own and were then followed by a smile, bright with red lipstick, that came unswervingly at you with all the certainty of a homing missile. There was no escape from those eyes or that smile, or indeed Benazir's voice, which was projected in clipped, well-modulated tones to the accompaniment of the hotel's harpist.

The missile comparison was apt, as was the presence of the harp, because news had just come in that morning that India had detonated two nuclear devices, sending tremors of rage and anxiety around the world. Benazir Bhutto, former leader of India's nearest neighbour and greatest enemy, admitted she was seething over India's perfidy.

'With three wars in the background, Pakistan has to protect itself,' she said, matter-of-factly. 'Obviously, I believe that Pakistan must have the capability to defend itself. I was Prime Minister when I received reports that India was frustrated over its inability to crush the Kashmiri uprising, which has been going on since 1989, and they've talked of war as a serious option. There was a division in their ranks as to whether Pakistan was bluffing when it said it had nuclear capability and, at that time, one of the arguments that was put forward was that India should detonate to see whether Pakistan could detonate or not.

'But I tell you it is absolutely appalling what India has done because, if a coalition government can do this two months after coming into power, such a rash act, one wonders what other rash steps they could actually take. I may have my disagreements with Nawaz Sharif [the Pakistani Prime Minister], but I'm not going to say he's going to do anything rash. But tomorrow we could have another person like this Vejpayee [the new Indian Prime Minister] and a rash decision could affect the whole world. So this is a black day in the history of mankind.'

As the harpist played a soothing Andrew Lloyd Webber melody in the background, Benazir Bhutto paused to sip her Coca-Cola and explained how she coped with the pressure. 'I find that ordinary people in extraordinary positions find extraordinary reservoirs of strength,' she said. 'I think I was an ordinary person and if somebody had told me before the events unfolded in my life that this is what I would have to endure I would have said that it was impossible.

'I was a first-born and first-borns are more responsible and tend to be achievers and tend to want to win the approval of their parents by doing well, or win the approval of authority figures. But if somebody had told me when I was president of the Oxford Union zipping around in my little yellow sports car that a time would come when I would go to prison and have to stay in solitary confinement and face the threat of facial paralysis, I would have thought I would not have been able to endure it. What I'm trying to say is that, in fact, each one of us has that capacity within which lies untapped until an event occurs that acts as a catalyst to bring out the extraordinary.

'I think God has given each one of us the resilience, but we don't know it's there until it's tapped and it's the event that leaves us with the choice of either collapsing or rolling up our sleeves and saying, "Well, I've got to get on with it." That's the crucial point. And anybody who decides, "I've got to get on with it," finds that strength somewhere inside. I have been through many ups and downs in my life, like a roller-coaster, and there have been times when I've just found it impossible to continue.

'When I was Prime Minister, my brother [Mir Murtaza Bhutto] was murdered. This was a dreadful situation: to be the sitting Prime Minister and to hear that your brother has been killed in a shootout. A brother who had been estranged from you for three years and who had just started coming close to you suddenly *goes*.

'You can't turn back the clock, you can't make greater efforts to bring him closer to you sooner. It was a terrible situation to be in and I don't know how I had the reserves to continue because I had to run a country of 140 million people. I wasn't given time to breathe. The Indians had just held farcical elections in Kashmir and I had to get on a plane and fly to New York to expose those elections and I didn't know how I was going to get on the plane – I really did not know because I needed time to grieve.

'Then I was hearing reports that the President [of Pakistan] was plotting against me. He'd been like a brother to me and I'd also physically lost a brother. These were people with whom I had strong emotional ties, so it was not just a political problem and it was in this period, when I just didn't know how I was going to get on to the plane, that it was as though I was on automatic.

'You go through things because you have to go through them and you push emotions to the back and concentrate on the work in hand. Of course at night everything comes back, but during the day one just focuses on the task at hand and that's what I've done. I also have the capacity at a time of crisis to remain very calm and not to feel tired and just continue, again an automation. Once the crisis is over, I'll suddenly find myself *drained* and wanting to collapse and rest, but during a crisis something comes out which gives one the ability to stay calm in the eye of the storm and to get on with the job in hand.

'I feel that people have two choices when confronted with a challenge: either to collapse, or to say, "No, I'm not going to buckle under," and if they say, "I'm not going to buckle under," it's there in them. I think all human beings are made more or less the same way and I think all of us have these reserves within.'

BENAZIR BHUTTO was born in the Sind province of Pakistan on 21 June 1953, and grew up with two brothers, Mir Murtaza and Shah Nawaz,* and a sister, Sanam. Her father nicknamed her Pinkie and accepted her as though she had been a son. Zulfiqar Ali Bhutto, scion of a feudal landowning family and an Oxford graduate, founded the Pakistan People's Party and served as the country's President from 1971 until 1973, when he was elected Prime Minister.

At 16, Benazir went to Harvard-Radcliffe to study comparative government. She didn't wear her woollen, silk-lined *shalwar khameez* on campus, but dressed like her American contemporaries in T-shirt and jeans and, with her long, straight hair, friends said she looked like Joan Baez. At Radcliffe, she had been initiated into the women's movement.

Benazir said: 'I've just been on a tour of North America and I met three bright young Pakistani women at McGill's and there are many more. When I went to Radcliffe, there were five foreign students and I was one of five – of the others, one came from Belgium, one came from England, one came from India and one came from France. Now when I see so many Pakistani women going to the West and seeing the rights that people have in these countries I have a great hope for the future of Pakistan and what these women will do when they go home. I think there's a much larger social base being created of women who have travelled the world and broadened their horizons.

'I lived in the West at a time when the United States was bringing down its own president. I saw the freedoms there, people making choices: choices about their lives, their careers, their marriages, their government and I wanted to go back home and see that my people had choices, too. I was there at a time in America when woman authors like Betty Friedan and Kate Millett and Germaine Greer were coming out with their books; it was a time of great, fierce, intellectual debate about the role of women and, being a woman, I was much affected by that debate. I took part in that debate; we used to sit up all night having milk and cookies and talking about what we women were going to do.

---

* Shah Nawaz Bhutto died mysteriously of poisoning during a family holiday in the South of France. His niece, Fatima, became one of Benazir Bhutto's harshest critics.

'I remember at that time there was a great fascination among some of my friends with the Mitford sisters and we'd talk about whether this group of us would get to be as well known as the Mitford sisters. One of my friends was very fond of reading Anaïs Nin and she knew a lot of intellectuals in the cultural and the literary world and she used to wonder whether she would become famous.

'My own interest was in foreign relations and not in culture and literature, and we wondered whether we'd both succeed in our own fields. She is now bringing out a cultural and literary newspaper, so it was really a time of women dreaming about achievement, not about marrying a rich husband and running a lovely home, which I think my predecessors in Pakistan wanted to do. They wanted, mostly, to get married and have a home and a family and their idea of success was marrying a successful man.

'But at Harvard it was very different, so it was a real awakening for me and I was lucky that I had a father who also wanted me to have a career. Politics was not my chosen career; I had hoped to join the diplomatic service and to serve my country and to have the intellectual stimulation which I felt was necessary for me to feel self-fulfilled.

'I read Kate Millett's book, *Sexual Politics* — that was one of the main books in my first year that all the young girls at Radcliffe were reading, along with Erich Segal's *Love Story*. So for me being a woman was very important and being a working woman was very important. I derived great inspiration from the fact that the Holy Prophet, Peace Be Upon Him, had married a working woman* and for me she was my inspiration; I felt that if the Holy Prophet could marry a working woman, why couldn't all Muslim women be working women and why did the clerics say that we couldn't work? This was something I couldn't understand. Why did they say we had to stay in the four walls of the house?'

Benazir left Harvard in the spring of 1973 and arrived at Oxford in the autumn of that same year. She read politics, philosophy and economics for three years, then returned for a fourth year to take a postgraduate course in international law and diplomacy. In her final year, she was elected to the prestigious post of president of the Oxford Union Debating Society.

---

* The Prophet Mohammed's first wife, Khadeja, ran a trading business for which he worked.

In Pakistan, her father had been imprisoned by General Zia and, returning home, Benazir campaigned unsuccessfully for his release, only to suffer long periods of detention herself. When Zia eventually released her after her father's execution, she was forced into exile and spent two years back in Britain, but received a tumultuous homecoming in April 1986 when a million people turned out to greet her in Lahore. In July 1987 she married Asif Zardari, a member of a landowning family from her home province of Sind, and began to raise a family while waiting for a political opportunity to present itself.

Her chance came after General Zia was murdered when a bomb exploded in his plane in August 1988. All that remained of the dictator was a set of dentures and his abrupt departure paved the way for free elections, which the Pakistan People's Party won. Although it did not obtain an absolute majority, Benazir became Prime Minister of Pakistan on 1 December 1988. She was the first female ever to lead a Muslim country.

'Pakistan is a complex country with different religious groupings, different ethnic groups, long legacies of military rule, a lack of respect for the rule of law, so it's a very difficult country to govern,' she said. 'But I found it was far more difficult because I was young and the élite institutions found it very difficult to accept working for a woman because they tended to be more traditional in their outlook, tended to come from those areas of the country where tribalism still held sway. So I found it difficult, but not impossible.

'Women can be the kindest of supporters and then they can also be the most savage of critics. But I think by and large the women of Pakistan felt liberated by my election because, in the past, a working woman did not enjoy the same kind of social status. When I became Prime Minister, it made it legitimate for women to want to work and when men were voting for me their daughters would say, "But if you can vote for a woman why can't you let your daughter run? If she's your sister [because people in the country used to look upon me as a sister] and you can let your sister work, why can't I work?"

'And I've had many men come and tell me that: that their daughters are now demanding to go to college, to make choices in their life, and that they are acceding because they do not have an answer to their questions. I remember when I was very young little boys used to run after my father's car when he travelled. Now I find that women come out in very large numbers all over the country to see me, so I think my very election liberated a large number of women in Pakistan. It also liberated women in the Muslim world because, when I travelled, I found that male leaders would tell me, "Our families would like to meet you, too."

'When travelling, I've come across working women who say, "It was your example that was an inspiration for us and allowed us to break out of our own moulds within Muslim societies." So I feel my own election had a far-reaching impact, not only in Pakistan but across the Muslim world.'

Benazir never felt that the welcomes she received in the male-dominated Arab world were anything other than genuine. 'The Arab leaders had known my father and, when they met me, they thought they were meeting their daughter,' she said. 'So I found that I was always received with a great degree of love and affection and a proclivity towards wanting to help Pakistan because their own daughter was in a challenging situation. Conversely, instead of it being an impediment, or an obstacle, I found that Arab leaders really treated me like a daughter; the doors would open, they would be warm with me, they could discuss anything with me.

'With Western leaders, somehow, I found that some of them were unsure of how to proceed and it was a strange situation to be in because one expects the West to be so much more advanced. But there would be a certain degree of reservation; they would be unsure how to proceed: "Is this lady just a lady, or does she know what she's talking about?"

'I'm speaking from my experience as a woman and from my experience as a woman leader surrounded by male leaders. I felt as a woman I wanted power to transform society; I wanted power to make changes which I thought were necessary and popular and all the reward I looked for was the love and affection of my people. When I was slandered, I found it awfully hurtful and painful, but with male leaders I found it was different: they're not so bothered about slander – they might worry about it, but they're not so bothered.

'So I think for male leaders, or for men, the pursuit of power and winning power is more important than love and affection, whereas for a woman leader the regard that one has is more important. I'm speaking only from my experience as a woman leader and the male colleagues I've known – I'm not trying to extend this to other countries. To me power never meant anything because I was the daughter of a Prime Minister and from the time I was born I remember being famous and not wanting to be famous. What moved me was the desire to change my society.

'I think in the urban areas after our reforms – the establishment of the Women's Bank and the deregulation of society – more and more women are coming out to work. In the rural areas, women work anyway, but they work in the fields with their menfolk. In urban areas, especially in big cities like Karachi, most women now work and, as urbanisation grows, more and more women will work and I feel that women are a moderating force in the politics of a country like Pakistan. It's an exciting time to be a woman in a country like Pakistan because the tussle between tradition and modernity continues. I have a great faith in the new generation of young Pakistani women.

'My own example certainly liberated the women of Pakistan. I've had so many women come up and tell me that and I've seen it in the social *milieu* of our own society in the rural areas. A few years ago, I opened an English-speaking school for girls in one of the rural areas of Pakistan in my constituency and many people told me that I wouldn't find any students to go to it, but, no, the men are sending their daughters, so it's a *remarkable* transformation; women were *never* sent out to the schools or to study.'

Benazir's first ministry brought her into headlong conflict with Nawaz Sharif, chief minister of the Pubjab, and ethnic violence broke out between rival factions. Citing the breakdown of law and order, President Ghulam Ishaq Khan dismissed the Bhutto government on 6 August 1990, and Benazir was charged with corruption and misuse of power, while her husband was arrested on a kidnap charge.

Nawaz Sharif held office after the elections in October 1990 and there was prolonged hostility between him and Benazir until she was elected head of the National Assembly's Standing Committee on Foreign Affairs. Zardari was released on bail shortly afterwards and Benazir returned to power following elections in October 1993.

General Joe Hoar, former commander-in-chief of the Middle East Command of the United States Army, provided a fascinating insight into Benazir's feminine power at that time. 'The first time I met Benazir privately was in Karachi after she had been elected for the second time as Prime Minister,' he said. 'She was beautifully turned out, coiffed, manicured, and wore a lovely, multi-coloured *shalwar khameez*. What was so interesting was that the Prime Minister had a scarf on her hair and during the 45 minutes or so that we talked the scarf slid from her hair a centimetre at a time, so that after a period of 30-odd minutes the scarf was down around her neck.

'I personally found it distracting and very exciting. She was clearly aware of it, but made no effort to replace it, or to adjust it, and throughout the conversation, which was all business, I felt there was this certain undercurrent of tension between us. I found her a most engaging person and I admire her and her political abilities greatly.'

BENAZIR'S political abilities had never really been in doubt, but what, we asked her, did she consider to be her greatest contribution to Pakistan as Prime Minister? After taking another sip of Coke, she replied: 'My single greatest contribution has been bringing down the population growth rate. According to official figures, the population growth rate was 3.1 per cent and, due to the efforts made by my government, we brought it down to 2.6 per cent.

'We started a plan of recruiting lady health visitors. We recruited them on a stipend because we didn't have enough money to pay them a salary and a pension. I thought that women would speak to women about women's problems and contraception *is* a woman's problem because it's *her* body and it's *her* choice, whereas men feel embarrassed talking about such matters, even to other men in traditional societies. So the cornerstone of the policy was to involve women in the villages.

'At first, the international aid agencies didn't assist us because they thought that these women weren't going to do anything. But we trained them for three months and sent them out into the field and this changed things dramatically. The women went back to the villages with money, so they had power, and they also had access to other women and they would sit there and talk to them. Now, we run free medical camps and we ask women how many children do they have and if they say four or more we ask them if they want a contraceptive injection and eight out of ten women say yes. So it's not that women don't want to plan their families, it's that women don't know how to plan their families.

'Actually, the single most important achievement has to be the emancipation of women because my election had a very dramatic effect in the Muslim world – it started a whole new debate. So let me rephrase that and say the single most important thing was my struggle as a Muslim woman leader in a traditional society where tribal taboos still held sway and my second most important achievement was bringing down the population growth rate.'

Explaining why there have been women leaders in Pakistan, India and Sri Lanka, Benazir said: 'None of our subcontinent women would have been able to succeed if we did not have name recognition, if we did not have the nationwide political platform, and if we did not have a ready-made constituency which believed in the ideas articulated by that political platform. But having said that, I also do not feel that we would have succeeded if we did not have the stamina and the endurance and the perseverance to face the trials and tribulations that we did.

'Conversely, we may have had the stamina and the endurance, but if we didn't have the name recognition, if we didn't have the political platform nationwide and if we didn't have a constituency wedded to a certain set of values and beliefs, it would have been impossible to succeed. So we were lucky to have the platform. I think that is why women in the West find it more difficult to succeed because they don't have that ready-made platform to catapult them to the top. They have to work their way up the ladder.'

However, Benazir's own political platform was dramatically cut from beneath her after some of her actions during her second ministry alienated her mother, Nusrat. The tight-knit Bhutto family was further divided when Benazir's brother, Murtaza, returned from exile in 1993 and claimed his father's political legacy. Widespread civilian unrest, set against a background of economic chaos, had already made her position untenable when, in September 1996, Murtaza was gunned down by police guards in a shootout outside No. 70 Clifton, the Bhutto family's home in the suburbs of Karachi.

In November of that year, Benazir was dismissed by President Farooq Leghari, her former friend, after being accused of corruption, and her husband was jailed on a charge of murdering Murtaza. When the Pakistan Muslim League came to power in February 1997, the new government immediately launched an official investigation into Benazir's second term of office. The authorities claimed that a total of $1.5 billion had disappeared from the public purse and that Asif Zardari had received kickbacks from airline, power station and pipeline projects, rice deals, customs inspections, defence contracts, land sell-offs, even government welfare. There were also incredible allegations that he had benefited financially from drug deals. In some published reports, it was claimed that Benazir and her husband had plundered a total of $3 billion.

On 10 April 1998, Benazir received permission from a Pakistani court to fly to Britain to prepare their legal defence, but a month later, while she was still abroad, the Pakistani government issued a warrant for her arrest on a charge of having improperly authorised the recruitment of a thousand employees for Pakistan's state airline. The campaign of harassment against her never stopped, she said, 'and that's why I think that one has to take a decision, sometime, to have a transition and hand over to somebody else. My party wants me to be there; they want me to be Prime Minister again, but I have deep reservations. I've been Prime Minister twice and I would like to convince them that we should have somebody else. Of course, if we can't find anybody else that we all agree on, I'll probably be forced to run again and become Prime Minister again when our party wins, but personally I feel it never stops in Pakistan.

'We've had martial law for most of the country's history and there are people who still support martial law. It's basically the democratic parties on one side and those parties who support martial law on the other. The ones who support martial law want to have strict, authoritarian rule. They don't have respect for the judiciary, or the electoral commission, or for the

Opposition, or the Cabinet, so the cycle will continue until there's a generation that grows up without martial law. That's why I think it's better to continue with this imperfect democracy to enable that generation to grow up.

'I'm the victim of a criminal conspiracy by the government of Pakistan, which has spent $15 million of government money through secret service funds to steal documents, and to forge documents, to try and say that my husband got kickbacks when he didn't. I just feel absolutely outraged when the *Sunday Times* and *Time* magazine come out with BENAZIR'S BOOTY on the basis of documents that were forged. When a government can steal documents, when a government can forge documents, when a government can arrest people to make them commit perjury, I consider that a criminal act.

'My husband is a businessman and he used to transfer money. Pakistanis are allowed by law to hold foreign exchange; we're given tax relief and tax incentives to keep our money in foreign currencies. So I'm simply outraged that they're involved in this criminal conspiracy. They've come to England saying, of all things, that there is a narcotics investigation against my husband. Thank God for the British courts because they gave us the papers, which showed that the statement was unsigned. We went back to the man's lawyers and they said he never gave the statement. So not only did they forge the documents showing kickbacks, but they forged the document implicating my husband.

'The government called a press conference at nine in the morning and it went to court at the same time, making a request to seize all my assets in Pakistan. I hadn't been indicted, I hadn't been issued with notice, and yet the court acceded to the government's request and froze all my assets. Before the judge even wrote the order, the senator who was holding the press conference said that all my assets had been frozen. The press said, CORRUPTION COURT FREEZES BHUTTO ASSETS. It didn't say without showing cause, it didn't say without an indictment.

'The only thing I will be indicted for when I return is the appointment of stewards and stewardesses and they've issued an arrest warrant without serving me with notice because I was out of the country. They all knew I was out of the country, yet they issued notice knowing I'm not going to get it. Their goal is to destroy me. They think that if there's an election I'm going to win, so they want to disqualify me and that's what everything is about. I have to go back and defend myself. If I don't go back, people will assume the charges are true.'

Benazir had last seen Asif Zardari in prison on 9 April just before she flew to London. 'He's been in jail for 18 months, solitary confinement, denied a public trial,' she said. 'My husband has been charged with the murder of my brother, although a judicial inquiry said that the state's allegations against him were without any legal basis. And the judicial inquiry went further, saying that the state had been unable to prove that there had been a conspiracy to kill my brother and, in fact, they felt that my brother had died accidentally. I, however, feel that the state never gave the evidence to show that my brother was killed as part of a plan to overthrow his sister's government.

'That's what I believe and that's why I got independent detectives from Britain to come and investigate this case and their interim report showed that they were looking at *all* three possibilities and they wanted to interview my brother's bodyguards, who were refusing to be interviewed. If they've got nothing to hide, why?'

The most difficult part had been telling her children about the death of their uncle.'I had to bring them together and explain to them that he'd gone to God, he'd joined my father and my other brother, but he loved them very much,' she said. 'And my daughter said, "I know", and I said, "How do you know?" And she said, "He sent me rabbits on my birthday." I thought that was so good because when he sent her rabbits she was four years old and I thought it was remarkable she had remembered. But it was a very difficult decision to tell them.

'My son's birthday celebration had been cancelled and I started by saying, "Do you know why your birthday had to be cancelled? I didn't want to cancel it; I wanted to be here, but something sad happened and you know mumma's been very sad." And he said, "I know." And I said, "How do you know mumma's been very sad?" And he said, "Because mumma's been crying." So there are a few things when you have to tell children and it's always very, very heart-rending and wrenching for me when I have to tell them any of these things: like their father going off to prison.

'First, I didn't tell them about it at all. I was taking them to see their father and wondering how I was going to tell them and I said, "You know, darlings, we're going to see your father." They said, "We know." And I said, "How do you know?" They always seem to know; this is the thing with kids. They said, "Because it's the same road you took us on last time." Last time, they were two and one – how they remember I don't know.

'I explained that these wicked people had come and taken their father and they were scared of their father and mother and that was the reason they did it. Now I'm concerned because I have to tell them that I may be arrested. They're in Dubai with their aunt and my mother and I'm not sure whether I should tell them and frighten them beforehand, or whether I should ask one of my friends who's living there to explain it to them if it happens. They're looking forward to my coming; they want me to come back and they want a toy and a mummy.

'I'm flying to Dubai tonight because they've frozen everything I own abroad and inside the country and frozen everything that my family and 33 of our supporters own just to make sure that I can't get support. I'm trying to get a loan, so that I can at least make arrangements for my children's school fees, then I'm going back to Pakistan. My party wants me to come to Lahore. I don't know whether there's a flight going into Lahore, or whether I'll be going into Karachi. I just hope they don't arrest me until I meet my husband.'

Benazir gulped down the last of the Coca-Cola, collected her Gucci handbag, smiled at the harpist on her way out, then walked down the marbelled corridor towards the hotel lobby. Like another famous handbag lady, she walked with a bustling, purposeful gait, with the bag resting on her right forearm, the left arm crooked, the fists clenched, the feet slightly splayed in their flat shoes. Several of the hotel's guests recognised her as she descended the steps and, out on the street, other heads turned.

In that moment, standing on the Knightsbridge pavement directly opposite Harvey Nichols, 'Pinkie' Bhutto somehow seemed the loneliest woman in the world. Then she hailed another ordinary black London cab and headed for her next appointment with destiny.

3

Manhattan Maverick

MADAM DEWI SUKARNO, the most perfumed Eastern legend since Madam Butterfly, opened the door of her Park Avenue apartment herself. The revolution was about to start in Jakarta, but the diminutive widow of President Sukarno, Indonesia's first president, had no bodyguards, not even a maid, at her beck and call in New York City. Dewi opened her own doors (and, for that matter, her own champagne), answered her own telephone calls, sent her own faxes, and ran her own businesses. So the first thing to record was that she was independent and the second, purely for curiosity value, was that 'Dewi' was pronounced 'Day-we'.

She ushered us into a red-and-gold reception room whose walls were covered with photographs in which her ageless face was the common denominator. She bobbed up, smiling, alongside Farah Diba, Prince Sianouk, Chou En Lai, Gorbachev, Margaret Thatcher, Imelda Marcos, Benazir Bhutto, Ted Kennedy, and Bill and Hillary Clinton. It was the suitably eclectic collection of the political maverick who had insisted on living a high-profile life ever since the death of her husband in 1970. No one was going to be allowed to forget Achmed Sukarno, not while his widow still drew breath.

Dewi Sukarno led us through solid mahogany doors into the study where, she said, she spent 'sleepless nights' putting together business deals for clients in the different time zones of Asia and Europe. 'There's a 14-hour difference with Tokyo and I'm here working like a horse throughout the night,' she said. The study was small, but very lush in golds and greens, with huge, tiger-pattern cushions.

Dewi's face was exquisitely made up, an art she had learned in the theatre, and she wore a lilac suit from Rue Faubourg St Honore, pearl earrings, a sapphire ring and a tiny, very simple, gold band which, she said, she had been given as a young actress in her native Tokyo. Her nail varnish was clear and she had an even more clearly defined femininity, tremendously powerful yet as subtle as willow pattern.

The glamorous image of Dewi Sukarno in the glossies did not do justice to her intellect, nor to her vast experience in world politics. 'The *New York Times* wrote about me and, in a two-hour interview, I tried to say that I'm not a social butterfly,' she said. 'I spoke about my business, but not one word of that came out. On the contrary, they said, "self-described social butterfly". You know, it's heartbreaking. I participate in a social life because I have invitations, but please don't think that I am there every night. One photograph goes around the world and they create this false image of me.'

Describing Dewi Sukarno as a social butterfly was like confusing a samurai warrior with a bowl of sushi. She might be Madam Butterfly in some respects, but never the frivolous social variety. For the next two hours, she was amusing, vivacious, coquettish, combative, talkative, excitable, sorrowful and, in her views on the West's interference in Asian politics, fearlessly opinionated. Pouring chilled champagne from a closet bar in her study, she said, 'Bon! Okay! Cheers!' and, having spanned three cultures in as many words, raised a glass to her lips.

'People should use whatever God gives you – charm, beauty, intelligence,' she said, answering a question. 'I am against women being manly. Real emancipation is not for a woman to be in an equal position to a man, or to have an equal salary. That has nothing to do with it. The aim of emancipation is to be competely independent and free *spiritually*. It has nothing to do with equal power.

'I like a man who stays like a rock on his own belief; that attracts me very much. When you meet someone like that you get scared. Fear and respect are like the front and back of a piece of paper: you have fear, so you have respect; you respect, so you also have fear. And that is sexy for me, so sexy. My husband had it and it was very sexy. When you meet such a man you want to be conquered; it's our nature to be conquered.

'A woman should be protected and loved and my husband spoiled me with his love. He was a man who reminded me of his love every second of the day. "I love you, darling, I love you." I was *fulfilled* by his love. Men today are so lazy that they think one telephone call is enough. I have 500 love letters from him. I kept them all. That's my treasure. He loved me. I was totally spoiled by his love. So I know what happiness a woman can have to be loved and taken care of and protected.'

After that testimonial, names, dates and stories rolled off Dewi's tongue like a printout from history. Time slipped backwards and, suddenly, we were in *The Year of Living Dangerously*:* The place: Jakarta; the date: 1 October 1965.

The murder of five generals during the night unleashed a bloodbath throughout Java and the hundreds of other islands that make up the archipeligo of Indonesia, triggering widespread civil unrest which led to a military takeover under General Suharto and, ultimately, to Sukarno's overthrow after 22 years in power. Dewi had been at Sukarno's side that bloodstained night and had sustained him in the difficult days that followed, even working hard to achieve a *rapprochement* between Sukarno and Suharto to try to retrieve the situation. That she failed is a source of great distress. Sukarno was placed under house arrest and remained a prisoner until his death in 1970 and Dewi had become Suharto's most vehemently outspoken critic.

'For ten years, I was not able to go back to Indonesia, most probably because of the book I published against President Suharto,' she said. 'I said that he had committed high treason and that he was a criminal for killing over one million people between 1966 and 1969 – in those three years, he killed 1.2 million people. He called these people Communists and he justified the massacre by calling it "a Red hunt", so if you were supposed to be a Communist, you were supposed to get killed.'

It had taken many years for the true story of Sukarno's downfall to come to light and Dewi Sukarno's version of events leading up to the apocalyptic night of 1 October 1965, had the ring of truth about it. She had met Sukarno six years earlier when he visited Tokyo to discuss war reparations with the Japanese Government. 'He had been invited to Japan during the war by the Japanese army, so he considered Japan like an elder brother country,' she said. 'His idea was that Indonesia had all these magnificent, rich natural resources and all she needed was technology and finance from Japan. He also had this very romantic thought about a Japanese wife. He had read a book on philosophy popular among Japanese women and he was imagining Japanese women through this. He wanted a Japanese wife because Japanese ladies had a reputation for being faithful and loyal.

---

* The movie *The Year of Living Dangerously*, directed by Peter Weir, told the story of Suharto's military takeover in Jakarta and starred Mel Gibson as an Australian radio reporter who was caught up in the conflict.

'Japanese people were throwing receptions and tea parties in his honour and I was introduced to him at one of the receptions. I was an art student and I wanted to become a great painter, but I was also at drama school and playing little parts on television. A friend in my acting class was the girlfriend of an important gentleman and he invited her "to bring some beautiful friends to make a party". I got a call and was very honoured to be asked, so I tried to make myself nice and I went. Sukarno was His Excellency the President of Indonesia and I never thought he was the man for me, yet something attracted me.

'In his beautiful presidential uniform, he looked so dignified; his eyes showed his purity and, when he smiled, he was very charming. One could feel his humanity; it was overflowing. Once you met Sukarno physically, you were completely a prisoner of his charm. But then, when he was leaving the reception and turned his shoulders, I saw a lonely man.

'I said to myself, "He's a president and I'm nobody." But, after all, we were two human beings who had been through the same experience of hunger and poverty. He was fighting for independence in Indonesia and we were fighting for our existence in Japan. Japan had been completely destroyed. They talk about the atomic bombs at Nagasaki and Hiroshima, but American air raids against Tokyo were bigger. Tokyo was flattened and more people died in these air raids than at Nagasaki and Hiroshima.

'One day after the reception, I got a call. He said he was leaving the following day and asked me to come to the airport. After he returned to Indonesia, he wrote me a very simple letter and asked me to send him a photo of myself and I sent one. We exchanged correspondence during the month of July, 1959. Then, in August, there were times when I heard nothing from him; that was the time when there were big political riots against him in Sumatra, so he was very busy.

'Come September, through an intermediary, he sent me an invitation to come to Indonesia for two weeks. My mother wanted me to marry a Japanese man to give us security. I was the eldest child and I was supporting my mother and my brother, but it might have taken years and years to become a great artist and my acting career was uncertain. I'd never been abroad, so I thought it might give me an idea of how to get out of this slum. I was delighted to go.

'I arrived in Jakarta and it seemed to be very fresh and beautiful, with white houses and orange roofs and lots of green everywhere. But what impressed me most was how people worshipped Sukarno – he was a godlike figure. In one village, a pregnant woman stopped him and asked him to touch her stomach to keep her baby safe and whenever he saw some children he stopped to talk to them.

'Just two days before my departure, we were alone for the first time on the terrace of the presidential palace. We were overlooking long lines of coconut palms, a huge sun was going down and the sky was red. The coconut trees were turning into black shadows and it was so quiet, so solemn, and he said I could be his inspiration and I could be his strength and I could be the joy of his life. Something exploded in my head. I thought I would never hear such a beautiful proposal in my life. He didn't say, "Please be my wife." He said, "Please be my strength, please be the joy of my life."

'I thought God had chosen me to be with him. My childhood, my school years, my youth had been hard and I thought this hard life must have been a preparation for me to be with him. I was strong enough to cope with anything because I was a student activist, too. I was brought up with anger: why was there no social justice, why was there no equality? Why? I was such an unsatisfactory child. I was so stubborn. I wanted to change the world on my own. Of course, I was of a more socialist mind in those days – I was against power, I was against richness, I was against everything. So it did not take any time for me to follow his political convictions: spiritual independence first and material independence after that. And then bring a balance of power in the world; otherwise, there could be no full independence and no social justice. I became a Muslim and married him.

'As he was the president, he could not go into a crowd and the only reports he'd get were from the armed forces, or from his ministers, or from the director-generals of this department or that department. Some of those reports might only be pleasing him, especially in a developing country – don't say undeveloped country; *developing* country – so I went to the people myself. Sometimes I even disguised myself and tried to catch what people were saying, and then I gave him the information from my own research. I gave no personal opinions, just objective information. And I tried to keep the cronies away.

'You know, Marie Antoinette's mistake was that she was trying to be happy as a woman instead of trying to be happy as a queen. I never loved my husband as a woman, never. I thought it would be too egotistical of me to love him as a woman. President Sukarno was for the country, for the people; he belonged to the country, he belonged to the people. I knew I should not try to have him for myself. It would have been most egotistical of me to try to love him for myself as a woman, so I loved him as one of his people. I admired him, I worshipped him as one of the civilians. When he was playing on the world stage, I was the manager behind the screen. I wasn't the prima donna; he was the star.

'In the sixties, there were only two dominating powers: Russia and

America. Sukarno was bringing about a third force of non-aligned countries in Asia, Africa, Latin America and the Middle East and he was becoming the leader. He called it the Third Force – afterwards, it was called the Third World – to balance the power of the world. The White House hated him for that because he was succeeding. The Asian countries, the Africans, the Arabs, the socialist countries, Tito, Nehru, Castro, Nasser, they all worshipped Sukarno. He always said, "A hero is a product of the time." Time produces heroes, and these people were heroes. But the White House hated him and they attempted to kill him five times. So then, of course, they supported Suharto with money and everything.'

SUKARNO was a dictator but, the way Dewi Sukarno told it, he was St Francis of Assisi compared with Suharto. She sensed that Suharto would have a great impact on her life the first time she ever set eyes on him. 'In 1963 I'd gone to Bali on my own and, on the way home, I stopped over in Surabaya,' she said. 'At the airport, I saw a military man with two men at his side, walking very strongly. He was walking with such confidence, as though he was cutting the air in front of him. You understand the expression? Cutting the air? I was impressed and I came back to Jakarta and immediately told my darling, "I saw some general at Surabaya airport who impressed me so much. He looked super."

'It was the first time I had spoken with some admiration about a man to Sukarno; how impressed I was with this man's silhouette. I wanted to find out who he was. My husband said, "Was he handsome? Were you attracted?" A joke. So he discovered who that army general was: Brigadier General Suharto. I forgot about him and never saw him again until 1965.

'On the evening of 30 September, Sukarno was delivering a speech to veterans at a sports stadium and I went to the Italian ambassador's reception and, afterwards, I had dinner at the Hotel Indonesia with the Iranian ambassador and his wife. I had my own palace and, when I came home, he joined me. Overnight, between 30 September and 1 October, five generals were killed – from number one to number five. In the morning, as usual, Sukarno left for the presidential palace. That same afternoon, I advised him to communicate with General Suharto, who was the only survivor – the only general who had not been attacked. But Suharto announced that the murders had been carried out by the PKI, the Communist Party of Indonesia. He brainwashed people and, of course, they shouted for revenge against all members of the PKI.

'I have to explain: in those days, the Indonesian Communist Party was not like the Russian Communist Party or the Chinese Communist

Party – please believe me – they didn't even know what a Marxist was. They were just simple Sukarno followers; could have been simple fishermen, simple farmers and, like in Pakistan, every man went to mosque. They believed in God. If you're a Communist, you don't believe in God.

'Sukarno said, "We have to find the truth about who did these murders and, if it's true that the Communist Party has done this, then we'll condemn them, but first let's have information from every side." Suharto did not wait. He said it was a Communist coup.

'When I heard that Suharto was the one who had resolved the situation on 1 October, I immediately knew it was the man I had seen at the airport. I had a huge sense, huge. So, when it happened, I made so much effort to get my husband and Suharto together to rebuild the country. I did so much to bring these two men together. Suharto's popularity was growing every day and he was becoming a hero, so I really tried to make my husband and him be friends. I praised God for Suharto. I contacted all the widows of the generals who were killed and I made afternoon tea to consult with them, and also invited them to the presidential palace. What happened was so disappointing.

'When you think that this great man Sukarno sacrificed his life for his country and they turned against him like that and disgraced him and put him under house arrest for three years until his death! How could they do this? I was in Japan giving birth to my daughter and was not allowed to go back. I broke into the country one day before he died because I knew he was dying, risking my own life.

'In reality, he was under house arrest in my palace. Suharto said he was guarding my husband for security reasons, but in fact he was isolated from his wife and children. Nobody was allowed to contact him, he was not allowed to read newspapers, not even allowed to have proper medical treatment. I was in Japan with my daughter when he was completely – and I don't like the word – stripped of all his power. He was life president and then the same People's Congress, MPRS, who decided he should be life president took away his title and chose General Suharto to be acting president on 11 March 1967.

'Ever since Suharto became acting president, I could not go back to Jakarta. I couldn't go to England or America because those two countries had helped him. I could not stay in Japan either, because Japan, England, America, Canada, Australia and all European countries, led by Poland, were welcoming Suharto. France was the only country that would give me political asylum. I arrived in Paris without any visa and they said, "Okay, madam, you can stay two years. After that, if you decide you are comfortable in France, you can stay – otherwise, go somewhere else." So

I stayed in France, but twice I attempted to rejoin my husband. I went as far as Bangkok. Twice I failed. The Indonesian ambassador would say, "Madam, you cannot go to Indonesia. It's regulations."

'In the meantime, I heard the voice of Sukarno in the air – his voice was sent by the wind – and I was so restless. I was nervous about how he was being treated and one day I saw from a photograph in the *Herald Tribune* that his face was swollen. It was taken by his second daughter on his 68th birthday, the only day they allowed children from the first marriage to see him. She took the photograph secretly and gave it to Associated Press. I knew immediately from his swollen face that he was not well.

'I was thinking about how to get back when I received a call on 18 June 1970, from Associated Press saying, "Do you have anything to say about your husband's death?" I said, "What? Is he dying?" and they said, "We heard he has fallen into a coma." I took this telephone call in the entrance of my apartment and I thought the house was breaking into two pieces and I was falling. My knee was starting to tremble, my voice was already trembling; I don't know what I said. I think I almost cried out. It was so difficult to hold myself.

'I said, "Thank you very much. I have nothing to say to you now, but if you have any other news please call me." Immediately, I asked the fastest way to reach Jakarta. I found that Air France went to Bangkok and I could change there to a Japanese plane for Jakarta. I had a little bird for my daughter and a little fish and these were the only two living souls I had in my apartment and I gave them away to friends. My friends said, "Dewi, don't do it. You are going to get killed. Please don't go." I said, "My life was nothing. My husband gave me a life. If I'm killed, it will be an honourable death."

'When we landed in Jakarta, some uniformed military men arrived and one said to me, "Would you kindly read this and sign?" The letters were dancing in front of my eyes and I could not read them. I said, "Calm down, calm down." The few words I could read said, "Now you are in Jakarta, your security is in our hands. You have to obey our instructions." So I signed.

'Then the officer said, "I guess your wish is to meet your husband?" I said, "Yes." So they put us in the car directly from the plane. I said, "Where are we going?" They said, "To the military hospital." The car started to move into the jungle and I realised that we were driving to Tanjung Priok, the port of Jakarta. I said, "This is not the direction," and all the time I'm thinking, "There's nobody here. It's all so dark in the harbour. We're going to be killed here. Maybe they're going to put me in an empty drum with cement and put me in the sea." In fact, some of my friends were following in another car and the soldiers had been trying to lose them.

'Finally, we arrived at the hospital and journalists and photographers were covering the entrance, so we had to go around the back, and the first word I heard was "morgue". But my husband was not dead – we just entered through the morgue to avoid the journalists – and I finally met him just a few hours before he died.

'Then Suharto put everybody in jail who'd worked for Sukarno, including a servant in the presidential palace. I was interrogated, too. Indonesian citizens weren't allowed to mention his name. If you were caught as a Sukarno follower, you'd get killed. While we were in office, he was worshipped like a god by people. Every house, every restaurant, every movie house, every airport had a portrait of Sukarno. He was so much loved; he was really a father; he was the founder of the nation. Yet for ten years nobody even dared to put his portrait up and no newspaper dared to publish his name.

'It is so disappointing it hurts – physically hurts. You spend so much time, you give your soul, your heart, time, energy for the country and the people and then people you thought were loyal friends turn against you – of course it hurts; it's hurting like you have no idea.

'The press has been very unfair to me. So horrible. I'm sick and tired of this journalism. They hurt me so badly. You know, most of the journalists know what they want to write – just to knock you down so it sells. They never write when I'm seriously working; it doesn't interest them. They're only after a picture at a party. They think I'm a jet-set socialite doing nothing.

'When my husband died, he left nothing. I was not educated to become a businesswoman. I'm not a university graduate. I married at the age of 19. I had to run businesses from scratch. You have a phone and it becomes your asset and a big company employs you as an agent. When I went back to Indonesia from 1980 to 1990 I represented five major companies from America, France, Italy, Spain and Japan. Who will make you an agent if your performance is not good? It is not because I am a Sukarno or because I am pretty. In business, the name Sukarno hurt me. Being young and beautiful hurt me. Being famous is a disadvantage.

'Look at Indonesia today: President Suharto has owned the country for 32 years. Everybody jokes about Indonesia Company Limited, or Indonesia Corporation and President Suharto is president of Indonesia Incorporated. His three sons and his three daughters and his Chinese friends and his general friends own the country; they own everything; there is nothing that they don't own from oil to natural gas to iron to gold to diamonds; from forestry to fisheries to agriculture, even to the flowers, even orchids.

'For over one quarter of a century, Indonesia was enjoying prosperity and business was booming and now, with one stroke, they collapse. We had forest fires that went for weeks and then the currency dropped 80 per cent as if God is angry against Suharto. With one stroke, the Indonesian economy is completely collapsing, food prices are four or five times more and I read in the *New York Times* something like $50 billion left Indonesia between October and January. It is like having an empire on the sun.'

TWO weeks after our interview with Dewi Sukarno, Suharto's 'empire on the sun' started to melt away when Indonesian students rose in open revolt against his presidency. Hundreds were killed in street battles with the armed forces in Jakarta before the moment Dewi had been praying for came on 20 May 1998, when Suharto, bowing to international pressure and the threat of civil war, finally resigned as president. 'That afternoon I was with Indonesian students on United Nations Square requesting Suharto to step down,' she told us. 'Then I saw it on television, but he has not really stepped down, he's only stepped back. He and Professor Habibie [his chosen successor] are close friends and have been partners in business for at least 25 years. He announced a new Cabinet, but most of them stayed the same and they all have Suharto's fingerprint on them. So nothing has really changed.

'We have only just started the long struggle of revolution, if you can call it a revolution. We have to get rid of the Suharto system and it's a long-term project to clean up the country. I supported the student activities from here, together with the Indonesian community in New York. I am now requesting our first free general election. We've never had one and, if there is an election, Sukarno's daughter, my stepdaughter, Megawati, will be elected. Now is the time for the Indonesian people to awaken and correct the history of the past 32 years.'

4

First Lady of Peace

NO WOMAN crossed more man-made boundaries or stepped through more political minefields in the Third World than Rosalynn Carter. She had power, real power, and she used it every day of her life in a quest for international peace and racial harmony. 'You have personal power when you don't feel like you're anybody's victim,' said the wife of Jimmy Carter, 39th President of the United States of America. 'It's when, whatever happens, you can handle the situation without blaming other people. Personal empowerment is when you understand that you have this power; you might not be able to change the world, but you understand that you have power and that you can use that power: that is empowerment.'

We were talking at the Carter Center, international headquarters of one of the most remarkable enterprises of its kind anywhere in the world. It was to be found off Freedom Parkway on the outskirts of Atlanta, Georgia, and we had been driven from the airport by an East African cabdriver who said: 'Jimmy Carter is a good man, a man of peace. He achieved peace all over the world.' These sentiments were typical of the high regard that Jimmy Carter had achieved in people's minds ever since he and his wife had started to cut through racial and political divisions in search of peace.

Set in tranquil, landscaped parkland like the campus of a well-endowed provincial university, the Carter Center consisted of several modern buildings, one of which housed the Presidential Library. Security, like everything else here, was understated and the atmosphere welcoming. The reception area, painted in muted corals, was spacious and high-ceilinged, with clear glass walls giving the impression that you were in the centre of a garden. Very much like the Carter presidency, there was no overt glamour or flashiness and only a small bust of Carter himself, discreetly placed beside a column, indicated the provenance of the place. However, it was not Jimmy Carter we were here to see, but his wife.

Rosalynn Smith Carter was born in Plains, Georgia, on 18 August 1927, and, five weeks short of her 19th birthday, she married James Earl Carter Jr, a 21-year-old United States Navy officer whose eternally boyish grin ensured that he would be known, locally at first and then globally, as Jimmy Carter. Even when he was President of the United States and, later still, America's Great Mediator dashing from one world trouble spot to another, he was still plain ol' Jimmy Carter from Plains, Georgia.

In Washington, Rosalynn's soft, lilting voice, feminine demeanour and apparent lack of ambition led many to mistake her for a submissive Southern wife, but during her years at Jimmy Carter's side she earned the nickname of 'the Steel Magnolia'. Before we flew to Georgia, Mary King, who had worked in the Carter White House, warned us: 'Mrs Carter is known for her gentleness and grace, but it would be a mistake for anyone to be deluded by her lack of obvious armament. She has an iron grip, she's tenacious and there's great depth to her thought processes. I think she's the most active woman in the world – she has the energy and determination to move mountains.'

Rosalynn Carter's workplace – to call it an office would be far too formal – was large yet cosy, the decor a pale yellow Georgia peach. She sat at a desk with the garden showing through glass panels behind her and a portrait of her daughter, Amy, on one of the other walls. Now 70 but looking 20 years younger, Rosalynn was petite and slim and blonde, with a flawless complexion and pale blue eyes that seemed to see inside you. She wore a peacock blue-green trouser suit and her only pieces of jewellery were simple gold earrings and a gold wedding ring.

She had, she said, started her own journey of self-discovery soon after her marriage to Jimmy and had arrived at a point at which very little had the power to disconcert her anymore. 'I admire women who have a real sense of themselves, of who they are and what they can do,' she said. 'They're ambitious, they have goals, they know what they want to achieve and they're successful in achieving it. Some women are interested in staying at home and raising a family, but I think that having a real sense of "who I am" is so important and, when that happens to a person, she can do whatever she wants to do.

'I developed a sense of what I could do not too long after we were married. Jimmy was in the Navy after graduating from the Naval Academy and he was gone to sea for long periods of time. I had a baby and I was very young and really not very secure, and I had to do things myself. It was important to me, over a period of time, to do the things I had to do to develop self-confidence, but it never occurred to me then that I might be First Lady of the United States one day. In those days, I thought Jimmy might rise to CNO – Chief of Naval Operations – which is as high as you can go in the Navy, because he had always got *the* best jobs; whatever he asked for in the Navy, he got.'

The long and winding road that took Jimmy and Rosalynn Carter to the White House began in 1953 when Jimmy's father, James Earl Carter Snr, died of cancer and Jimmy inherited the family peanut-farming and fertilizer business. Rosalynn said: 'Jimmy had been in the Navy for 11 years when his father died and we went home. I wasn't very happy with the thought at that time, but I never regretted it later. I'd been living all over the world and it was exciting, and I was going home to Plains, Georgia, which had a population of 680. I thought I was going to be bored, but it didn't work out that way at all.'

The Navy had instilled the principles of justice and equality in Jimmy Carter and he soon showed that he wasn't afraid to put those principles into action. When civil rights became an issue in Georgia, he stunned local people by becoming the only white male in the Plains area to refuse to join the racist White Citizens' Council. He also started to take an active interest in politics.

'Jimmy's family had always been political: his grandfather on his mother's side was postmaster through both Democratic and Republican administrations, so he was a *real* politician to be able to hold on to that job,' said Rosalynn. 'When Jimmy's father died, he was in the state legislature and had been involved in all kinds of community activities. He'd been on the local school board so, when the person who had taken his place was accidentally killed, Jimmy stepped in. His father had been on the hospital authority and they asked him to take his father's place. He was asked to be on the library board, so he became really involved with civic affairs. He ran for the Georgia Senate in 1963 and one of the things that caused him to run was the condition of schools at that time, but it kind of ran in his family to be in politics.'

Jimmy served two terms as state senator during which he developed a countryman's healthy disrespect for the big shots and lobbyists in Washington, DC. Then, in 1966, something happened that left the doors of the Governor's Mansion in Atlanta wide open. Rosalynn said: 'Our leading Democratic candidate for governor had a heart attack and dropped out of the race very close to election time. Jimmy came to

Atlanta to see who was going to run for office because there was no obvious candidate. He called me and said he'd been to see all the top officials that he worked with in the State Senate and they couldn't find anybody. "Nobody's going to run for governor," he said. "So I'm going to run."' Jimmy, however, lost the nomination to the segregationist Lester Maddox, who was elected governor.

Jimmy took a break from politics and returned to the family business. His experience in the cut-throat political world had only strengthened his beliefs in equality and fairness, and it was at this time that he became a Born-Again Christian. The Carter family had grown until there were four children – three sons, John William, James Earl III and Donnell Jeffrey, and a daughter, Amy Lynn.

Jimmy returned to politics when he contested the governorship again in 1970, this time successfully. 'Back in those days, I was not as independent as I am now and I don't think I would ever have told him that I didn't want him to run,' said Rosalynn. 'That was my position at that time; but, as you grow and learn, you develop your independence. At that time, I was just overwhelmed and excited and I went out and campaigned.

'We didn't have much time, so we spread out across the state. We didn't have schedules, we just got in the car and drove with one of my sons, who was then 14 years old. We'd just stop and pass out brochures and try to get Jimmy's name before the public because nobody knew him outside the one senatorial district he had represented. But that was really exciting for me and I learned just from walking down the street, passing out brochures, going into the stores, going to the newspapers, the radio stations, the television stations. And I learned about people's problems from the questions they asked me. I'd come home and share these with Jimmy, and that's how I got involved with issues for the first time.

'There were many people who didn't like that sort of pressure and it was hard on some families. I have friends who couldn't take the criticisms of their husbands and they were either soon out of office or they were divorced. But, in our family, we all campaigned in all directions over the state and when Jimmy was elected governor we all came home. One son was in the Navy and the two other boys were at college and we hadn't been together for a long time. So the Governor's Mansion was immediately home.'

THEY'D never seen a family like the Carters in the Governor's Mansion before and nor had they seen a governor like Jimmy Carter. He challenged the hidebound attitude of the state legislature by rallying public support for a number of progressive measures, including an increase in the number of blacks appointed to public office. Sweeping aside patronage, he forced through reforms in every area of government, then undertook ten trips abroad to counter Georgia's negative image as a backwoods, racist state and to improve its appeal to potential investors.

In 1974 he announced his candidacy for the 1976 presidential election and became the front-runner by winning the vital first primary in New Hampshire. He received the Democratic nomination and, in a closely contested campaign against Gerald Ford, went on to win the presidency by a slender two per cent margin. The Carters moved to Washington and Rosalynn became *chatelaine* at 1600 Pennsylvania Avenue. She also broke with tradition by becoming the first President's wife to sit in on Cabinet meetings.

Rosalynn said: 'The White House was just home for normal, natural people. The first day Amy went to school in Washington everybody told me how beautiful she looked with all the press around and this little girl going into the schoolyard. Amy had been three years old when Jimmy was elected governor and the Governor's Mansion had an 18½-acre allotment with a fence around it and we had tourists downstairs five days a week. We lived upstairs and, to get to the kitchen, you had to go through the tourists. Amy learned to walk through that crowd at three years old without seeing anybody. When we got to the White House, it had an 18-acre allotment with a fence around it, tourists downstairs every day, and we lived upstairs. When somebody asked her, "Amy, what's it like living in the White House?" I heard her say, "Natural."

'For us, upstairs at the White House was the one stable place in our lives because every member of a president's family is in the same situation when they go out. People crowd around, they want autographs, they want photographs made with them, and you can't feel like a normal, ordinary person except when you're with your family. We really cherished those times in the White House and it brought the family close together because we were all in the same situation.'

It was a different story downstairs in the Oval Office, however. The Carter Administration was bedevilled by the OPEC oil embargo which pushed up the price of gasoline and everything else. Jimmy's Energy Bill and many other measures became mired down in Congress, even though the Democrats held a sizeable majority. Jimmy had placed his own people, 'the Georgia Mafia', in executive positions in the White House, which only increased his isolation from the traditional powerbrokers on Capitol Hill. With runaway inflation devaluing people's earnings and eroding their savings, an economic malaise spread across America.

Rosalynn said: 'I was concerned because I didn't know what kind of questions concerned people outside of the State of Georgia. The first trip

I took as First Lady was to Florida – I just drove in and stopped along the way and talked to people. I learned that people everywhere felt the same about the things that are important to them. I'd also read the newspapers and watched the news on television and, when Jimmy stepped off the elevator, I'd come in and say, "Why did you do this? Why did you do that?" One day he said, "Why don't you come to the Cabinet meetings and you'll know why we make these decisions?"

'So I started going to Cabinet meetings. He was having them weekly at that time and I sat around the room – not at the Cabinet table – but around the room with government officials who were not at the level of Cabinet. I usually sat by the door because I couldn't always arrange my schedule properly and sometimes I had to slip in and out.'

Rosalynn claimed that her attendance at Cabinet meetings was nothing more than a natural development of her role as First Lady; that she simply grew into the job. But beneath the chiffon she had a steely resolve to become involved in political matters. Mary King had told us: 'Rosalynn understood it was symbolic for her to attend Cabinet meetings, to be well informed, but not active. This caused a storm of protest, but within the parameters of that symbolism she understood that she could move heaven and earth.'

Rosalynn said: 'I was criticised for going to Cabinet meetings, but that didn't bother me because we'd *always* discussed the issues of the day in the afternoons anyway. I stopped my schedule at 4.30 because Jimmy would call and say, "Let's play tennis" or "Let's jog." We'd take some exercise, then we'd sit on the Truman balcony and I would tell him what I had done in the day and he would tell me what he had done in the day. If I had been travelling out in the country, I could tell him something I had learned about particular issues and share that with him.

'I could learn more about how people felt than the President could. It was very difficult for people to tell the President anything because they felt very complimented just to meet him. But I could go into things like the world energy crisis and worldwide inflation. I could go into a couple's home in New Hampshire and talk about the high cost of fuel oil. I could meet with older Americans and talk to them about their problems. I could do those things and come back and report to him. He could never have done that kind of thing as President: if he'd tried to talk to a young couple, everybody would be crowding around, but they'd talk to me because I had no entourage. The President can't get that close to people to get that kind of information.'

FRUSTRATED at home by Congress, Jimmy Carter was determined to make a greater success of his foreign policy. Rosalynn said: 'Jimmy wanted to work on Middle East peace – it was very important to him. The Christians, the Bible and the Holy Land were very important and he wanted to do what he could to bring peace to that area. One day we were walking around Camp David and it was so peaceful and wonderful that he said, "If we brought them here, something good would have to happen because it's such a wonderful, peaceful place."

'So he invited President Sadat of Egypt and Prime Minister Begin of Israel to Camp David and they came. After the first day or two, President Sadat and Prime Minister Begin didn't see each other again because they argued whenever you got them together, so Jimmy would meet with one and then he would meet with the other. And it was really hard on him because, when he was meeting with one, the other could rest, but he didn't get any rest and it was just as tense a period of time as I have ever been through.

'Most of the time, I took notes and sat in. After meeting with one of the principals, Jimmy would come back to our cabin and tell the advisers what had happened and I was always there. So I kept up with the whole negotiations. It was exciting, but it was traumatic. Sometimes you would be in the depths of despair, thinking that nothing would happen, then sometimes you'd be elated because you'd think, "This is going to work." That range of emotions from despair to elation was constant; it was the most emotionally exhausting experience I've ever had.

'The thing that I like about the First Lady's position is that you can do whatever you want to do with it. People used to ask me if I thought the First Lady ought to be paid and I said no because if you were paid there'd be certain responsibilities and you'd have to do these things and I liked being able to do what I was interested in.'

WHEN the Iran hostage crisis precipitated Jimmy Carter's defeat by Ronald Reagan in November 1980, the Carters returned home to Georgia with many of their dreams unfulfilled. Inspired by the Christian principles that had sustained them in the White House, they founded the Carter Center to carry on the work that Jimmy couldn't complete as President.

Asked about her husband's international peace initiatives, Rosalynn Carter said: 'It makes me very proud. It's something Jimmy has pursued for as long as I can remember. When we built the Carter Center, we were trying to decide what we could do with the rest of our lives. One night, I woke up and Jimmy was sitting straight up in the bed. I thought he was sick because he sleeps all night long every night.

'But he said, "I know what we can do with the Carter Center – we can have a place to resolve conflicts. If there had been such a place, I wouldn't have had to take Prime Minister Begin and President Sadat to Camp David." So that was the idea when we first began the Carter Center, but you don't just go out and solve conflicts and so we started agricultural programmes in Africa and those programmes that we had – and still have in 33 African countries – give us an entrée to the leaders of those countries and if a conflict evolves, or if there is a conflict, we can say, "Maybe we can help you with this."'

From that beginning, Jimmy Carter travelled the world as a private human rights ambassador, often with Rosalynn at his side. He mediated civil strife in Somalia, Ethiopia and Bosnia-Herzegovina, and monitored elections in Panama, Nicaragua, Haiti and Mexico. Despite resistance from the State Department, he made an unprecedented private visit to North Korea in 1994, where he brokered an agreement between Kim Il-sung and President Clinton which enabled talks to resume between the two countries over North Korea's nuclear capability. In Atlanta, the Carters worked on an anti-violence programme in the community, set up a loan fund for small businesses and sought ways to co-ordinate mental health facilities for families. This last project was one of Rosalynn's greatest concerns.

'I have worked on mental health issues since my husband was governor in the early 1970s,' she said. 'A few years ago there was a study done by the World Bank, Harvard University and the Carnegie Foundation to determine the burden of disease in the world, including disabilities. The burden of disease had always been measured by how many years you lived. This young man at Harvard developed a plan for measuring disabilities and what they learned was that of the top ten causes of disability in the world five are mental illnesses.

'By the year 2010, depression will be the leading cause of disability in the world. So in talking with the people who had done this study I worked out a programme of action. I'd worked for a long time with a committee of the World Federation of Mental Health called First Ladies in the World. They wanted to know if I could disseminate the information to these women, but we had to change the name of the committee because we had two queens, so we named it Women Leaders of the World.

'The increase in depression in the West has a lot to do with the stress we live under today, but depression in the Third World is also growing fast and a lot of it is caused by wars, traumas and poverty among refugees and displaced persons. Depression has been there a long time, but we just haven't recognised it as such. I don't think people understood that they have an illness which can be controlled in the overwhelming majority of cases. It's just that, in the last few years, we've learned so much about the brain and we have new medications and new treatments, so the recognition and treatment of mental illness is fast developing.

'I hope we're beginning to overcome the stigma, but a lot of it is that nobody understood mental illnesses in the past and if somebody had a mental illness they were shut away in an institution. Now, as we learn more about the cause of illnesses and how the brain works, we are realising that most of these mental illnesses are biological and they can be diagnosed and treated, just as physical illnesses are. As we learn more and more, the stigma goes away.'

As we were leaving her office, Rosalynn Carter casually mentioned that she was flying to Africa later that day. From all the nervousness she displayed, it might have been a trip to the supermarket, but she had travelled too many miles on her globe-trotting missions in the Third World to let anything bother her these days. After all, she was nobody's victim.

5

My Father's Daughter

THERE is a quiet corner just off Pall Mall in the heart of imperial London that is forever Egypt. High above streets lined with bronzed statues and blue plaques commemorating Britain's warriors and statesmen, Kitchener and Curzon among them, President Gamal Abdel Nasser gazed like a visionary across a garden of jonquils and leopard oak towards the Grecian frieze adorning the Athenaeum Club. It was in the Athenaeum that the great explorer and Arabist, Sir Richard Burton, translated *The Arabian Nights*. And it was here, across Waterloo Place, that the spirit of Egypt's greatest warrior-statesman lived on in the heart of his daughter, Mona Abdel Nasser Marwan.

Nasser's body might be buried in Cairo, but his memory survived in a single colour photograph in his daughter's fifth-floor apartment. He had been middle-aged when the photograph was taken, but his military bearing was still intact and there was a slight smile beneath the famous moustache. The eyes seemed to seek out some distant horizon but, from this vantage point in SW1, found instead the Union Jack flapping over the roof of the Institute of Directors.

Nasser, the man who had nationalised British interests in the Suez Canal, would have greatly appreciated the irony of finding himself in such pukka British company and the words that Mona spoke about him might well have moved him to tears. Shunning the prevailing attitude among some children of the famous that they carry an unfair burden from their illustrious parents, Mona said: 'I feel so proud because I think it's a gift from God that I am the daughter of Nasser.'

The drawing-room of Mona's apartment was rich in Impressionist paintings, although there were few other concessions to Western culture; the furnishings were in gold and beige and the overall effect was a pleasing blend of Egyptian and Oriental. Family pictures in silver frames were dotted about the room, with the portrait of Nasser – the first official photograph of him in colour – on a table flanked by the Three Wise Monkeys and a collection of carved elephants in turquoise, rock crystal and coral.

Mona Nasser was a beautiful, raven-haired woman, with eyes set like dark emeralds in the classical, high-cheek-boned features of a screen Cleopatra. She also possessed an inner calm that was frequently shaken, though never quite shattered, by an engagingly deep chuckle. Mona Nasser laughed a lot, mainly at her own little foibles, and when she spoke, either in English or Arabic, her voice had the same good-humoured richness as her laugh. She wore leggings, a jumper and simple gold earrings, and only the most *au fait* would have appreciated the rarity of the small, yellow, emerald-cut diamond ring on one of her fingers.

Mona's upbringing at a time when the Middle East was undergoing one convulsion after another had given her an unparalleled insight into the politics and powerplay of the region. She was also the subject of snide remarks by Egyptian aristocrats living in London whose land and businesses had been appropriated for the state by her father's regime, although some of these had later been returned by President Mubarak. Mona had heard the criticisms, but her dignity remained unassailable. Throughout the interview, she was diplomatic and thoughtful and it was evident that her father's philosophy was deeply ingrained in her.

'I have two personalities – Mona who is the daughter of the president and Mona who is the wife and mother,' she said. 'I was born in Cairo and educated at an Arabic public school, not an English school like all of the upper classes, but I had a private teacher to learn English. At that time, education was free for boys and girls – there were no fees for government schools or universities.

'Women were liberated in Egypt under the King – even before the Revolution – so women went to university; that was no problem whatsoever. But many people in the poorer classes did not send their daughters to university; they married young or went out to work for economic reasons. It was boys first, of course, and I find that a lot of girls do get educated and then don't work. A girl goes to the faculty of engineering and trains as an architect, then she gets married – and that's it. In Egypt, half of the girls don't work or they're looking for a job where they don't really need to do a lot of overtime so they can go home and take care of the house and the children.

'I believe in equality of opportunity for men and women – of course I do; but I don't like women who force themselves to work and then develop a complex that they have to compete with men. She competes with her husband; she competes with her brothers. You know, it comes from women being frustrated from lack of opportunity in the past and some of them are overreacting. Some of my friends work just for appearance sake.

'I have an older sister and three younger brothers and we were brought up in a villa on the outskirts of Cairo in the fifties. The villa was in the presidential barracks and, after that, was the desert, so we had a very big garden for the security forces to guard. But it was a house – never a palace – although we did live in a palace in Heliopolis for three months while they were enlarging the villa. The palace was very elaborate and my father said, "I don't want my children to have such a life that they won't be able to go on after I die." So we went and lived in the president's second house in the Barrage, a village in the country, for the next seven months while they finished the villa.

'In the war of 1956 I was in Cairo and I remember aeroplanes going overhead and the lights blacking out, but I didn't see any fighting because we were 45 minutes away from the Suez Canal. All my childhood I was aware of attempts to assassinate my father, but I only heard about them when they were reported on the radio; we didn't have a TV at the time and I used to listen to my father's speeches and then I would know. Now, after raising my own children, I would say that we were very obedient, but it was unconscious – nobody ever told us to be. We had a fear inside us that we might do something wrong and cause his death, so we were very cautious children without being forced to be. It was out of love for our father.

'He was a very tender, very affectionate man towards his family. During vacations, it was sacred that at three o'clock all the family would gather at the table for lunch, or a quarter to four during schooltime. He was never late; he liked to sit with his family every day – something that most husbands don't do now. He was the president of a big country, but I spent a lot of time with him. Speaking with hindsight, I think he expected high intelligence from me; that I would understand everything and, since I was the daughter of Nasser, I would be very brave You know, bravery was always expected of me and I *was* very brave, but now I'm not. Then, it was expected.

'I met all the important guests from 1955 until 1970: Khrushchev, Kosygin, Tito, Nehru, Mrs Gandhi. Everybody who visited Egypt at that time was a head of state and my father was very proud to introduce them to his family. I always felt that they were like friends and we never had to wear uncomfortable clothes to the receptions because my father would never wear a black tie. The man who impressed me most was Pandit Nehru. He was so kind and I remember his voice – it was very, very soothing. I was so young that I'm just telling you about feelings; at the time I did not make any judgments, it was all feelings and all my responses were natural.

'President Tito came to Aswan every winter. I used to meet him with my father when he came to Egypt and we used to go to Yugoslavia. He was a very good friend of my father and I was close to him. For the last year of his life, he was on a life-support machine and I was praying for him to die because I had seen him in his powerful moments and every time I saw him on television he was just a vegetable and yet he was still President of Yugoslavia.

'He was getting sicker and sicker and that touched something inside me. It was a very touching experience for me and made me feel that if you are healthy, you exist and if you're not healthy you don't exist. After that, I started to become very health-conscious. Now I exercise and watch what I eat.

'I remember that my father's wish was to go to Paris. He used to say, "If I grow old and leave the presidency, I want to see Paris." We all studied Napoleon at school – it was obligatory – but he was educated during the English occupation, so he studied the English version of French history; the stress was on the history of the occupying countries – *the bastards*!

'You read in some psychology books that children of very famous, powerful people have an inferiority complex and hate being called "the daughter of . . ." They try all their lives to prove to the world that they are somebody else. I don't believe in this. I believe that you are born with gifts like the name of your family, and this is a gift from God. If I'm stopped in traffic and the policeman sees the name on my driving licence, he says, "Oh, you are the daughter of President Nasser. I'm so *honoured*." Instead of punishing me, he becomes *honoured*, so this is a gift. But I don't really go on trying to prove to the world who I am. I am happy. God chose me to have this name and I'm very grateful.'

Mona said she had never considered going into politics because she would always be compared with her father. 'I can have a role in charities in the social world, but politically I was never encouraged. I feel that we should give a chance to others. If I'd gone on carrying the name, people would never accept what I was doing as Mona because I am the daughter of Nasser. So I don't really do anything except very low profile things because of respect for the name; my father has done what he has done and that's it. He has opened so many doors and these doors are still open and so many things came through these doors. Life is going on. The English did not come back. People say, "If he was alive, he wouldn't have done this or that wouldn't have happened," but if he was alive he would have been 80 years old.

'Now there is no Soviet Union, for example, so you can't go on with the same thing. He used to play with the two powerful forces together: the Soviet Union and America, Communism and capitalism. How can you play two powerful forces together if there is only one? He did everything that was good at that time and I don't think that the second generation of a very important man who changed the history of our country should go on like that.

'It happened in India. Indira Gandhi was trained by her father and, when he died, she was mature enough to continue. I met her many times. She was a powerful woman. I met her with my father and, after he died, my mother and I went to India and we stayed there three weeks as her guests. She met us twice and she was really so nice to my mother. She treated her as if my father was still alive and he was the official guest of India. It was gracious. My mother was sick and she sent her a doctor and she used to phone every day to see how she was doing.

'The most important thing my father did was that he liberated the peasants in Egypt. If you read in history how badly peasants were treated, he eliminated the slavery of the peasants. This is a door which has been opened and which cannot be closed. This was after Farouk was deposed; the first two years were just getting into power and then he started the reforms and he shaped the classes very well. I notice now in Egypt a great difference between rich and poor. The population has increased, prices have gone up, but salaries have not kept pace. There is a very small middle class. There is so much poverty I feel guilty when I spend money, although my husband is wealthy.'

Mona's husband, Ashraf Marwan, was recognised as one of the most powerful men behind the scenes of Egyptian politics and there were unsubstantiated rumours that his huge fortune had been based on arms dealing. Mona shrugged off such accusations and talked instead about their relationship. 'I met Ashraf on Miami Beach in Alexandria. My aunt had a cabana and I used to go there to meet young people. At that age, you are attracted to handsome boys and Ashraf was handsome. I was friends with his sister and we started to play rackets on the beach. We started talking and we got along.

'Then I started thinking about my bodyguards, and it was a problem. When Ashraf told me he'd like to see me after the summer had finished, I told him it was impossible because, on the beach, you see people as equals. But after Alexandria we started to be closer anyway and I told him I had to tell my father instead of him finding out from Intelligence. So I told my mother and my father. Ashraf was in his final year at university in the faculty of science. My father said, "Wait until he graduates and gets a job and then we will talk about it." And that's what Ashraf did; he graduated with honours and worked for the army doing chemical research.

'His father was from upper Egypt, so we followed all the traditional procedure, which is for the father of the groom to meet the father of the bride. I booked an appointment with my father to meet Ashraf and his father. I remember that day very clearly: my father was dressed and he was waiting for them to come to ask for the hand of his daughter. And they were late. This was really something. Usually in Egypt and the Middle East, the groom would be punctual, but if he's going to ask for the daughter of President Nasser, then he should be even more punctual. My father started to get nervous. Then I remembered I had forgotten to tell security that they were coming and they'd been stopped outside. So I said to my father, "I didn't tell security. Did you tell them?" Of course not. So we called them and they let them in. Ashraf hasn't forgotten that, even now.

'We were married in a religious ceremony at my father's house in Cairo in July 1966, and spent a ten-day honeymoon in the north at Mersa Matruth. My father bought some land and was building a villa for me, but it was not finished, so I lived in one of the president's rest houses until I had my son, Gamal, who was born nine months and ten days after the wedding.'

Mona had been married for just one year when peace in the region was shattered by the Six Day War in which Israel inflicted a punishing defeat on Egypt and her Arab allies. It had a profoundly depressing effect on President Nasser. Mona said: 'I remember going to his room to ask him what was happening. He used to open his door and we could go in any time. It was a privilege that many children didn't have, which was having the office of our father in the house. He was so sad. I can remember only sadness. After that, he resigned, but it was not accepted. I remember people crying, millions on the streets, but if you're living it you just watch events happening and try to cope. Then, after that, he was sick. He had been diabetic since 1958. He rebuilt the army, but it was more difficult to rebuild the morale of the people. It was horrible – the loss of everything. He wanted to get back the land – that was his aim; to get back what was lost.

'I was still a student studying economics and political science at university and it was a little bit difficult for me to go on with my studies, so my son and I moved in with my father. I'm so happy I did because they were the last years of his life. He loved children and he was so attached to my son that every morning he used to have him with him at breakfast; he was part of breakfast. The butler would come and tell me, "The President has asked for breakfast, can we have Gamal?" Even when I moved into my own house, I used to send my son to be with him at breakfast. We lived in the President's residence for two years and I moved to my own house just months before my father died on 28 September 1970. I was pregnant with my second son and he was born less than nine months later on 13 June 1971.

'I was the only one of his children who was with him that day when he was taken ill. He had been at the Black September summit meeting with the Jordanians and the Palestinians* and he was very tired. After he had said goodbye to the Emir of Kuwait at the airport, he came back to the house and we were all gathered together as usual to have lunch because, even after my sister and I were married, we had to have lunch with him every day. He appreciated it very much and we loved it.

'After lunch, my sister went home and I stayed with my mother to have a chat. The house became quiet and my father said, "I feel that my sugar is going down. I don't feel well. Would you go and get me something sweet?" So I ran and got him something sweet to eat and he still wasn't feeling well and he asked for his doctor. The doctor arrived and I was in the living-room with my mother when another doctor came up the stairs, followed by another doctor. I went into my father's bedroom to see what was happening and he seemed well; he was sitting in his bed with so many doctors around him, but I started to suspect there was something wrong.

'My mother also started to get suspicious and she started reading the Koran and I was looking at her, but I still had denial that something was happening. Then we moved to the room beside him with the door open and we saw the doctors running about and I went in and he looked alive. I saw them with my eyes doing resuscitation; I saw them doing this and I still had denial. Then one of the doctors said, "The President is very ill. Call your brothers."

* King Hussein of Jordan took military action to drive the PLO out of their bases in Jordan in September 1970. Thereafter, Palestinians called this month 'Black September'.

'It was dark – it might have been six or seven o'clock; it was September and it gets dark around that time. So I called my brothers and they came and then the doctors closed the bedroom door and wouldn't let us in. Members of the government arrived and I suspected that something was wrong because nobody was ever allowed to come up the stairs to the first-floor living quarters, not even a minister, and I found these people coming to the first floor.

'So I started reading the Koran with my mother and then they let my brother, Khalid, go in and he came out and told us that my father was dead. I didn't believe it until my brother told me bluntly. He had to say, "Your father is dead." Without him saying that I would have been in denial for weeks. He died of a heart attack from overwork; he had been working so hard from 1967 to 1970. The doctors were the only people with him when he died, then they called the government into the bedroom, which was the first time in history that had happened. They let only important ministers in, the close ones, and after that we all went downstairs and had a meeting and they decided how to tell the people.

'After that, the Koran was recited on TV and radio and everybody was suspicious that something had happened to the President. Then it was decided that the Vice-President, Colonel Sadat, should go on the media and announce the death of Nasser and this is what he did one or two hours later. Sadat was very close to us. He had his political differences with my father, but he never changed towards us.

'I was more aware of the war in 1973 than in 1967 because my husband was involved. He was working with President Sadat as Secretary of Information. He was very close to President Sadat and he used to send him every day to a different country with messages to the kings and presidents of these countries. I didn't have first-hand information this time. I used to go and ask my father directly in '67, but in '73 I had to listen to the radio. We are a generation that is used to war and, in war after war after war, you just feel you will survive. I knew that we would survive all wars because we have always survived; Egypt has always survived. But for us it was always a world of war.

'I was in London when President Sadat was killed. I had been with him from the beginning of October, like five days before he died. I went to Egypt for my father's remembrance day on 28 September and I told Sadat we were moving to England with our children. We had dinner on the terrace of his bedroom. I had a chat with him and Jehan Sadat and it was very friendly. Then I came back to London and three days later he was shot, so I went back again to be with his family.

'Jehan had started social work and charity work while President Sadat was vice-president. She'd had this wish to work like that before. It was in her personality to have this role and she got it. She has opened a door with all these religious sheiks and fundamentalists that they couldn't really close fully. When you get some rights, you don't lose them easily and she has opened that door.'

Mona said that Suzanne Mubarak, wife of Sadat's successor, had continued to push at the opened door with her social work. 'Suzanne is very, very intelligent and very influential.' She said: 'When she gets into a project, she studies it and gives it all her time – she never does things vaguely and that's what I like about her. She loves children and her programme of setting up libraries has encouraged children to go back to reading.'

Mona denied accusations that her father had stashed away millions of pounds worth of assets during his presidency which had left the family wealthy after his death. 'I inherited 380 Egyptian pounds from my father,' she said. '[He also left] some life insurance, which he had taken out before the Revolution because he thought he might die, and some shares he used to buy in new companies as a promotion.

'I'm sure he didn't leave any more. Inside me, I am sure and then it's their problem. And being sure makes you walk with your head high. I know that as I know that I am Mona. So if they tell me, "You're not Mona, you're Mohammed," then it's their problem.' And with that Mona Nasser Marwan gave one of her engagingly deep chuckles.

6

Jewel of the Nile

AS SOON as Imelda Marcos, former First Lady of the Philippines, arrived in the Valley of the Queens in Upper Egypt, she started to experience a strange sense of *déjà vu*. When she entered the tomb of Queen Nefertari, who died circa 1255 BC, the feeling became overpowering.

Imelda whispered to her guide, Jehan Sadat: 'You know, Jehan, this is *me*.'

'No, Imelda, this is Nefertari,' replied Jehan Sadat, widow of President Anwar Sadat.

'No, I feel as though I was here many thousands of years ago.'

'Well, Imelda, I don't think so. She was the wife of Ramses II and you are Mrs Marcos. Look, there's not a single pair of shoes anywhere.'

Imelda, however, had become convinced that she was the reincarnation of Queen Nefertari, whose name means Beautiful Lady. She inspected the brilliantly painted tomb and was distressed by its state of decay. The tomb had been discovered in 1904 and salt water seeping through the limestone had reacted with air to crack many of the most beautiful murals.

Jehan Sadat told us: 'When we went outside, Imelda opened her handbag and she wrote a cheque for $1 million to renovate Nefertari's tomb. I looked at her and said, "You know, Imelda, you were right; it's *you*!" One million dollars! We renovated the tomb and it became one of our most colourful monuments.'

Jehan Sadat was as animated, unaffected and effortlessly charming as

Imelda Marcos was grandiose. A religious sheik noted for his devotion to Islam told Jehan during a speech at al-Ahzar University, 'When God distributed beauty, He gave half to you and half to the rest of the world.' Coming from a respected religious figure, this compliment caused quite a stir, but it was nothing more than an expression of the high regard in which the widow of President Sadat was held.

In the 11 turbulent years of Sadat's presidency, Jehan Sadat carved her place in Arab history as the first head of state's wife to become an active First Lady, fulfilling the sometimes incompatible roles of loyal spouse and social reformer. Until she arrived as the power behind the presidency, political wives were neither seen nor heard in Egypt. Yet with unflagging energy and great devotion she shared the intrigues and intricacies of presidential life, while still pursuing her own agenda in the highly sensitive area of women's rights.

Jehan's emergence as a women's liberator was due in no small part to the formidable task that faced her husband when he took over as president following Nasser's premature death in 1970; not only did he have to live up to the Nasser legend, but he was also plagued by Soviet interference in his country's affairs and crippling economic problems. Respecting his wife's deeply held beliefs about inequality, however, he gave her his full support in her campaign for women's rights. He also encouraged her when she decided to go to university at the age of 41, even guiding her choice of studies. She graduated top of her class and later became a professor.

That Jehan Sadat was able to lead a traditional life with a modern outlook was a tremendous achievement in itself, considering the sensitivities of the Muslim world. But she went much further. Her initiative in taking up women's causes and having laws changed to protect women and their families continued until her husband's assassination in 1981, despite the controversy that these changes inevitably provoked among fundamentalists. Other Egyptians criticised her use of power and resented the fact that she was not an elected politician. 'She should not have taken an office next to the President,' said one critic. 'She should have understood the delicacy of her position and taken things slowly, but she was in a hurry.' Not surprisingly, perhaps, many of the laws that Jehan was instrumental in bringing to the statute books were rescinded after Sadat's death; many, but not all.

Now a grandmother ten times over, Jehan Sadat entered the salon of the villa in which she and her husband had lived and in which she still spent half the year. She spent the other half at Great Falls, Virginia, not far from Camp David, scene of her husband's greatest political triumph. Dressed casually in striped trousers and a silk shirt, she was slightly plump, with only a little make-up emphasising her flawless skin, and green eyes that reflected warmth and good humour. She wore a pair of open-toed mules which looked as comfortable as she seemed to be with herself. She was like someone receiving a friend into her home, and it was clear that the thought of trying to impress never crossed her mind.

Built in French colonial style beside the River Nile, the Sadat villa was in a walled compound surrounded by dirty, crowded streets. To reach the huge, double doors, we walked through the compound's grounds, which had none of the manicured formality of a European garden. A butler ushered us along a high-ceilinged hallway towards a picture window with a view of the Nile. There were reception rooms to the right and left, and we were led into a salon decorated in muted gold, and offered tea. The salon was a large room with an alcove that, again, had windows overlooking the Nile. A large photograph of a uniformed President Sadat took pride of place on a table in the centre of the alcove, and photographs of their four children were dotted on occasional tables placed on either side of an antique sofa.

Born to an English mother and an Egyptian father, Jehan had several qualities that one associated with the British, like *politesse* and prompt time-keeping, yet her sense of hospitality was entirely Arab. Despite the six months she spent in the United States every year, she remained something of an enigma in the West. A former British diplomat recalled that he had been taken aback by the reverence which Egyptians afforded her. 'They treat her like royalty,' he said, 'but she is still very approachable.'

In common with other First Ladies in this book, Jehan Sadat's power was a potent combination of femininity and strength, mixed with a tenacious dedication towards her husband and a complete understanding of his ambitions and anxieties. A friend of hers also remarked on her loyalty: 'After Sadat became President, I thought Jehan would be too busy to keep up our friendship. But she made every effort to keep in regular contact and, when I got divorced, she could not have been more supportive, inviting me to receptions and making sure I was all right.'

Jehan's recollections of how she met Anwar Sadat were vivid and her lack of pretension in describing their humble backgrounds was endearing. 'My mother was from Sheffield and she was completely against us because the British don't understand marrying that young,' she said. 'I met my husband when I was on holiday from secondary school. I was 15 – no, actually, he attended my 15th birthday party, so I was 14. I was spending the holiday at my cousin's house at the Suez Canal and her husband was a close friend of Sadat.

'Sadat was in prison and he was talking about him all the time: how he was very devoted to his country and opposed to the British Occupation. My mother had taught me to love my country, Egypt, as she loved her country, England, and I was fascinated by this hero who was from a poor family and wanted the best for his country. I met him when he came out of prison.

'I fell in love with him – it was a love story – and when he came to ask to marry me, my mother started asking him one question after another until she came to the question, "What do you think about Sir Winston Churchill?" Without hesitating, he said, "Well, I think he's a thief." My God! I can't tell you – I still remember the print of the carpet; my eyes went down and I couldn't bring them up again. I said, "Well, that's the end of that – she'll never agree."

'After a while, he left and I called him on the telephone and said, "Why did you tell my mother that? You know she's British. You know she worships Winston Churchill. How could you tell her that?" He said, "Jehan, I can never say something which I don't feel. Maybe he is a hero, but he is a thief, and he robbed my country. We were occupied for 70 years and they robbed our country." I said, "Don't you know how to be diplomatic?" It took me a long time to prepare another meeting – two months at least.

'My mother was a teacher who used to read many books, and Sadat had been in prison for two years with nothing to do except read. They met again and my heart was beating. I knew if anything happened it would be the end. But he started talking about Charles Dickens and Somerset Maugham, authors she had read, and she fell in love with him and said, "Well, he's an honest man. Even what he said about Churchill was honest because he didn't want to please me." From that time, they respected each other and became very close friends.

'My father knew from the beginning that I liked him so much and wanted him. When my husband came into my life, he was poor – he was just out of prison with no job, no money, nothing. My cousin told him, "Anwar, tell her father that you are rich and you have branches of oranges and they will accept you." I said, "That's a very good idea," but he refused. He said, "No, I will never cheat your father."

'I said, "Anwar, I know you are poor and I am the one who's going to marry you, not my father. But they will not accept you if you say you are poor." He said, "You never, never cheat." I said, "Okay, but please don't start saying it. If he asks you, then you can say whatever you want." Of course, my father never asked him whether he was rich or poor. My father told me later on, "I knew he wasn't rich, but I respected the man so much and I know that you love him." He asked him not to get involved in politics, so that I would not be worried.'

Jehan said that she had never experienced any conflict growing up with mixed parentage. 'My father was Muslim, but he was not that religious,' she said. 'My mother was a Christian, but she wasn't religious either. She didn't go to church every week. But, as Muslims, we used to fast at Ramadan. He loved her so much that she left her country and came to Egypt to be with him. They had their family and were devoted to their children; it was such a lovely, warm atmosphere. My eldest brother was born in Liverpool, then the second one was born here, and then there were seven years between my brothers and me, and then my sister was born.

'My mother had lived with my father's family and she tried to bring us up as Egyptians, not British, although there was porridge for breakfast and at three o'clock she always had cookies or cakes for us. But she tried to speak Arabic. When World War II started, she couldn't go back to England, but after the war we went to England for a visit.'

Jehan said that even as a young woman she had had political ambitions, but had no idea where her political conscience came from. 'My father was not a politician and nor was anyone in my family, but I was always concerned about the situation in my country,' she said. 'My mother never forgot her country, even during the Second World War when she would never put sugar in her tea. She used to say when she was young during the First World War there was never enough sugar for the people. She instilled in me a love of my country by talking about her love for her country.'

Despite her husband's intense interest in Egyptian nationalism, Jehan had no idea that he would ever be president. 'He wanted to go back into the army, but the Minister of War had to decide whether he would accept him or not because he had been in prison several times,' she said. 'He was very tense and we went to a restaurant in Giza and there was a fortune-teller going around. He looked at my palm and said, "You will be the First Lady in this country." At this stage, we didn't have the money to pay the rent of the flat, the electricity, the water, the maid. My husband was very tense because it was his responsibility, and while we had nothing at all this man tells me, "You will be the First Lady in this country." At that time, we had the King, and I said, "Oh, I am going to be the Queen, am I?" It was a ridiculous thing to say and my husband was just listening, not even commenting. When we were walking over a bridge on the way back, I said, "Even if the army won't take you, I will give you a wonderful job with a high salary because I will be the First Lady in my country."

'He was laughing and that was at a time when we were wondering how we were going to pay the rent. Then there was a telephone call for him to see the minister and he was accepted back into the army on the understanding that he gave up his political work. He rejoined Gamal Abdel Nasser and all this time they were preparing for the Revolution. He couldn't take me with him because they were living in camps in the desert.

'I was dreaming if God gave me the opportunity, I would do something for children. I was too young at the time, but I was trying to help my husband to reach the people. I would sit with people and listen to their problems and tell my husband; acting as the liaison between them. The support of the wife is very, very important; it doesn't reflect only on her, but on him, and it helps the role of the man. My friends were still in secondary school and I wanted to go back and he encouraged me. So I started taking lessons, but then I became pregnant. I said, "My role as a mother is more important than any other thing." I had four children. I think I was a good mother; I gave them time, listened to them, tried to be friends, solving their problems, and that's why I didn't have any problem when they were teenagers, which so many people have. I was always with them, always.

'I married very young – not quite 16 – and after that I had my children and I was always dreaming and hoping and looking for my education. My husband said, "Jehan, it is not a certificate that matters – read, read That is real education." But I wanted to go to university and graduate. I went to university and I graduated at the top of my class. I have my MA and I have my PhD. I studied Arab literature at first, but my MA and my PhD were about comparative literature. The MA was about the influence of Shelley, and my PhD was about the influence of British criticism. My husband encouraged me so much, but when I was studying Arabic he was always telling me, "This is a very difficult thing for you to do. Why don't you study history – it's much lighter." But I insisted on studying Arabic because that is my language and I thought if I was to give speeches to people here it was better to know my language well.

'I wanted to help women to stand up for themselves, to live on their own, to fight, work, to go out, to teach themselves. When I went back to university, I was not young. If you can imagine when my husband was the President it was very difficult for me. At the beginning, maybe the professors thought I was just making a show, but I was always on time and did my best. My children were in the same university, although not, thank God, in the same classes. It was very hard because I had so many obligations as the President's wife. But nothing stopped me because I believe that where there's a will, there's a way. It's not easy, but at the end it's very rewarding.

'I always did things step by step. I didn't want to shock people. I started working in social activities before my husband became

President. I started in a rural area, helping women to depend on themselves and to feel their identity. That was when my husband was the speaker of the party. I was also involved with war refugees in '67. Once you do social activities, it's very hard to quit. Once you feel it, you will never quit because every day you feel that you have done something good for others. It's tiring, but it's very rewarding. At the beginning, people were shocked because they'd never had a First Lady working in social activities. I was the first.'

Jehan was aware that her campaign for the rights of women under Islam would bring her into conflict with Muslim traditionalists. She said: 'I would never do anything against Islam, but it was difficult because there are Muslim people who are narrow-minded and who want us to stay at home; they feel that is our role, just to bring up children and be good wives, and that's it, which is wrong.'

Echoing the view of Benazir Bhutto, she continued: 'Islam gives many rights to women and they never talk about it. But I believe if God gave me the opportunity to help others, why not? It's also something in my nature. Here in our country, and not only here – everywhere, even in the United States and Britain – there are so many things which need the help of women. When I was teaching at Cairo University before going to the United States, I used to take my students to see the welfare societies to feel the blessing of God. I used to take them to the disabled, which is one of my favourite causes and which I started here in Egypt, and orphan children and let them see how they live and go to school.'

Jehan then described how President Sadat had envisaged sitting down with the Israelis to hammer out a lasting peace in the Middle East. 'As a military man, he knew we had gone to war against Israel many times,' she said. 'The last time – in 1973 when he was President – he was the one to stop the war, actually, not the Israelis. He knew his soldiers, he knew that they could do something if they had a plan, if they prepared for it, and he was sure, almost sure, of winning. The day before he left home, he told me, "I know I'll win. I'm sure." I was surprised because we had been defeated several times.

'He didn't want to wage war for war's sake, he wanted to restore confidence in his troops and in the Arab world and to tell the whole world, "I want you to listen to me. I want to make peace." But he didn't want to go through the negotiations while we were defeated; he wanted to be on the same level as the Israelis. And this is what happened after we took Sinai.'

Declaring that he wanted a permanent peace deal, Sadat addressed the Knesset in Jerusalem, then, in September 1978, he met Prime Minister Begin at Camp David. Jehan said: 'President Carter played a wonderful role, especially during the peace process. He made such a wonderful effort.' The Camp David accord, however, was regarded by many Arabs as an act of treachery and Sadat was assassinated in front of his wife at a military parade on 6 October 1981, when four Muslim fanatics jumped from an armoured car, hurling grenades and firing automatic weapons.

'Even when I think about it now, I'm very surprised at myself,' said Jehan. 'I always reflect very calmly, not shouting, not screaming, even at the time of the assassination. I was with him and, when the bullets came, some of the ladies screamed and shouted and I said in a very firm way, "Please don't do that."

'It was a very confusing situation. I knew he was killed and yet I still had hope that maybe he would survive. I knew it, I knew it because I saw it, but they took him away very quickly in a helicopter to hospital and then I took another helicopter and came here. I took a car from here to go to the hospital. I had a feeling that maybe, maybe he was alive. When I went to the hospital, I found my children there and I looked at their faces. Every one was sitting, doing nothing, just looking. I wondered why a doctor didn't come out and tell me, "We're doing our best" or something. When nobody came, I felt it immediately and walked into the room. The doctors were standing there, crying, doing nothing.'

Many of Jehan's social reforms were rescinded after Sadat's death, 'but they weren't completely overturned,' she said. 'All of the projects which I started are not working as before, but recently the new Minister of Social Affairs has been giving attention to them and starting to change members and bring new blood into these projects to work as they were in the past. Now they are looking to bring in another law which I would love to see because of the continuity. We are better than other countries.'

Jehan said that she was aware of the hostility towards her in some sections of the community. 'Not everyone knows that I am half British and they were criticising me as a very forward woman,' she said. 'They hadn't seen someone like me before – that's why I was criticised severely, especially when the family law came out. There were demonstrations from one university against me, but it didn't stop me because you can expect something like that. But it hurts sometimes, the way they can talk about me. It hurts, but I never stopped. It's better than if we look back 30 years. I wish the rights would come quicker, but it is going on much better than before. In Arab countries, women are involved in so many activities. It is changing.'

Jehan said that women could evolve in Islamic societies 'by knowing their religion well, by knowing Islam, by educating themselves. I respect my religion and I follow it, yet I'm still working and travelling and meeting men and women and it isn't harming my religion at all. As long as I respect myself – that is the most important thing in Islam: our behaviour and our attitude.

'I wish every women knew her rights and behaved well and educated herself as much as she could and knew her religion well. When she knows her religion, she will understand that there is nothing against her working, against her being involved in activities or helping her country, helping her people – these are the things that God wants us to do.'

7

Star of David

A SCULPTED dove of peace sat like a talisman on the desk of Leah Rabin's office in Ramat Gan on the outskirts of Tel Aviv. White canvas blinds were drawn against the morning sun and Mrs Rabin was standing beside the desk dressed for work in a beige top and brown trousers. Having undergone a thorough check by a young security guard – testing the tape recorder for Semtex, a body search with an electronic metal detector and questions such as, 'Are you carrying any nerve gas?' – it was an immense relief to discover that Mrs Rabin was as unpretentious as her small, narrow office.

The first thing you noticed about this proud Jewish matriarch was her eyes, a piercing shade of blue, which were set against the long, raven hair that framed her Renaissance face. She had several gold bracelets on her arms and numerous chains, including a gold and lapis lazuli flower chain around her neck, but the piece that immediately caught the eye was a gold medallion of her husband, Yitzhak Rabin, the Israeli Prime Minister whose life had been sacrificed in the cause of peace.

The overflowing bookshelves, the numerous artworks and the framed family photographs in that tiny office signified an intelligent woman with an artistic temperament and a great attachment to her loved ones, but that, perhaps, was only to be expected in the woman who had twice been Israel's First Lady. It was, however, Leah Rabin's unbending political stance since her husband's murder that had made her a deeply controversial figure in Israel. While many respected her loyalty towards her husband's memory and his work, and admired the tremendous courage she had displayed in adversity, she was extremely unpopular with the government of Benjamin Netanyahu and his supporters, and it was not difficult to see why.

Coming straight to the point, Leah Rabin said: 'In Israel, things were tough because at the same time as my husband was conducting the peace process, the opposition – the Likud – and the religious groups started a campaign against him. He was the target of that campaign. He said, "I know peace has enemies from the Arab Muslim fundamentalist groups, the Jihad, the Hamas, the Hezbollah, and I know that there are enemies of peace in our society, yet I don't see an alternative road and so this is the road I am going to follow."

'And he also said – and this is something I want you to quote – he used to say, "I will continue the peace process as if there is no terror, and I will fight terror as if there is no peace process." In other words: yes, fight the terror, and, yes, continue the peace process, believing that once the peace process comes to its final destination, terror will lose its *raison d'être*.'

Do you feel the efforts of Prime Minister Rabin are now being let down by the people of Israel?

'Not the people of Israel, the Prime Minister; he's destroying the political process. He thinks the biggest achievement will be to destroy Oslo. Oslo was a terrible agreement, he said, it didn't take into account the security of Israel. Now, who are you, Mr Netanyahu, to put a question-mark on Yitzhak Rabin's concern for the defence and security of Israel? The man's crazy; he is crazy to challenge Yitzhak Rabin's integrity about the defence and security of Israel. He knows better?'

Do you think Mr Netanyahu has the support of the people?

'He has, unfortunately. He's a big demagogue and with a demagogue's ability you can influence many people who are naive or with very low education. And those are his followers. He has a following; there's no question about that. Yesterday there was a poll that shows he probably has over half [of the electorate] if there was an election tomorrow. This is frightening because this man is really leading us to disaster by denying the peace process. He doesn't want peace because his constituencies don't want peace. He's really trying his hardest to preserve his power and his seat and, as for the security of Israel and the peace of Israel, that is just talk.'

Leah Rabin's life and the politics of Israel had undergone a violent convulsion after the signing of Oslo II, the historic agreement between Israel and the PLO which required Israel to withdraw some of its military forces from the Occupied Territories, as well as extending Palestinian self-rule and setting up the first Palestinian elections. Anti-peace demonstrations among right-wing Israelis had taken a savage turn in the autumn of 1995 when Yitzhak Rabin was labelled a traitor to his country, and effigies of him in the uniform of a Nazi officer were hoisted in front of the TV cameras. One man shouted at Leah that she and her husband would be hanged from their heels in the town square after the next election 'like Mussolini and his mistress'.

Leah Rabin knew the risks at the sharp end of Middle East politics, but she had no forewarning of the tragedy that was to take her husband from her so brutally and decisively on 4 November 1995. The Prime Minister just had delivered a rousing speech to 200,000 supporters of the peace initiative at a rally at Kikar Malchei Yisrael – the Kings of Israel Square – in Tel Aviv and, with chants of 'Peace! Peace!' and 'We love you' ringing in their ears, the Rabins had prepared to leave. Leah wrote in her book, *Rabin: Our Life, His Legacy*: 'Yitzhak and I headed towards the car. I started down the stairs behind the stage on my husband's right. The crowd continued to press close, and Yitzhak stepped ahead of me. I was still on the stairs as Yitzhak moved to get into the car. "Where's Leah?" Those were the last words that Yitzhak uttered before the gunshots . . .'

Calmly producing a 9mm Beretta from his pocket, Yigal Amir, a right-wing law student at Tel Aviv's Bar-Ilan University, had fired three shots at Rabin from point-blank range. Two of the bullets struck the Prime Minister, mortally wounding him; the third hit one of his bodyguards. In the elections that had followed the assassination, Benjamin Netanyahu swept to power on a wave of hysteria and extremism and Leah Rabin found herself cast not only as the guardian of her husband's memory, but also as the defender of his beliefs.

LEAH RABIN was the daughter of Augusta and Fima Schlossberg, who had emigrated to Palestine from Nazi Germany in 1939 when she was nine years old. Her memories of that period are full of colour and happiness. Her father had acquired the lease of the Palatine Hotel in Tel Aviv and, with no austere German nanny to scold her, she recalls playing in the hotel's corridors and making friends with two waiters from the Sudan. Her mother, a middle-class woman from an affluent background, upholstered chairs and stitched new eiderdown covers. It was Augusta's stoic acceptance of their new life and Fima's love of music, art and poetry that instilled many of the qualities in Leah that became her trademarks.

She was still a high school girl when she met Yitzhak Rabin at an ice-cream parlour in Tel Aviv in the summer of 1943. He was then a 21-year-old officer in the Palmach, the youth branch of the Haganah defence league. He wrote in his memoirs: 'It began with a chance encounter in a Tel Aviv street, a glance, a word, a stirring within, and then a further meeting . . .' Leah remembers him as looking 'just like King David himself. His hair was a rich auburn, and his eyes were somewhat grey, somewhat green, and incredibly intense.'

They were married in Tel Aviv on 23 August 1948, during a ceasefire in Israel's first war with its Arab neighbours. When the rabbi arrived half an hour late, the groom, used to precise military time-keeping, announced: 'This is absolutely the last time I'm getting married.' Yitzhak's own upbringing as the son of politically active Russian immigrants, Rosa and Nehemiah Rabin, set the pattern for the union.

'Very early in our married life, I realised my husband's profound desire that I should not be a committed career woman,' said Leah. 'Really deep down in his heart he wanted me to be at home with the children. He grew up in a home with a working mother, both parents were working, and he had very strong memories of coming home from school and his parents not being there. They were not only working, they were also very active in other levels of life – in security, in social affairs – so they were often out for meetings in the evening and the children were left alone. He was the elder brother and felt responsible for his younger sister and he did appreciate that part of his childhood memories very much.

'What he had in mind was that, in his life, when his children came home from school, their mother should be there. So it was not a question of a dispute between us, but I was teaching school – I didn't have my own car and had to take two buses – and he said, "What is the point of killing yourself for so little money? There is no sense in that – you should give up your job." I sensed that it was beyond the question of the money; it was really his profound need that I should be at home as long as the children were young.

'I accepted it with no resentment at all and after the Six Day War he was asked in a very popular radio programme [My Parents' Home], "You were raised in a home where the parents were always away and you emphasise that you felt uncomfortable about that and now you yourself are never home for your children." He was the commander-in-chief of the Israeli Army and, even before that as a military man, he was rarely at home, really. And that was the reason he so very much wanted me at home. So his answer was, "Yes, but my children have their mother at home with them."

'At that point, the way he said it, I said, "Leah Rabin, this is the essence of what it really means to him." And I also sensed that as he was fulfilling such important roles – at that time, it was defence; later, it was other things – he deserved this little luxury. We didn't have money to have a housekeeper or a nanny, so it was either me or nobody. Today, it would have been a different option. Today, young women go out to work; they don't stay at home. The norms have changed very much and there are alternatives: there are day-care centres for young children and maybe the pay is different and the wife of the commander could more easily afford for someone to be at home with the children.

'Forty years ago, this was the scene. However, later, when the children grew up and weren't so dependent or, for that matter, left home, I took all kinds of social work and responsibilities upon myself. He was immensely supportive of me playing any role I wanted and not only supportive – I also think he was very proud of me. He realised that I accomplished things and that people wanted me very much.'

Leah became active in several organisations, primarily the Autistic Society, the Shiba Medical Centre and two important museums. 'Whenever we asked him to a charity function or important gala, he was always there,' she said. 'He always came for me because he realised that I was always there for him. So from time to time I needed his support, and it was enormous support if the Prime Minister came to a function. He was very, very generous in that way. Finally, it gave me the ability to meet the challenges of public speaking, of dealing with the public, which unfortunately after the murder, I'm constantly exposed to.'

When did he decide to go forward with the peace process?

'It was always on his mind; from way back this man knew what we needed was peace with our neighbours. Unfortunately, we were so unwelcome when Israel was reborn that we were invaded by seven Arab nations and barely made it through that first year of 1948. After 1948, my husband came to the conclusion that we had to build a very strong army if we really want to survive in the area. He realised that we would be attacked again; that our neighbours would try to destroy us again and again, and only when they realised that it was impossible, that we were indestructible, only then could we aspire to peace.

'So on the one hand he was fully aware of how desperately we needed a strong army, but at the same time, he was always thinking of the day when our neighbours would realise we were indestructible and come forward for peace. After the Six Day War, a huge victory when we occupied the whole Sinai desert, the whole West Bank and the whole Golan Heights, he went to the Prime Minister, Mr Eshcol, and said, "I think I've done my share with the Israeli Army and I want to go to Washington." As ambassador in Washington, he could expect support for a peace process and, from then on, he really started working on it.'

In Washington, Leah developed the skills of a political hostess. 'I put into practice several rules of entertaining, such as taking great care in seating arrangements and avoiding serving the same menu,' she said. Secretary of State Warren Christopher liked dining at the 'Rabin restaurant', but Henry Kissinger thought the food prepared by their Hugarian cook was 'too heavy'. Leah understood the value behind the tedium of diplomatic functions. 'While courtesy visits and dinners are usually assumed to be superficial affairs, important signals can be communicated through these channels.'

Although Leah would not necessarily describe herself as a politician, her instincts and understanding of what was going on around her contributed greatly to her husband's political success. 'The first thing he had on his mind was finding avenues to Egypt because he realised that Egypt was the strongest Arab nation, the leading factor, and peace with Egypt would mean a lot,' she said. 'But the first attempts failed. Then after we returned from Washington and after the October war in 1973, he became Prime Minister a year later in 1974 and the first thing he started was trying to come to an interim agreement with Egypt. Together with Dr Kissinger, this materialised in September 1975. So the interim agreement was already the vision and the decision of my husband and his sense of commitment.'

With no established protocol for the Prime Minister's wife in the young country, Leah had to create her own role. At a particular low in German-Israeli relations, she organised an official dinner on the patio of the Prime Minister's residence for Chancellor Helmut Kohl. After dinner, she asked the Israeli singer Ora Zitner to sing songs about Jerusalem, which prompted Israeli guests to sing along. Leah knew that Jerusalem was a controversial issue, but she wanted to make a point. Afterwards, Chancellor Kohl said: 'I am a very experienced, long-time politician, but you have moved me to tears.'

'Later, when Sadat came to Jerusalem, my husband wasn't Prime Minister any more; he had resigned and Labour had lost and it was Mr Begin. But I can tell you he was such a patriot that he celebrated; he was so patriotic he didn't mind, he didn't say grudgingly, "Why not me? Why am I not the one to meet Sadat?" No, he was happy that Sadat came. We were in America and he rushed to Israel to be there for President Sadat when he arrived in Jerusalem and, later, he was invited to the White House when they signed the Camp David accord. I watched him – and he had no role in that – and I was so happy and so proud of him. The country was always bigger and more important than himself.'

How did you feel playing a part in history?

'I didn't realise that I played a part in history. Not that I was playing; that my husband was playing and I was privileged and fortunate to be with him.'

What were the most memorable moments in the peace process?

'First of all, the handshake with Yasser Arafat on the White House lawn [on 13 September 1993] was a wonderful moment, a wonderful moment that I shall never forget. But the handshake was only a symbol and then after that you started working on it. Then we came to Cairo to sign some maps to make a step forward with the peace process, but we anticipated problems with Yasser Arafat in the discussions towards the agreement the next day. We, the ladies, took a ride on the Nile, and I went to sleep around midnight and my husband came in at three o'clock in the morning and he said, "No problem. Everything went very well." And he was very happy.

'So the next morning we got up and got dressed and it was such a feeling of something festive: another stage of the peace process was going to be completed. And I remember we were standing on the terrace at the Hilton and taking a picture with the Nile behind us and we were really happy that morning. As we were arriving at the Congress Centre for the ceremony, I said, "I feel more excitement today than when we were going to the White House for the handshake because that time it was like a beginning, and a symbolic beginning, but now you have the feeling it materialises already. This is the realisation of the symbol and therefore it has maybe much more meaning."

'So I was really bubbling all over from joy. Then there was a difficult moment. All of a sudden, on the stage, my husband discovered that Yasser Arafat hadn't signed where he needed to sign. There was a big struggle on the stage and then Suzanne Mubarak, whom I sat next to, said, "They should get off the stage. They'll never solve it on the stage." And when they did get off the stage the problem was solved in five minutes and everything was okay.

'But there was always tension and long discussions and long dialogues; it wasn't easy. But, yes, they signed in Cairo and then there was Oslo and then we came to Washington again and then, in the presence of the whole world and all the prime ministers and all the foreign ministers, it was officially signed in Madrid. There was a sense of wonderful achievement and wonderful joy; we were opening a new chapter; we were looking forward with so much hope to a better tomorrow in the Middle East.'

Did your husband have any contact with King Hussein?

'All the time. He used to meet Hussein very discreetly from time to time, or Crown Prince Hassan, and they were on very good terms; you can say they were friends. But each time he used to come back and say, "It was wonderful, but no case to answer because King Hussein said,

'Give me everything or nothing.'" Only when the peace process with the Palestinians started and King Hussein realised he may miss the goals, then peace with Jordan was easy.

'They say, "You make peace with your enemies, not your friends," and I always repeat this about Yasser Arafat. I say, "Why do you accuse my husband of shaking the hand of Yasser Arafat? Was it better to shake the hand of Sadat? Were his hands not stained with blood?" Okay, he was head of state and not a terrorist and remember how many battles we had to fight and how many people we lost on the battlefields with Egypt, so this was an enemy and when he came to Jerusalem we welcomed him; we were so overjoyed when he came. But with Hussein it was different; he was never an enemy. He was always like a latent friend.

'I remember we were standing in the White House and we were about to go out for the ceremony of the first official handshake between King Hussein and my husband [to end the state of war between Israel and Jordan]. I was standing with Queen Noor and Tipper Gore and I said, "I'm so excited because this is really the first time I've laid my eyes on the King." I knew about all the meetings he had had with my husband. He was always "the neighbour from over the border" and we never felt any particular animosity towards him.

'I will tell you a story to the contrary: in September 1970 King Hussein ousted the PLO from Jordan. At that time, there was a situation that was a little tricky for Jordan because Assad of Syria was threatening, "If you don't stop, I will move my tanks into your country." They called my husband, who was ambassador in Washington, and said, "Ask your government if they will come to the support of King Hussein."

'He contacted Golda Meir and the answer was yes and that was enough. Assad withdrew his tanks and King Hussein ousted the PLO. That was September – the Black September – and two months later I was at a cocktail party in Washington and the Chief of Protocol, Ambassador Andrew Mossbacher, came to me and asked me, "How is the food at Sisco's place?" Joseph Sisco was American deputy secretary of state at that time and we sometimes dined at his home. I said, "Why do you ask such a question?" He said, "Because I'm invited to a stag dinner there tonight in honour of King Hussein." So a few moments later, I decided to send a message to the King. I told Ambassador Mossbacher, "Please tell the King that I'm sending our regards and that we have great admiration for the courageous and wonderful way he handled himself with the PLO in September."

'I thought, "Who knows if Ambassador Mossbacher will really give him that message?" The next morning at 7.30 a.m. – now 7.30 in Washington is five o'clock anywhere else; you don't call people at 7.30 –

he called me at the ambassador's residence. A voice said, "Mrs Rabin? Ambassador Mossbacher wants to talk to you." This made me realise it was for real: if he just wanted to tell me something he could have waited, but he was so excited – 7.30 in the morning! He had such a very low voice, "Mrs Rabin, we all have our problems. Probably King Hussein has more problems than most of us. You made the man so happy last night." He said that when he saw the King to his car, before he said goodbye, [Hussein] said, "Please remember to send my regards to the Rabins." So you see there was a latent and hidden relationship. I wonder if he remembers. But for me it was a very daring decision to send my regards to the King. I was very impressed with him – he's a wonderful human being. He's everything: he's brilliant and he's warm and he's charming and he's a friend. I really love the man.'

You mentioned the incident about Mrs Mubarak. Did you feel there was some kind of unity among the leaders' wives?

'Yes, in a way. We got together several times, Suha Arafat and myself; for instance, we used to go out together in Spain. There was this prizegiving ceremony at Oviedo when the Crown Prince of Spain gives awards to people who excel in science, art, literature, education and philosophy and that year they decided to give this award to Yasser Arafat. So we were there together. We had lunch with King Juan Carlos and Queen Sofia in the palace at Moncloa near Madrid, then we went to Oviedo for this ceremony.

'The Queen comes but the King does not come because it is the Prince's day. We spent a whole afternoon together, and we were sitting, [Suha Arafat] and I, and we didn't understand Spanish, so we were quite bored. Later, we were together in Oslo when they got the Nobel Peace Prize and I saw her again in Washington. She didn't come the first time for the handshake, but she came for the signing of Oslo II, and there was Mrs Mubarak and Queen Noor. I met Queen Noor several times, once at the handshake in Washington, then the signing of the agreement in the Arava desert near Aqaba, then we came again when my husband had an interview with the King.'

Would you say the relationship among the women was warm?

'Yes, very warm. It was lovely, they came for the signing. I remember we were standing on the second floor of the White House with Hillary Clinton waiting for Queen Noor who was stuck in traffic, so in the meantime she showed us around her home. But about Suha Arafat: she is wonderfully accessible and a very natural, disarming person. Not for one moment does she set aside her role as representative of the Palestinian people. Nor does she forget that Palestinian women are still sitting in Israeli jails. I must say that there wasn't one time when she met me that she didn't say, "Your husband has to release the Palestinian women." She never skipped one opportunity to remind me.'

She is rather controversial among the Palestinian women. There are those who are very supportive of her, but there are those again . . .

'Why?'

Well, a lot of people feel that she pushes herself to play a role. You know how Arabs are? They like the woman to be . . .

'In the kitchen.'

. . . in the kitchen, but they don't like it that she's . . .

'Too outspoken?'

What qualities do you admire most in women?

'First of all, intelligence, a certain level of culture, because I myself like art. I love art, and I love to talk about books and I love to talk about art so this is something I appreciate in women if they are well read and if they are in the circles of art and music and those are qualities that are appealing. I don't want to say what I like in women because I like the same in men. Integrity and warmth and standing for certain values that I appreciate like family.

'I'll put it this way: I judge women maybe even more than men by their priorities. What role in her life is more important to her: to be a mother, to be a wife, to be a good friend, and then her career and her education. For a woman *nothing* should be more important than her children or her husband for that matter. Then you see if you can then function on other levels.'

What effect did your husband's political career have on your children?

'It didn't have much effect on my children because we were very modest and we never exposed them. They always realised that to be the children of their father was a commitment and a responsibility rather than a privilege; maybe they are privileged to have had such a wonderful father who very much loved them, but in society this doesn't give them any privileges; to the contrary it puts them in the position of extra commitment, extra responsibility and extra realisation that we are being watched and we must not fail.'

Do you feel that's a burden for them sometimes?

'Unfortunately, since the murder, they all emerged into the public eye and into public encounters. We are constantly in demand to attend various ceremonies to accept various awards. We share it because not one person can do it all, so sometimes my son goes, sometimes my daughter goes and sometimes I go and we all go quite a lot. I may go most because I don't work and they have to work, but they do a lot with their work. But all of a sudden they are in the frontline.

'The other day we were together on a television programme and the anchor said, "You are actually the Kennedys of Israel." I didn't have the chance to respond to him, but if I had had the chance to say anything I would have said, "Yes, the resemblance between the Kennedys and us – and there isn't much resemblance – but if there is one it is that we are very strong together. We are very close and we feel a great commitment and responsibility one towards another." And I think that is the nice thing about the Kennedy family. There is a feeling "we are the Kennedys" and the Kennedys stand for something and, of course, Teddy Kennedy who is now the head of the family feels a great responsibility for every one of the Kennedys. So whenever, God forbid, a tragedy happens they are always together.'

Do you feel your children can play an important political role?

'Yes, I think so. I would like to see that. I am sometimes asked, "Would I?" and I say I would.'

But why not? You are an international figure.

'If someone came to me and offered me, shall we say, a diplomatic job, I think I would accept to represent my country. It's out of the question right now with this government who will never offer me anything. But under different circumstances this might be a reality. But I would not enter the political arena because in politics you need to fight for every position. They don't come to you and say, "Would you please become this or that?", you have to fight for it. I say, "For 50 years I lived with a man who had to fight for every position and I was part and parcel of this struggle. Would I start all over again now that I've lost him? No way." If they had something that would be appealing to me, if they come to me and offer me something, then I might accept it, but not if I have to struggle for it. Except for the image of my country and the memory of my husband, for that I'm struggling; I'm struggling all the time.

'Since this horrible murder and since I am travelling so much in the world, I am constantly – but really constantly – approached by Arab people, Muslim people from all over the region, no matter if there are relations between the countries or not – people from Saudi Arabia talk to me on the streets of London or in a restaurant in Paris. The other day I was standing in the entrance of the Churchill Hotel in London and there was a princess from Kuwait and she said, "May I shake your hand? Your husband was a wonderful man." You know, even Arafat made a discreet visit to our home to pay his respects. He was very upset, he was very shaken.

'I think I did play an important role in the peace process. I don't think I was ever so popular as I am now since I lost him. That puts me on a different level of popularity, support of the people and love of the people. For instance, I visited a school that carries my husband's name and they had a big ceremony prepared, with dancing and singing and quoting things that he had said over the years, and there was this lovely, lovely togetherness between me and those children who are in their teens – 13, 14. You should have seen the outpouring of love when the ceremony was over. They all came to me – the girls – and said, "Can you hug me, I love you so much." With tears in their eyes; boys as well. It's a new generation – boys kiss!

'Whenever you go to this place where he was assassinated you see people there most of the time, you see flowers there, you see candles there. All the time people pass because it's in the centre of town. Also people come all the time to the cemetery and to the tomb. We have a weekly meeting on the spot where he was assassinated. There is a memorial that was done by an architect and a sculpture and he chose an earthquake as a symbol. Where he fell is where an earthquake was.

'We are there every Friday afternoon; it varies between 50 and several hundred poeple who come together. We sit and sing and sometimes a politician will come and say a few words to the people, sometimes I say a few words. Always someone opens the book and reads quotations of what my husband used to say. So it is a very interesting phenomenon that since his murder two and a half years ago people do have the need to come and be there on that spot. They were strangers to me and now I know most of them.

'I still go through hell, actually, most of the time. I miss him so much. He was uprooted from our house, from our life, so abruptly, so suddenly, from a good, productive, active, wonderful life that we shared for . . . we would have now celebrated our 50th anniversary this year.'

8

Fatah's Secret Weapon

NIDAL, a two-and-a-half-year-old child, slept soundly in his cot while his 16-year-old sister, Hanan, read in her bedroom down the corridor. Their parents were downstairs in the small room that served as a makeshift office. The mother was urging her workaholic husband to retire to bed, but he stubbornly refused. There was simply too much work to do and his responsibilities rested heavily on his shoulders. The simple white villa, protected by a lone security guard, was located in Tunisia, far away from the Middle East flashpoints. Yet it was to be the scene of a violent murder that would result in recurring nightmares for the sleeping toddler Nidal.

'My husband, Abu Jihad, had a meeting outside our home and he came back at about ten to eleven at night,' his wife, Umm Jihad, told us in the first interview she had ever given about the events of that April night in 1989. 'I arrived after he did, within minutes. We stayed up, talking and joking, and Hanan, our daughter, was with us. She was telling him about a dream she had which was a bit disturbing. In Hanan's dream, she saw her father going to Jerusalem on a white horse. Then she went to her room.

'It was past 12.30. He was still asking me to make telephone calls for him, but I felt tired and I got ready for bed. I asked him to come and get some rest, too, but he was still at his desk, writing and making calls on the phone. He told me he had a lot of work to finish.

'Suddenly, I heard a noise. Abu Jihad shot up from his desk to reach for his gun. Then I heard, if you like, a cry let out by people who were breaking in. I asked him what was going on, but he did not reply. He walked out of the study to investigate. I was right behind him when I saw four armed, masked men. Abu Jihad had his gun in his hand, ready to fire. He immediately fired one shot, which made them retreat a bit. By now, both of us were at opposite ends of the corridor. Abu Jihad was trying to keep me away from them.

'Suddenly, the first armed man shot at Abu Jihad, aiming at his arm. His gun fell from his hand to the floor and broke, then the man shot Abu Jihad all over his body. His body turned as he was falling to the floor and I rushed over to him to embrace him, to hold him. The armed man directed his machine-gun at my back and, without speaking, signalled an order with his hand that I should go back and face the wall. The machine-gun was still pointed in my direction and at my back. Every time I tried to turn my head left or right he would signal me once more to turn my face back towards the wall. At that moment, I started to recite Qura'an [the Koran] and say *al shahadatine* [a Muslim prayer] as I knew my life was about to be over any second.

'Suddenly, another armed man broke in and shot at Abu Jihad while he was still on the floor. I was terrified. Then a third armed man came in and fired his gun; I was petrified. And a fourth armed man came in and fired; I was terrified once more. I felt that they were heading towards our bedroom as I could hear the guns being fired all around the room. There was not anybody there but my youngest son, Nidal, who was in his bed, so I believed they had killed him, too, and my resistance, or endurance, began to falter. I started screaming out loud, "*Bas!*" I let out that cry after a fifth armed man broke in and proceeded to shoot at Abu Jihad while he was stretched on the floor. Enough, I thought, you have already killed him. What more do you want? Then I heard a female voice yell at them from the bottom of the staircase in French, "*Allez, allez! Vite!*"

'They ran down the stairs. At that moment, Hanan, woken up by the noise, came face to face with them when she came out of her bedroom. She was shocked and asked what was going on? They told her in broken Arabic, "Go to your mother." She started screaming because she was terrified. I held her to my bosom and told her, "You are 16 years old and your father has been made a martyr. You know that your father is a good man."

'The Tunisian mortician said there were 75 bullets in Abu Jihad's body. Why so many? I asked myself that question at the beginning. It is said that each of the responsible authorities who participated [in the assassination] had a representative. Each of the Israeli security forces had one man, yet they are supposed to be one authority. The Israelis have confessed in one way or another because the decision was taken in a small cabinet meeting under Shamir.'*

Umm Jihad, or Mother Jihad, aka Intissar Al Wazir, sat in the dilapidated Ministry of Social Welfare at Ramallah – bare, whitewashed walls, a desk, the Palestinian flag and a few wooden chairs. As is customary in Arab tradition, some women were airing their grievances over cups of coffee. Umm Jihad saw them to the door with promises that she would do everything in her power to resolve their problems.

Petite, slightly plump and dressed in a black linen dresscoat relieved by a black-and-white chiffon scarf and simple pearl costume earrings, this unassuming woman had played an important role in Palestinian politics since the age of 15. Assured and self-possessed as a teenager, she had showed fearless courage in breaking away from many of the Arab conventions that shackled the women of the region.

'People are sensitive in different ways,' said Umm Jihad. 'Some are pioneers in their own field and I consider myself as such – one of those who believed in struggling for the sake of our homeland. Of course, when I joined Fatah, I always believed that I could be made a martyr at any second; I could be captured or wounded. I was not looking for status or a title. My homeland was occupied, my people were dispersed, so I was struggling for the right of these people to return to their homeland and win the freedom to determine their own destiny and to establish an independent Palestinian state with Jerusalem as its capital. Those were the goals that I had built my beliefs upon from the beginning.'

Shunning the limelight, and virtually unknown in the West, Umm Jihad had struggled to bring up a family by working as a teacher to supplement her husband's income in various parts of the Arab world. Fatah had been founded as an underground cell of Palestinian activists by Yasser Arafat/Abu Amar and Khalil Wazir/Abu Jihad in 1957. (Abu means Father in Arabic; Umm means mother). 'As a Palestinian girl, I had witnessed with my own eyes the disastrous *Nakabe* [catastrophe] and its effects on the lives of Palestinians,' said Umm Jihad. 'I also lived under the Israeli occupation in the Gaza strip in 1956. I lived all these experiences which directed me towards working actively with the movement or *Thawra*. So I joined Fatah in 1959 soon after it was established. I met my husband there and I continued to work with him in a consistent, systematic way until we got married in 1962 and I continued working with Fatah after that. I did not stop for one day.

---

* Yitzhak Shamir was Prime Minister of Israel at the time of Abu Jihad's 'assassination'.

'It was difficult for my children and there was great pain as a mother to see them disrupted by the continual moves. I was deeply saddened each time we left or moved. In Lebanon, I always felt secure and stable. My children were happy there and had their own friends. They were surprised each time we moved, although they understood it. We did not have a normal life. Even when we all moved to the same country, we lived in separate homes for security reasons. It was important for both myself and my husband to make sure that our children lived as much a normal life as possible under the circumstances, so that their own lives did not suffer because of our own. But they understood. We were Palestinians in the Diaspora and we had no choice.'

Her voice was firm but gentle, her commitment to the cause of Palestinian rights absolute. Having initiated social welfare programmes in the PLO, including pensions and other assistance to the widows and children of the men killed in the struggle, she was now determined that Palestinians in the new, emerging entity should have a social programme that protected them and served their needs. Her vision, coupled with her abundant energy, had already ensured successful programmes for former detainees of the Israelis. A total of 25,000 former prisoners had completed these programmes, which consisted not only of counselling, but also practical training for a trade, as well as university courses.

Yet despite the practical nature of her work and many disappointments, Umm Jihad's power was vitally evident and, like Jehan Sadat in Egypt, she was committed to ensuring that Palestinian women knew their rights and she was very active in her support of campaigns against violence towards women (a taboo subject in the Arab world), as well as actively encouraging women to work.

'Work is an essential element of an Arab woman's life, as is education,' she said. Even in the confines of Arab tradition, she saw no contradiction. 'By organising her time well, she can fulfil her role as a mother and as a working person in any field. If she is organised, she can prove herself at work and be a good mother. The two do not contradict, or do not have to contradict each other.

'Arab women have reached high degrees in education, despite the fact that we still have a degree of illiteracy. And because of recent economic hardship in Arab society, Arab women have gone to work and found their place. The Arab woman is not, and should not be, restricted to certain fields of work.'

INTISSAR means Victory in Arabic and as a teenager she was active in the struggle for liberation, acting as a courier for her cousin, the dashing Khalil Al Wazir. Her job was to pass on messages and to distribute propaganda leaflets in Gaza, which had become a refugee camp for displaced Palestinians. 'My mother discovered once that I was carrying grenades in an orange basket,' she said. 'She was very frightened. She said I'd be killed by the Israelis, but I said to her, "Mother, we will have no life unless we fight back for our homes."'

She did not see Khalil again for three years after 1956 when he moved to Egypt, where he was jailed for his political activities. When they did meet again, it was purely by chance. An acquaintance in Gaza asked her if she would like to meet an important Palestinian leader, an invitation that she readily accepted. 'I was taken to a secret meeting place,' she told Yasser Arafat's biographer, Alan Hart. 'There were quite a few people there. Most of them were talking in small groups. It was like a cocktail party without drinks. Then I saw Khalil. We were pleased to be with each other again and we talked. After some time, I whispered to him, "Who is this very big leader I am supposed to be meeting?" Khalil was serious and he began to search the faces. I followed his eyes. Then he said to me, "Don't you see him?" I said, "No, tell me." Then he smiled. "It's me, Khalil Wazir, that you have come to meet!"'

Khalil asked Intissar if she was prepared to fight for the freedom of Palestine and when she replied, 'Yes, of course,' he insisted on explaining that this was not a game, that there would be sacrifices, torture and even death. But for Intissar, these were not issues. She had seen too much of what it was like to be occupied in her homeland: the indignity, the continual humiliation. Khalil then asked Intissar to marry him and she accepted.

From 1959, she travelled with Khalil Wazir/Abu Jihad as his assistant and fiancée. She was privy to the entire Fatah underground network, the names of its members and the various codes they used in messages. At any time, she could have have taken over if Khalil had been arrested or assassinated. They had planned a summer wedding in 1960, but Khalil was under pressure from Yasser Arafat and Fatah's new central committee to delay the nuptials because it was felt that this would distract him from his political work. Intissar hid her disappointment and carried on as Abu Jihad's assistant. Her continued presence at his side was perceived as scandalous by traditionalists in the community because respectable young girls simply did not travel unaccompanied with a man. But Intissar ignored the gossip, believing that her mission was far more important than any damage to her reputation.

Intissar and Khalil were finally married in Gaza in the summer of 1962 and spent their honeymoon on secret missions in the Arab world. The young couple's purpose was to build up support for Fatah. 'I spent my honeymoon in meetings and more meetings,' said Intissar. 'Most of the time we slept either on planes or in cars.' She met Yasser Arafat in Kuwait during this period when Abu Jihad introduced her to him as 'Fatah's secret weapon'. Arafat, who was living in the kingdom ostensibly as an engineer, came to pick them up at the airport. 'He was courteous, warm and friendly,' Intissar said. 'In time, he became like a brother to me and a father to the children.'

The relationship that developed between the young couple and Yasser Arafat grew deeper in the coming decades. Abu Jihad told Alan Hart: 'We believed, Arafat and me, that it was only military actions that could fix the Palestinian identity. That was our slogan. What did we mean? We were convinced that our first task was to prove to the Arab regimes that we Palestinians still existed and that our problem could not be swept under the carpet. We were young and naïve about many things in those days, but we knew that guns spoke louder than words in the world of big powers. You can say that we had to speak the same language as those that wanted us to disappear.' Leah Rabin had made exactly the same point in describing her husband's attitude towards the defence of Israel.

No sooner had Intissar settled in Kuwait as a young wife for six brief months than it was decided by the central committee that her husband should proceed to Algeria, which had been newly liberated from French rule. President Ben Bella had promised Arafat that an office for the Palestinians could be established in the capital, Algiers. This was an important step for the young Palestinian movement because it gave them their first chance to break free from the clutches of Arab states that tolerated their activities with great reluctance and often with open opposition.

It was decided by the committee that in order to save expenses, or, more accurately, due to the lack of funds, Abu Jihad should proceed alone and that Intissar should return to her family in Gaza. Changing his appearance and adopting a new identity as Ala Ben Amar, Abu Jihad proceeded to Algiers on his own. Intissar's return to her father's home once again exposed her to gossip from the neighbours and concern from her family, who assumed that the marriage had foundered. Intissar had to keep her own counsel, assuring them that her husband was working in Beirut.

For six months, the Algerian authorities came under tremendous pressure from other Arab states over the Palestinian presence in their midst and would not allow Abu Jihad to enter his office. Finally, he was informed that he had to leave the country. Unperturbed, Abu Jihad refused to go. 'I am sitting here because President Ben Bella gave us his word,' he said. 'If I am now to be thrown out into the street, the President must come here and do it himself.' His cool reaction resulted in the establishment of the first-ever Palestinian office, known as the Palestine Bureau. President Ben Bella accorded it the full status and privileges of a political mission. This was the breakthrough that the movement had been waiting for because it gave them a window to the world through which to promote the Palestinian cause.

Intissar joined her husband in Algiers and found work as a teacher during the day. 'At the time, I was a teacher involved in arabization as it was the days of the arabizing campaign or T a'areeb in Algeria,' she said. 'I was therefore the breadwinner because his work was voluntary.' At night, she continued with her role as Abu Jihad's assistant. Khaled Hassan, a member of the central committee at the time, said: 'Not many people knew it, but we could not have kept the bureau going without her. Without the money she earned as a teacher, we could not have paid the expenses of running the office. In those days, and for some years to come, we were flat broke as an organisation.'

A turning point in the Palestinian struggle came when Khalil was invited by Chinese diplomats in Algiers to visit China. Yasser Arafat went with him, but the two leaders failed in their request for Chinese arms to begin an armed revolution. The Chinese did not believe that guerrilla warfare in the occupied territories was a viable proposition, but promised to assist the Palestinians should they start their armed struggle independently. Seeking support wherever they could find it, Arafat and Abu Jihad started running the alliance that was to become known to the world as the PLO. The first meeting of the Palestinian Liberation Organisation had been held in Jerusalem in 1964 and five years later popular support among Palestinians for Arafat and Abu Jihad's commando activities against the Israelis had propelled Fatah into the most dominant position inside the PLO.

Often used as a tool to suit other people's agendas, the PLO soon became notorious in the West as 'a terrorist organisation'. It tried to emulate the Israeli terrorist organisations of the forties, which had fought a tireless campaign to drive the British out of the Protectorate of Palestine in order to establish the State of Israel. Like Prime Minister Rabin, Abu Jihad believed in military strength, but his view was not shared by other members of the central committee and caused friction within the eight main cells that comprised the PLO. Umm Jihad's role was pivotal to her husband's aim.

She said: 'When I first started in Fatah, I started at the very bottom as an observing member, then as an active member of the movement, then I was responsible for a whole cell, then in turn for a whole wing. So I went through all the leadership steps of the movement. By the time Abu Jihad was martyred, I was deputy under-secretary of the revolutionary council. After he was martyred, I was elected as a member of the central committee of the movement. In that era, I had worked in various fields. I worked for the General Union of Palestinian Women and was secretary from 1980 to 1985. In 1966, I set up the Social Welfare Establishment to look after the families of martyrs and the wounded from the beginning of the revolution until the present time and it is still functioning now.

'I never experienced any difficulties with men because joining the movement was understood to be about sacrifice and *Nidhal*, or fighting for our cause, and this sacrifice and *Nidhal* were appreciated by everyone. On the contrary, in 1966 the leadership was imprisoned in Syria, so I had to take control of the Fatah movement and was the general leader of Fatah. Whenever I gave orders, they were carried out and everybody respected that.'

Having moved to Lebanon, her Beirut apartment became the *de facto* headquarters of Fatah, the most powerful faction in the PLO, and she was appointed as Fatah's first chief of staff and co-ordinator of military operations. As she had two young sons, Arafat had discussed her appointment very seriously with Abu Jihad before giving her the job. Umm Jihad said: 'I did everything. I prepared the military communiqués, I received the leaders of the groups to give them their orders for each military operation, I was the contact between one group and another. You can say that I took care of all the needs of our fighters. I was even the one who gave them their weapons.'

She was fully aware of the risks involved, knowing that she could be killed at any time, either by the Israelis or by her own bodyguards who were under instructions to shoot her to prevent her being taken prisoner. Her reputation grew in the Arab world, where she became highly respected by both sexes. She had proved beyond question that Arab women could have influence and power without undermining their traditional role in society. Her acceptance was all the more extraordinary because Arab society could be unforgiving of those who did not follow the conventional path. Arab women had emerged as a force in their own right and this was particularly true of Palestinian women.

SPEAKING in Arabic, Umm Jihad said: 'As Palestinian women, we have a different role to assume to that of other Arab women except for those whose land is under occupation like ours. Our efforts are streamlined towards national liberation, then social liberation. The latter cannot be achieved without the former. Through national liberation, the Palestinian woman can achieve her independence and the female role that she has achieved throughout the years of *Nidhal* is a vital one.

'Now she is asked to effectively resume that role towards achieving social independence which will only happen if national and governmental independence are achieved. For the individuals to be independent, the government and all its establishments and authorities have to be independent. This will allow for the democratic growth and building of society that would create such liberated individuals.'

Why were the Israelis after Abu Jihad in particular?

'First of all, because Abu Jihad was the founder of Fatah with Abu Amar [Yasser Arafat]. From the beginning, our lives were dedicated to the homeland. We knew quite well, like a vision, that one of us was going to be martyred any second, or captured, or wounded. We expected this from the kind of life that we led. Abu Jihad was a military leader who led major operations against the Israelis, so he was always on the wanted list. They always had in mind to assassinate him and he had been exposed to many such attempts.

'Probably their last decision to have him assassinated then was due to many reasons: firstly, he had attempted many military operations to reach the nuclear reactor base. Secondly, he was the engineer behind the *Intifadah*. These two reasons were sufficient and important enough for them to have him assassinated, but he was also a symbol of Palestinian unity. He fought for it. They regarded him as the man who had the last word. He was responsible for all that was happening inside the territories.'

Do they still think of you as a terrorist?

'No, maybe now that image has slightly changed because of the establishment of Palestinian authority and our efforts in the negotiations to reach a just peace. This fight for peace is much more difficult than fighting with arms because you are literally snatching everything from them that they are trying to hold on to.'

After the assassination, did you ever think of stopping because of your fatherless children?

'Never. I had to continue the path we started together. One has fallen or dropped, but the other had to carry the flag. I wanted my children to live in peace, so I had to continue the path we started.'

Umm Jihad's daughter, Hanan, interjected: 'What she did was for our sakes. But I knew that the only protection was by living in peace. This was a strain and a dream. I had a duty to my family and now we all have a duty to our countrymen. We had to follow our father's dream because it is our dream, too. We were expecting this to happen as we knew what our lives would be like.'

What was Abu Amar's reaction when he first found out?

'Certainly it was painful for everyone and particularly for Abu Amar. He lost the support of a brother and a friend. He was his right arm.'

Like Leah Rabin, Umm Jihad did not seek to glorify her husband's assassination, nor did she seek sympathy. But the tears were there. You felt them in the silences.

Were women jealous when Umm Jihad emerged in such high profile?

Her face visibly relaxed as the questioning moved away from the assassination to more practical matters. 'No, no. I always had a position and my role was cut out, so nothing has changed because I did have an active role already prior to him being martyred. But, of course, many tried to advise me to quit my work and stay at home and be protected and dignified. I would not have to struggle from day to day. I told them that I refused to hear such talk because it was against my principles and against what I had promised Abu Jihad from the beginning: that one of us would continue what the other had started until we delivered our people to freedom.

'Even at the time of Fatah's fifth convention when I was thinking about running for office as a member of the central committee, some had advised me against this as I might lose, which would then reflect badly on Abu Jihad's name. I told them that I was not running under his name, I was running under my name: Intissar Al Wazir, who is now the vice-president of the revolutionary council.

'There was also another vice-president and another treasurer, and the other vice-president was also running for election, so it was on those grounds that I wanted to run. And I also told them that if I did not succeed, I would have worked harder by the next convention and I would have also served my people better, and I would run again for election. In the end, I had won by a majority. The experience of running for membership of the central committee was a significant one because it was the first ally to the Fatah movement. It had always been restricted to men. I was the first woman to break that rule, even at the time when Abu Jihad was alive.'

Hanan, do you have any aspirations for a political career?

'Yes, of course. Since I was a kid I was in Palestine and I was preparing for that role.'

Did you ever feel that people were for you or against you because you were your father's daughter?

'They respected me since they respected my father and also my mother. But the way we were brought up was not to feel or be treated differently from the others. That is why we attended Palestinian training camps, just to live a normal childhood and to bear our responsibilities as other children did.'

How did you feel when you came back to live in Gaza?

'When I first came back, it was in April when the land was still occupied by the Israelis. So I was really scared. But I felt at home completely. Everything was familiar, although it was my first visit. But my body reacted to me being here. It was telling me that I belonged here, and that this was home. I was experiencing something like *déjà vu*. It was a great experience.'

Umm Jihad, how did the people receive you when you came back?

'It was such an exceptionally warm welcome. All the people came out holding pictures of Abu Jihad and Abu Amar, more than one million Palestinian people went out to receive us with Abu Amar. We arrived together, at the same time.'

How did you personally feel?

'I was extremely sad as Abu Jihad was not with us. I felt happy and sad at the same time. Tears were rolling down my face. I cannot really describe the emotions I went through the second I entered Palestine. You cannot begin to imagine what it was like. It was the feeling of homecoming at last, yet a beloved one was missing. It was a difficult emotion.'

How did you find a place to stay?

'I have family here in Gaza, so I stayed with them for two months until I rented a place.'

How did you find it once things had calmed down a bit?

'Thousands and thousands of people came to welcome me on my return. All the delegations or groups of people who went to welcome Abu Amar used to pass by my family's home and welcome me too. For two months, we were welcoming people by the busload. I felt they were very happy to see us return as it was the first step on the road to building a new Palestinian State.'

Did you find any discrimination between Palestinian Moslems and Christians?

'No, no. We, the Palestinian people, do not have such discrimination on religious grounds. There are certain foreign elements who are trying to fuel this discrimination. But we Palestinians never had any discrimination among us between Christians and Moslems, nor against Jewish people.'

Abu Jihad's mother was living in Khaleel [Galilee] in 1929 when some of the massacres took place. She hid three Jewish women in her house to protect them.

'We were never ever, either as Palestinians or as a political movement, in favour of racial or religious discrimination.'

Among famous people, whom do you admire the most?

'There are many.'

Let's start with the women; you have met quite a few.

'I admired the late Indira Gandhi and I admire Benazir Bhutto. As a Moslem and as a mother and as a woman working in politics as head of a party. As a former prime minister.'

Did you meet Mr and Mrs Tony Blair during their visit?

'No, I was in Syria visiting Abu Jihad's tomb. I very much admire Mrs Suzanne Mubarak. She is a wonderful woman. She is the foremost symbol of Arabian womanhood that one takes pride in, and one also admires her simplicity. She has a great deal to offer and has achieved a great deal as far as wiping out illiteracy and educating children and establishing libraries.'

What are your hopes for the future?

'My overall hope is that just and complete peace becomes a reality, and that the State of Palestine becomes independent. Also, for my children and grandchildren to live happily and securely in an independent and free homeland. To reap the fruits of my and my husband's struggle towards freedom.'

Leah Rabin said earlier today that Netanyahu's politics would destroy the peace process.

'And this is what we also believe: that under Netanyahu there will never be peace.'

Why do you think the Israelis went to the bedroom?

Umm Jihad paused and looked down at her hands as though seeking an answer. 'I don't know why,' she finally said. 'They just opened fire everywhere; and above the bed of the baby, too. Nidal still lives in a nightmare . . .'

9

Washington Wives

THERE was no more influential name in Washington, DC, than Roosevelt and no one was better qualified to talk about feminine power in the White House than Lucky Roosevelt. She had known every First Lady since Jackie Kennedy, who had been her classmate at Vassar College, and she was still a player in the Potomac power game in Hillary Clinton's time.

This was one very sharp cookie: tight-lipped CIA wife to her husband, Archie Roosevelt, Washington hostess, newspaper columnist and intriguer for countless causes. But Lucky Roosevelt's most important political credential was that, for seven years, she held the title of Chief of Protocol of the United States of America, reporting directly to the President.

When she swanned into the Regency Hotel in New York, there was nothing of the *grande dame* about her. She was shrewd and intelligent, with a lively sense of humour and friendly, long-lashed, brown eyes. She had flown in from Washington, she said, to hear her friend, Placido Domingo, sing at the Met and they had had dinner together after the performance. She was staying at the Colony and, after tea, she was heading for Bill Blass to order her winter collection.

In the meantime she talked about the eight American First Ladies she had personally known, as well as discussing her role as a powerbroker during the Reagan years. She had, she said, presided over the state visits of Mikhail Gorbachev, the Queen and Margaret Thatcher, travelled to summit meetings with the President, overseen the diplomatic corps and accompanied princes, potentates and prime ministers on their rounds when they visited the USA.

'I've known every First Lady since Mrs Eisenhower,' said Lucky Roosevelt. 'The first was Jackie Kennedy. A lot of people who didn't know her made nasty comments about her, but she was much more extraordinary than she was given credit for. People talk about her glamour, but Jackie was more than that: she had a lot of substance; she just didn't advertise it. She was very sharp and very witty and very artistic and she had a lot of strength; well, look at what she went through. This was a woman who made a big difference in our cultural life and I particularly respect what she did for the arts.

'When you consider that Jackie had only three years in the White House, it shows what an impact she made. She set the tone for the future in redecorating the White House because she showed us what we, as a nation, should preserve as our heritage. So many previous presidents' wives hadn't thought that this was something they needed to be bothered with, but Jackie made it impossible for people to think of the White House as anything other than one of the nation's great treasures.

'Jackie was a terrific woman. She lost a child, Patrick, and had to carry her sorrow in full view of the world. She really wanted children and she loved the idea of having a big family. She was a wonderful woman and I had great affection for her.'

After JFK's assassination, Jackie's successor in the White House was Lady Bird Johnson, who brought a simple approach to the role. 'The First Lady is an unpaid public servant elected by one person – her husband,' she declared. Lady Bird had been the sweet-talking Texas heiress Claudia Alta Taylor when she married Lyndon B. Johnson and, once installed in the White House, had proceeded to show that she was anything but a subservient wife. To Lady Bird Johnson went the kudos of cleaning up Washington, physically if not politically. An environmentalist long before it was fashionable, she founded the Committee for a More Beautiful Capital and became a model of civic pride for women throughout America.

'Lady Bird Johnson was also wonderful, but in a completely different way from Jackie,' said Lucky Roosevelt. 'She left her mark on Washington with conservation and beautification. Whenever I drive through Washington and see all these daffodils and other wonderful flowers coming up in spring, I say, "Bless you, Lady Bird." She is an extraordinary woman and I don't think LBJ was an easy person to live with.'

Rosalynn Carter, a fellow Democrat, also paid tribute to Lady Bird. 'I've always loved her,' she said. 'She had a sense of family and home, but she knew what she wanted to do: she wanted to beautify America. Clean up the litter. She did what she was interested in and she felt empowered to be able to do that because of her position.'

Lady Bird's replacement, the former Thelma Patricia Ryan, had worked as an X-ray technician in New York City before becoming Mrs Richard Nixon. To Pat Nixon had fallen the duty of standing loyally beside Tricky Dicky in his, and America's, darkest hour. She was the unhappiest First Lady of all, once commenting: 'I have sacrificed everything in my life that I consider precious in order to advance the political career of my husband.' Lucky Roosevelt said: 'I only met Pat Nixon a few times and I felt great sympathy for her.'

Watergate brought Elizabeth Bloomer, a dancer and model in New York City before she became Mrs Gerald Ford, to the White House. Betty fought breast cancer and an addiction to prescription drugs during her husband's presidency and once plaintively asked: 'Is there life after the White House?' But she made a full recovery and like her successor, Rosalynn Carter, made a huge contribution to the lives of American women after her husband had left office.

'Betty Ford was terrific,' said Lucky Roosevelt. 'I feel strongly about the subjects she had the guts to be gutsy about. They were a woman's right to have an abortion and being frank about breast cancer. She is a very gutsy woman. She developed breast cancer at the time she was in the White House and she handled that with a lot of courage. She was a good example to the rest of the world. That was the thing that broke the taboo against discussing breast cancer. It was something women didn't talk about and she changed all that and that was an *enormous* step forward for women. Any First Lady can make a difference, obviously, but she addressed an important and meaningful subject.'

Rosalynn Carter told us: 'I admire Betty Ford. She said she wanted to make waves for women and she did, and she was able to do so because she spoke out when she disagreed with her husband on the equal rights issue. No, I don't think it undermined him. My position was the same as hers and I think women everywhere were happy that she spoke out. It's kind of fun for the public to see that the First Lady has a mind of her own.

'She had breast cancer which gave her the incentive to want other people to know what she had gone through and to help other women understand what breast cancer was and get people involved in research into breast cancer. One thing that you learn in this equality movement is that most research has been done on men, so she was very instrumental in getting research into the causes and cures of breast cancer by making women aware of the issue.'

Jimmy Carter's electoral defeat of Gerald Ford put a Democrat back into the White House and Lucky Roosevelt found she wasn't quite so welcome. 'I met Rosalynn Carter a few times, but she was a Democrat and at that point I was a very big Republican,' she said, 'so I wasn't exactly somebody high on their guest list.'

Lucky's real rapport with a First Lady began when Ronald and Nancy Reagan replaced the Carters. 'I knew Nancy Reagan well and she was a very, very good First Lady,' she said. 'She had this protective manner with her husband – always. It was part of her love for him. I'd supported George Bush against Ronald Reagan in the primaries because I knew George very well. He was a friend of my husband Archie's family and their families were next-door neighbours in Hobe Sound, Florida. I'd observed George Bush for many years and I liked him, but I had no interest in a political job and it never occurred to me to seek one.

'The real reason I came to the attention of the Reagans was that, as a journalist, I got very angry about all these attacks on Nancy Reagan which I thought were very unfair. I sat down and wrote this piece in the *Washington Post*, saying, "Hey, back off. Give the woman a chance." There'd just been an assassination attempt on her husband's life and she was just starting to get over it.

'So I defended her and very effectively. There was such a dramatic reaction to that article that the *Post* had to publish 12 letters; they've never done that before or since. They wouldn't even tell me how many letters they got; they were, I think, embarrassed. It was very successful and it turned Nancy's image around. It made a difference. That was just an isolated incident, then Mrs Lee Annenberg, whom they had appointed as Chief of Protocol, found she couldn't do the job with her husband Walter being in Philadelphia, so she decided she had to leave.

'It was Mrs Reagan who had observed me. I'd had her to lunch at my house and we just became friends and I think she decided I was the right person for this job. It shows her perception because, actually, I was. I really was qualified for that job: I had followed Archie to three posts – Istanbul, Madrid and London – and learned everything I needed to know about protocol, about dealing with VIPs, about royalty – all the things that you had to absorb if you were going to do this job properly.

'And then, as a journalist, I'd covered the White House, the State Department and state visits – that was my beat. I knew how state visits were run, I knew what went on in the White House, I knew the diplomatic corps very well, so I had this fund of knowledge, and suddenly it all fell into place like a mosaic and made a beautiful picture. I realised my whole life had been spent preparing for that job.'

Barbara Bush had already served two terms as deputy First Lady before stepping into Nancy Reagan's shoes after George Bush fought what Barbara described as 'a fascinating, frustrating and *exhausting*' presidential campaign against the Democratic candidate, Michael Dukakis. Barbara told us that living in the White House was 'great' and added: 'The life was not difficult and it was a real family time. In spite of a full schedule, the thing I remember most are the giggles and voices of our children and grandchildren echoing down the hall.'

Barbara was remembered for her one-word response – 'Baloney!' – to allegations that her husband had had an affair, but she did not think that either she or her husband had been unfairly treated by the media. 'Our personal lives were pretty much an open book,' she said. 'Our children were hurt by criticism of us and certainly one of our sons was clobbered unfairly by us having chosen a political life. I can't blame this *totally* on the press – some of it was just the ugly side of politics. But I think we have brought up our children to make up their minds and to be responsible for their actions.'

The most difficult time during the Bush presidency was the Gulf War, which Barbara recalled with dread: 'One has to remember the dire and grim news reports, "Fifty thousand body bags are being prepared." It was horrid.' Lucky Roosevelt said: 'I'd known Barbara ever since I'd met George in Florida and we'd see each other at various times. She lives for her family. She never particularly wanted attention, but she did do a lot for illiteracy. That was her big thing, even before she was in the White House.'

Barbara said about her work in this field: 'The vision is easier, but we hope that we can stop illiteracy – and soon – by working with the family and by teaching the caregiver not only to read, but the important part he or she plays in his or her child's education. As to what we have achieved, we have opened the door to a literate world for many people.'

In 1992, the Democrats held the key to the White House once more when the Clintons moved in and Lucky Roosevelt found that the door was still open to her. 'I think Hillary Clinton is doing a great job, which may sound surprising because I'm a Republican, but I like her and my experiences with her have been very positive,' she said. 'I've met her several times and talked with her and she's a very bright woman. She maybe came to Washington with certain ideas, but she's learned and adapted to being First Lady very well. She is an impressive woman and very, very bright.

'Chelsea has turned out beautifully. They've both been marvellous parents. This child is unspoiled, nice, bright – everyone says nice things about her. She's a great credit to her family, considering all the difficulties. The adolescent years are the worst time for a child to be in the spotlight and she's handled that with such dignity and a maturity far beyond her years and that has to be a compliment to her parents.'

LUCKY Roosevelt was born Selwa Showker into a struggling Lebanese *emigré* family in Kingsport, Tennessee. She got her nickname at school and the story of her meeting with her husband, Archie Roosevelt, grandson of President Teddy Roosevelt, showed just how lucky she was: country girl weds one of the most elegible men of his time, travels the world with the CIA, then takes on one of the hottest jobs in American diplomatic life.

Lucky's partner on this incredible 40-year odyssey, Archibald Bulloch Roosevelt Jr, was born in Boston on 18 February 1918. After graduating from Harvard, he had been newspaperman, diplomat with the US Foreign Service and CIA intelligence officer in Beirut. A slim man with a little goatee beard that made him look older than his 32 years, he was chief of the Near East section of the Voice of America, based in New York City, when he met Selwa in 1950.

'I was graduating from Vassar and I went to Washington for the weekend because I wanted a job in foreign affairs,' she told us. 'I'd majored in international relations and the State Department gave me a list of five names of people I should talk to. The last name on the list was Archie Roosevelt. He was in New York and, as Vassar was in upstate New York, I thought I'd start with him. I telephoned Archie's office and asked his secretary if I could see him on Saturday morning.

'I put on my prettiest little red suit, I had a hat and a black veil pulled down over my eyes, and I thought I looked pretty spiffy. I walked into his office and he said it was love at first sight. He was considerably older than me and he was married, but getting divorced. We had lunch and the next day he drove me back to Vassar. He asked me to marry him and we were married three months later on 1 September 1950. We had a wonderful marriage. We were very happy and very compatible. He appreciated my background, which was very important, and I really became part of his: I sort of became an honorary Wasp.'

How did you deal with being a Lebanese girl in America?

'When I was a little girl in Tennessee I had all the problems of growing up in a totally Anglo-Saxon environment. I felt very American, but I realised I was different. It was not only learning how to cope with that difference, but what I learned at Vassar was how to turn it to my advantage. That's why I was able to go from a little country girl from Tennessee to a hostess in the very sophisticated world that I became part of. My most famous college friend was Jacqueline Bouvier, who was incredibly kind to me. I appealed to her intellectual curiosity – she had never met anyone of my background before.'

Did people resent you over your Arab extraction?

'Not among the Roosevelts because they were a very intellectual, sophisticated family that had always had foreigners in their midst. The reason Archie got interested in the Arabs at all was because an Arab prince had been a friend of his father. Archie was intrigued by him and the tales he told stirred his imagination about the Middle East. We were married in New York at the home of his aunt, Mrs Belle Roosevelt, who had a fabulous house on Sutton Place. My wedding dress was a wedding present from my cousin.

'My mother was a very educated and cultivated woman and she broke all the barriers to run off to America to marry my father because she was betrothed to someone she didn't want to marry. My Lebanese relatives also betrothed me to a Druze suitor, whom Jackie called "the Sheik". At the time I married Archie, she sent me a wedding present with a note saying, "I never really could picture you in veils on the back of the Sheik's charger."

'Archie was so supportive and his family were wonderful to me; they just accepted me. My father-in-law depended on me a great deal after his wife died. He called me "the General" and wanted me to run everything. His aunt, Mrs Alice Longworth, the famous hostess, was one of the legends in Washington and her pronunciation was, "This is wonderful. It will shake up that very stuffy family." They seemed to appreciate me and my background very much.'

Was the Roosevelt name a hindrance or an asset in journalism?

'Both. I never made a phone call that wasn't returned and you can always get a reservation in a restaurant or tickets at the theatre. The hindrance is that some people just hate Roosevelts: they either hate them because they see them as the establishment, or as rich, or as too powerful and then there are Democrats who hate Republican Roosevelts and Republicans who hate Democrat Roosevelts. Teddy Roosevelt was too far back to be controversial, but Franklin is still controversial. But now, we, the Roosevelts, the two branches of the family, have come together after years of being separated and we're all friends now.'

How did you deal with being the wife of a CIA spy?

'We were sent to Turkey; that's where I learned. It's easier to learn how to entertain, how to seat a table – all those things that a hostess has to know – in a small post like Istanbul and people were very helpful and nice. Archie wasn't great on protocol and I was fussing around wanting to get everything right as a young bride. He finally said, "Listen, try to remember something: whatever we do is right." Meaning that we decide, we set the pace, and that, of course, was true. And he wasn't arrogant and he wasn't socially ambitious – he didn't have to be; that wasn't said with arrogance, it was said to reassure me. First of all, it showed he had great trust in my judgment and taste, but he just knew I was going to be all right and not to worry. And that was very reassuring.

'That's why I'm not a feminist. Of course, I'm pro-choice. I feel so strongly about a woman's right to have an abortion I can't tell you. My life has been dedicated to doing as much as I could to help this cause and to see that this right isn't taken away. And there are other issues like equal pay that I believe in strongly. Femininity can be extremely useful. Let's be realistic: men still dominate most things in the world – the arts, well, less so the arts, perhaps, but they dominate business still, although women are coming right along, and all the professions. But a woman, if she is wise and not on the defensive, never has to apologise for being a woman, although there were times during my service as Chief of Protocol when being a woman was a complication. For example, the Afghans were coming to see the President and I got a message saying, "The leader of the Afghan resistance has asked would you please not shake his hand because he does not want to be photographed shaking a woman's hand."

'The other thing I found difficult was travelling with the President. His entourage were male, naturally, except for secretaries, but I had a different status: I was an official. It was one of the few times I had to subordinate myself. I wouldn't have wanted to intrude on the all-male clubbiness when the President takes off his shirt and puts his feet up – he'd never do that in front of me because he was an old-fashioned gentleman. So I had to be sensitive to that and I'd disappear.

'The advantages were that people looked after you, were anxious to please, were gallant, gave you lots of credit if you did a good job – more than you, perhaps, deserved. If a man did the same thing he might not have got the same credit. The President, Defense Secretary Shultz, the Vice-President George Bush, were always praising me. I was so appreciated that maybe I did do a good job.'

Some people say you were the most influential woman in Washington during the Reagan years.

'Hardly that, but this journalist wrote an article about the Kowtow Factor and referred to me as one of the ten most kowtowed-to women in Washington. I thought, "Oh God, I'm not going to have a friend left."

The combination of the job and the family background helped, and I think what I brought to the equation was my own heritage: I mean, being of Arab origin could, in this country particularly, be a real handicap. But in a funny way everybody wanted to show that they weren't prejudiced. I had also inherited this love of people and entertaining and receiving in my house, so I received for the nation.

'I did it with a real sense of pride and love, and being a woman made it a lot more effective. We have something men don't have: the ability to project warmth; men are a little embarrassed about projecting warmth, and rightly so because it's not exactly a masculine trait to be gushing around, but women can do that and they can do it effectively. In other situations, it seems to me that a woman doctor can be more empathetic than a man, a woman lawyer might do very well in a courtroom where she has to be dramatic to influence a jury. And why not? We *are* different. I don't believe women should be like men and I don't believe women should frustrate themselves in trying to imitate men. They should be themselves and damned effective.

'Women are equally intelligent and, often, they control just as much wealth and power – they are *being* more empowered; that's the big difference. We've always known – I guess it's a secret among women – that we have a lot of influence and that we're pretty powerful. Maybe now it's more generally acknowledged and more publicly acknowledged in our society and in every society except maybe in the Middle East. Fabulous women. I've got Arab friends in London and I've seen them being educated in America and then they go back and it's extraordinary the way they adjust.

'The Chief of Protocol carries the rank of ambassador and it was always a man's job. Shirley Temple Black was the first woman to get it and then there were others who were there just briefly. When I left my job, I advised President Bush, who was a good friend, to give it to a man. I'd been there seven years and I thought it would start to be regarded as "a woman's job" and I thought that was wrong, both for the position and for the modern world: this should not be a gender position. And he took my advice and he had two men, one after the other. Now it's a woman again.

'During the seven years I was in office, I orchestrated about 1,000 official visits of heads of state and heads of government; some were official and some were private, but they were all to see the President. I had 70 people working for me and I ran Blair House, the presidential guesthouse; in addition to having to run it, I also had to close it, redecorate it and reopen it again. That was a $16 million project and I had to raise $6 million because Congress gave me $10 million to do the structure because the house was collapsing and it's not just one house it's 110 rooms in four houses. When I opened the house in 1988 it was fabulous. That is my great accomplishment for my country – it is so beautiful. I know that I did it. It was my determination to see this project through and it took six years.'

How did you deal with people asking for favours?

'I'm a realist and the truth is that people use you, but I don't hold it against people because if you did you'd spend the rest of your life resenting everybody. You know who your real friends are after you've been in and out of important offices. When you're in, you've got a lot more friends, of course, but when you're out your real friends are the ones who've stuck with you. I'm not saying it doesn't hurt when someone you've regarded as a real friend, come hell or high water kind of thing, turns out to be a fair-weather friend. Of course that hurts. But I've become a realist and when you're disappointed in someone you just put them in a different cubbyhole.

'I'm wiser, I'm essentially an upbeat person, an optimist. I really believe that you look for the best in people. This might sound Pollyanna-ish, but that's what makes me what I am. I really believe in people, I love people and I'm happy. This isn't to say I wasn't heartbroken when my husband died eight years ago. He'd had some heart problems over the last ten years of his life. He gave me that wonderful support. I don't know about women who talk about men as enemies, but I just never experienced that.

'I had a man in my life and the other men who've come into my life since. One always meets a few cads in life, but you have to meet them to recognise the good ones and appreciate them. Being married to Archie gave me such an appreciation of how wonderful men can be, how kind, how loving and supportive, and how much they can enhance your life and make it right. When you have a disappointment, it's great to come home to someone who loves you. When I was working, some days would be really tough and the lilt in his voice when I walked in the house made me feel, "Well, here is my loving refuge," and I miss that.'

Who were the most impressive men you met?

'Mikhail Gorbachev and his Foreign Minister, Eduard Schevanardze. I suppose that was because we knew this was history in the making, but Gorbachev had this incredible magnetism and vitality. He called me "Comrade Protocol". I could see that this man was going to make it happen: Russia was going to change. And Schevanardze had this incredible humanity; he was – he is – extremely attractive. Those two men made an indelible impression on me, and so did the way they interacted with Ronald Reagan and George Shultz, who were two more incredible men. Shultz was extraordinary and I loved working with him. Again, here was a supportive man. I'd go to him and say, "Secretary, we've got to do it this way . . ." and he'd say, "Go ahead, Lucky." He had such faith in me and just let me do what I thought was right.'

Which women impressed you the most?

'Indira Gandhi was very impressive the way she handled power in her enormous country. This delicate little woman – I'll never forget the bright red nail polish on her toes. I saw them when we were marooned in a car for an hour and a half in a torrential rainstorm, barely able to move in New York traffic. I had heard how difficult she could be, a prima donna, but not at all. She didn't complain, she took my suggestion that she must be tired and just nodded off for a little nap.

'We all fell in love with Cory Aquino – so feminine and soft-spoken, but so determined to lead her country back to stability and prosperity after the years of Marcos misrule. I cherish the letter she wrote to me after her return to the Philippines, which said, "If you may pardon a bit of female chauvinism, I think what you and I proved is that, what men can do, we can do better."

'But the woman who really impressed me was Margaret Thatcher – she knew her mind and she had so much courage. You know, women have more courage than men about expressing what they really think. We make good politicians for that reason. She was also quite feminine. When we were together, she'd say "Oh, shoes! Isn't it the worst problem for a woman? Oh, my feet." Both of us found that so much standing for public ceremonies caused our feet to increase by half a size and we moaned over the difficulty of finding shoes that were both comfortable and chic. In my job I saw a lot of pompous people – it went with the territory. Margaret Thatcher not only eschewed the pompous, but she could shrink self-important types with a steely glance. She also knew when and how to stroke their egos. When someone like George Shultz called on her, she herself greeted him at the embassy *porte-cochère* and, when he left, escorted him to his waiting car.

'Unlike most male heads of state, Mrs Thatcher travelled light. Her entourage was the smallest we ever dealt with. She was so secure, both emotionally and intellectually, she did not need hordes of tom-tom beaters to impress people with her importance. She never brought a maid or hairdresser, but relied on local talent. She managed nicely on only four hours sleep – to the despair of her staff, who were normal folk. On almost every trip she began her days at 5.45 a.m. She could do four morning TV shows – ABC, NBC, CBS, and CNN – in an embassy drawing-room, moving from one corner to another so the backgrounds would be different for each show.

'She was so eloquent and she could express herself so well and there was never a hesitancy about what she wanted to say. She knew what she thought and she was more eloquent than any man around. Shortly before he left office, Shultz gave a luncheon for her at which he presented her with the Order of the Handbag – a handsome, black leather purse – in recognition of her talent for pulling just the right statement from her handbag at meetings of allied leaders.

'Mrs Thatcher was adorable with Denis her husband, but she started flirting with Ronald Reagan – there was a little electricity there. She was Reagan's first and last official visitor, and during his presidency she came to Washington at least once a year, maybe more. Her suits were conservative, well cut and of the finest English woollens. As time went on, she seemed to become more clothes-conscious, and on her last visit actually changed costumes five times on one busy day. I would guess that she was Ronald Reagan's favourite visitor.'

How did Placido Domingo come into your life?

'I left the protocol job in 1989, I lost my husband and I'd been a widow for a year when I suddenly said, "What am I going to do with the rest of my life?" I didn't think I wanted to marry again – and as you can see I haven't. When you've done something well, like a marriage, maybe you don't want to risk doing it badly. The passion of my life is music. I don't have musical talent, but I'm a great listener. I'd met Placido Domingo in my job, then one day in London a friend of mine was having a little dinner for Placido and his wife, Marta. I happened to be sitting next to him and we were talking about music and I explained how much I loved Spain, how much I loved music, how much I loved bullfighting. He said, "Why don't you come to Spain for Expo, I'm singing, and be my guest?"

'Well, that's the way it began. Placido and Marta took me into their lives and I became their pupil. We kept doing things together and I kept going to all these music festivals. I realised that music was filling the void and I was not sad, I was not lonely. We became very good friends. Then, because of my love of opera, I was invited to go on the board of the Washington Opera. I knew Placido would love to have his own opera company, so they asked me to approach him. After a lot of negotiating, Placido took over the Washington Opera Company – that is something I actually accomplished.

'We were at a festival in Verona when Placido said he'd do it and I said, "Placido, I need to do something big to introduce you into Washington –

I need to do a gala to raise some big money. Just give me a date." So he gave me a date – 10 March 1996 – I'll never forget it. Without telling him, I formed something called the Domingo Circle. I got 200 people to give $10,000 each to become members of the Domingo Circle – that was $2 million – and then I sold out the gala. I raised more money that night than has ever been raised in Washington in a single event: $2.6 million, maybe $3 million with bank interest. It was such a fun thing to do and I adored every minute of it.

'Placido didn't know about it and when we announced it at the gala he was absolutely stunned. Nobody had told him, nobody betrayed me. When you accomplish something like that, it's thrilling. You bring joy to people and leave something behind.'

PART TWO

SOCIETY, STARDOM & STYLE

10

Ivana's Secrets

AT FOUR o'clock one languid Saturday afternoon, Ivana Trump was sitting at home at Mar-a-Lago, the Trumps' sprawling, palm-fringed, Florida estate, when her private phone rang. It was the New York-based Greek financier Alexander 'Alecko' Papamarkou, 'an absolute sweetheart' according to Ivana, calling from his private jet.

'Ivana, I'm with Prince Charles and King Constantine and we're coming to Palm Beach,' said Alecko. 'Prince Charles would love to see Mar-a-Lago. Can you arrange it?'

'What time are you landing?' asked Ivana.

'In an hour.'

'Come for tea,' said Ivana, as though entertaining members of European royalty was an everyday event. Mar-a-Lago, the former home of heiress Marjorie Merriweather Post, was a Florida legend. Set in 20 acres facing both the Atlantic Ocean and Lake Worth, the palatial pink hacienda had 58 bedrooms, 32 bathrooms, 27 servants' rooms, a theatre, a ballroom and three bomb shelters. Donald Trump had bought it for $5 million and spent three times as much turning it into a showplace of Spanish-style grandeur.

When Alecko Papamarkou rang off, Ivana briefed the staff, then got busy on the phone. Her first call was to the country club where Donald was enjoying a round of golf. 'You have to find my husband and tell him he has to be back home in an hour,' Ivana instructed the steward who answered the phone. 'Tell him it's an emergency, but not to panic – it's not a death or anything like that.'

Then she phoned Estée Lauder and several other 'influential' female friends on the Palm Beach A-list and asked them if they'd like to pop around to take tea with the heir to the British throne. 'I have never seen these girls dress so fast,' Ivana told us. 'They were all into full gear in an hour. Prince Charles arrived and spent three or four hours with us. He had tea and was most charming. He said he was in Palm Beach to play polo, but he'd heard about Mar-a-Lago and wanted to see it for himself.'

Ivana had no idea, however, how deeply her husband detested the aristocracy, or how little he thought of her for entertaining bluebloods like Prince Charles. Donald Trump was New Money Man personified and his towering ego simply couldn't tolerate a wife who kow-towed to old-world privilege. People with hereditary titles made him seem less important.

'Ivana is what I'd call a traditionalist. She aspires to the aristocracy,' Donald wrote in his memoirs. 'Down in Mar-a-Lago, she used to keep a fancy, leather-bound book in which guests signed their names, and she would hand out printed schedules telling you when you'd play tennis, play golf, eat and get a massage. I understood, but always hated that kind of lifestyle. In my opinion, the social scene – in New York, Palm Beach, or anywhere else for that matter – is full of phoneys and unattractive people who often have done nothing smarter than inherit somebody else's wealth – the Lucky Sperm Club, I call it.'

Ivana's reign as mistress of Mar-a-Lago and the rest of the Trump empire came to a sudden, heart-wrenching stop when Donald walked out on her in February 1990. She already knew he had been having an affair with Marla Maples, a 26-year-old blonde beauty queen. Ivana was disbelieving at first that an affair with a bimbo could seriously threaten her 13-year marriage, but she soon discovered that Donald was serious about trading her in for a younger, blonder model.

When the stress of the impending divorce became overwhelming, it was to Mar-a-Lago that Ivana fled with her three children, Donald Jr, then 12, Ivanka, eight, and Eric, six, from the family's New York home, a 50-room triplex atop the black-and-gold Trump Tower on Fifth Avenue. Trying to come to terms with the break-up, she walked alone in the estate's orange grove, and, she admitted, shed a lot of tears.

Eight years later, Ivana Trump wanted people to know how far she had come since those dark days. 'I'm a woman, I'm pretty, I'm colourful, I have intelligence and people are drawn to it,' she told us. Few people knew how hard she had struggled to make the transformation from dowdy, Communist-bloc brunette to stylish, Americanised blonde. She lowered her voice to a confidential whisper, but the accent remained as enchantingly Zsa-Zsa as ever. 'I had so many disdvantages to overcome,' she confided. 'If you're born in America or the UK and you're a *leetle* kid and you go to the school, you have the friends, then you go to the university and build relationships which go with you through life. I came to America with nothing, not knowing the language and I didn't have a friend, so I had, like, 25 years of disadvantage. I had to start totally from scratch.'

She was born Ivana Zelnicekova in Gottwaldov, Czechoslovakia, in 1949 and grew into a slim, dark-haired child 'with dark circles underneath my eyes from my father'. Her father was an electrical engineer and Ivana described him to us as 'my rock, my teacher, my friend and my inspiration'. Although the family was well off by Communist standards, Ivana was sent to work in a shoe factory at the age of 12 for two weeks. The experience 'petrified' her. 'I promised myself I was never, ever, going to do that kind of work again,' she said. Her temperament was much more suited to acting and she appeared in several Czech films as a child actress. 'My parents were middle class and I made it the old-fashioned way: I worked for it,' Ivana told us. 'Nana, my mother, taught me everything that was good in life, but I had no business training, just a masters degree in physical education from Charles University in Prague.'

Her father had encouraged Ivana to ski since the age of four and, as a young woman, she aimed her sights at a place in the Czech team for the 1972 Winter Olympics. She failed to make the team, but was named as a reserve for the downhill and slalom events. She was also secretly planning to escape from the suffocating rigidity of the Communist system. At the age of 22 she had gone through a marriage of convenience with Alfred Winkelmayr, an Austrian, 'for the sole purpose of getting an Austrian passport'. The marriage was never consummated, but, using her married name, Ivana Winkelmayr, and her new passport, she emigrated to Canada.

Ivana was working as a model in Montreal when she first saw Donald Trump, a floppy-haired, seriously suited young man, at a reception for athletes at the next Olympic Games in 1976. They met again at Maxwell's Plum, then the trendiest restaurant in New York, when she was on a modelling assignment in the Big Apple. 'It was his energy that attracted me to him,' she said. 'That he was handsome didn't hurt, either. I liked his values, his sense of reality – no smoking, no taking drugs, no cheating, lying or stealing.'

Donald John Trump had been born in New York City in 1946 of German ancestry. His father, Fred C. Trump, was the son of an immigrant couple who had opened a restaurant in New Jersey in 1905. Fred had gone into the property business and built flats in Brooklyn and Queens which were rented out to poorer sections of the community.

Fred was reputedly a millionaire several times over and Donald and his four siblings were raised in a 23-room Queens mansion. Donald was the only child to show any aptitude for business and, after attending a New York military academy, he graduated from the Wharton School of Finance in Pennsylvania. He had, however, been a spectacular flop in his first ambition, to be a Broadway producer. 'He liked to see his name on the billboard at the front of the house,' said one of the partners in his first theatrical venture. 'He was always going outside the theatre to look at it. The play closed after a week or so and Donald lost his money. It was then that he decided to go into real estate like his father.'

Ivana married Donald for love in April 1977. Her husband had yet to become the hottest property on Wall Street, but he was wealthy enough to ask his bride to sign a prenuptial agreement. The contract was drawn up by Roy Cohn, the notorious legal fixer who had advised Aristotle Onassis when he decided to divorce Jackie. Ivana signed on the dotted line after Donald explained that the pact was merely a legal formality required in his high-risk business. Unskilled as she was in the ways of Western commerce, Ivana probably never gave it a second thought. Not then anyway. She was living in the most exciting city in the world with the man she loved and she would soon be bearing their first child. From the beginning, she stood resolutely beside her husband on his hazardous climb to the top of the New York real estate pile.

Ivana's friend, Liz Brewer, said: 'Donald Trump hadn't started to get his fame and fortune and she definitely did help him. If you ask anybody who had dealings with him in those early days – and I actually have friends who did – they say it was Ivana they dealt with, even on the building sites.'

Donald's most audacious move was to gamble against the 'flight to the suburbs' trend that was turning New York into a ghost town after dark because of the rise in drug-taking and urban crime. He persuaded the bankrupt Penn Central Railroad Company to sell him the dilapidated Commodore Hotel, built above Grand Central Station on 42nd Street, for just $10 million. Then he persuaded City Hall to give him a $120 million tax break and the banks to lend him $80 million to rebuild the Commodore.

Ivana oversaw the construction side of the project, which entailed encasing the 1,400-room hotel in a gleaming glass shell. Renamed the Grand Hyatt, the dazzling monolith opened its doors to the public in 1980 just as the economy was picking up and New Yorkers were starting to reclaim their city from the drug dealers and muggers.

The huge success of the Hyatt enabled Donald to borrow heavily and expand his portfolio in the booming property market of the eighties.

With three big apartment buildings bearing his name – Trump Tower, Trump Plaza and Trump Parc – Donald finally had his name up in lights and not just along the Great White Way, but surmounting the whole of Gotham City. 'Everything is Trump something,' said London socialite Ira Kettner, a frequent visitor to New York. 'Trump Tower, Trump this, Trump that. He's a modest little man, isn't he?'

His next act was to get involved in the casinos that were turning down-at-heel Atlantic City, New Jersey, into the Las Vegas of the east coast. He operated two big casinos on the boardwalk, Trump Plaza and Trump Castle, which raked in $40 to $50 million a week, and was planning a third, the vulgarly opulent Taj Mahal. Ivana was appointed chief executive officer of Trump Castle and took to commuting by helicopter to Atlantic City each day, returning home to the children at night.

'In Atlantic City, I made a fortune for him,' she told us. 'I ran his hotels and his casinos for him, so I was definitely instrumental in his success – there's no question about it. We were a team and nobody could match us.'

The Trump name became synonymous with excess and luxury, a symbol of Reagan's America. 'We were definitely an unbeatable couple,' said Ivana. 'Donald had tremendous vision and he came up with the ideas and he would get the financing, then he would give the project to me. I'm a great manager, always have been, and I would take the project over. Donald's deals take a lot of time because he's always negotiating ten deals and nine of them fall out, but one of them comes through in a year, or two, or three, whatever it is. I was always catching up behind him to run the buildings and make them successful.'

Trump bought a Boeing 727 with a built-in bathroom, study and bedroom from a Texas millionaire for $8 million and a French military helicopter from Warner Communications for $2 million. When Adnan Khashoggi fell on hard times in 1987 Trump purchased *Nabila*, his onyx and gold-plated yacht, from its new owner, the Sultan of Brunei, for $30 million. He spent $10 million on a refit and relaunched it as *Trump Princess*. Very few women could have kept up with this cracking pace, but Ivana matched her husband stride for stride, as well as consolidating her place in New York society and raising three children. There was, however, an even bigger challenge on the horizon.

In 1988, Donald bought the Plaza Hotel on Central Park for $408 million and gave her the title of president. Ivana threw herself into the immense task of refurbishing the hotel in its original French-chateau style. In the fabled Oak Room, she lifted one corner of the worn-out carpet to discover that it was concealing an exquisite mosaic floor. With the help of the original contractors, she had this restored to its former glory. She also consulted a couple of friendly British aristocrats, the Duke of Northumberland and Viscount De L'Isle, and drew inspiration from the furnishings in their stately homes.

Everyone agreed that Ivana had succeeded in restoring the Plaza to its rightful place as New York's premier hotel, but some said it had gone to her head. Surrounded by gilt and grandeur, she was like a Bourbon princess, haughty, demanding and dripping with diamonds and *haute couture*. It was said that she shouted at staff and dismissed those who did not live up to her expectations. Answering this criticism, Ivana said at the time: 'I don't fire people on the spot and I don't shout at people who work for me. I run my business with dignity.'

Ivana was too preoccupied with the Plaza and her many other commitments to notice that Donald was going through a mid-life crisis. America's perennial whizzkid had passed 40, the age at which many men feared they had lost their appeal to young women and started blaming their wives. As a result, his eyes started to wander. When Ivana realised what was happening, she took immediate remedial action. 'I'm never going to look a day over 28,' she had once declared, 'but it's going to cost Donald a lot of money.' True to her word, Ivana worked out at a health club and spent many painful weekends in beauty clinics to recapture her looks. 'The incredible thing about Ivana Trump,' said a female TV executive who worked out in the same West Side health club, 'is that she never sweats. She'd really go for the burn, but come out looking fresh as a daisy.'

In 1989, Ivana took the extreme measure of reconstructing herself with the help of cosmetic surgery, including a facelift, silicone implants in her breasts and some enhancement of her lips. Her husband appeared to applaud the dramatic change. One commentator noted: 'At a New York charity party, Donald unveiled the '89 Ivana as if she were a new model car.'

'I'm a very traditional European wife and I don't mind that Donald is the boss,' Ivana said in an interview at the end of that year. 'I like it that way. I'm very happy – we have wonderful children, houses, wealth and a good marriage. We are lucky and we know it.' She was Donald's wife, soulmate, co-conspirator, business partner and emotional anchor – and, at the same time, she readily accepted that Donald was the boss. Instead of being grateful, Donald was moodily resentful about the way his private life was being conducted.

'My marriage, it seemed, was the only area in my life in which I was willing to accept less than perfection,' he disclosed in his memoirs. 'My nine-to-five day fascinated and energised me. But then, late in the

Hillary Rodham Clinton (Sygma)

Benazir Bhutto

Dewi Sukarno

Rosalynn Carter and Mona Bauwens

Mona Abdel Nasser Marwan with her husband Ashraf

TOP LEFT: Jehan Sadat

TOP RIGHT: Leah Rabin

LEFT: Hanan and Umm Jihad

TOP: Mona Bauwens with Liz Brewer

ABOVE: Ivana Trump and Count Roffredo

RIGHT: Ivana Trump and Sir Benjamin Slade

ABOVE: Marisa Masters and Mangal Kapur

LEFT: Mary McFadden with Mona Bauwens

BELOW: Ruth Harding and Richard Gist
(Steven Cleeve)

ABOVE: Shirley Bassey with Mona Bauwens

LEFT: Samantha Bond

Christina Estrada and Sol Kerzner (David Koppel)

afternoon, I'd get a call from Ivana, reminding me of that night's engagement. Sometimes I'd get angry and say I wasn't going and we'd fight about it on the phone. In the end, I'd almost always agree to go along. When I hung up the phone, though, I'd often say – loud enough, I suppose, for anyone standing in the hall outside my office to hear – "My life is shit."'

Donald installed Marla Maples in a suite at the St Moritz, a hotel just a few blocks from Trump Tower, and provided her with a chauffeur-driven limousine. Word of the liaison reached Ivana's ears when he started taking his mistress to society parties. The *denouement* came at Aspen on New Year's Eve 1989 when Ivana confronted Marla Maples at Bonnie's, a *chi-chi* mountainside restaurant, and exchanged some sharp words with her. Donald, who was also present, told his wife she was overreacting and they later embraced outside the restaurant for the benefit of photographers. That night, however, he took Marla to a party at the home of the oil billionaire, David Koch, and Ivana reached for the lawyers.

At Ivana's behest, the gossip columnist Liz Smith broke the story of the bust-up of New York's most glittering couple in the *Daily News* with a front-page splash, LOVE ON THE ROCKS, which announced that Ivana was leaving Donald because he had betrayed her with another woman. Donald's public relations fixer, Howard Rubenstein, fed the rival *New York Post* with claims that Donald had left Ivana, not vice versa, because 'her level of arrogance had grown steadily in recent years'. Donald was quoted as saying, 'The bottom line is I don't want to create another Leona Helmsley,' an unkind and unfair reference to the disgraced hotel queen who had been found guilty of tax evasion the previous year.

Liz Brewer said: 'When Ivana discovered there was another woman in his life, it was such a shock to her. She had three beautiful children and what she considered to be a great marriage, yet she was suddenly toppled. And what was Donald saying? "I wanted a woman in bed; I didn't want a woman running my empire." What an insult! Ivana had helped him to build it up, then he turned around and said that's not what he wanted at all: he didn't want to share the glory; he wanted a submissive Marla Maples in his bed. It was such a terrible thing to happen to Ivana and she was so distraught, so hurt, so damaged.'

Ivana celebrated her 41st birthday in February 1990 at a party arranged by the Ladies Who Lunch at La Grenouille, a French restaurant on East 52nd Street. Accompanied by bodyguards, she arrived in a black Mercedes to shouts of encouragement from wellwishers. Donald packed his clothes and moved to another apartment in Trump Tower and Ivana took the children to Mar-a-Lago, while the lawyers argued about how the pre-nuptial agreement would affect the divorce settlement. Although the pact had been updated three times with the birth of each of their children, it still limited Ivana to $25 million of Donald's estimated $1.7 billion fortune in the event of a divorce.

As a sign of things to come, Ivana flew to London and, looking stunning in honey blonde beehive hairdo, a pink and green dress and pink shoes, threw a thank-you dinner at Claridge's for the Duke of Northumberland and Viscount De L'Isle. 'To tell you the truth, I've made Ivana a very popular woman,' Donald told *Vanity Fair*. 'She can do whatever she wants.'

IVANA'S first move in overcoming her humiliation at the hands of her husband was to burst into tears on American television. Women viewers rallied to her and she received huge support when she launched her own designer label, The House of Ivana, using some of the $25 million she had finally settled for (plus the Trump estate at Greenwich, Connecticut, a townhouse on East 64th Street, and a few other expensive odds and ends). Donald Trump's rejection had, in fact, given her the opportunity to be independent and she had seized it with both hands.

Instinctively sharp to the tips of her French manicured nails, Ivana used the shopping channels on television to advance sales of her range of jewellery, clothes, make-up and accessories. Flouting Andy Warhol's First Law of Celebrity that everybody would be famous for 15 minutes, she became a symbol of feminine achievement in the New Age nineties. Her house on East 64th Street reflected her new, uninhibited *joie de vivre*. Nobody could compete with the marble-and-ormolu temple that her neighbour, Gianni Versace, had created for his fabulous art collection, but Ivana did the best she could with mirrored panelling, gilded cornices, cerise flock wallpaper and crystal chandeliers. 'Oh dear,' said a London socialite, 'have you seen her house? She's the laughing stock of New York society.'

But it was Ivana who was having the last laugh. She seemed to be everywhere, a hot-pink pimpernel, doing deals in New York and London, entertaining friends at the Connecticut estate or her new Palm Beach villa, shopping at the couture shows in Paris, writing a sex-and-shopping novel and relaxing on her ocean-going yacht, *Ivana*, in Monte Carlo. The yacht had 286 monogrammed sheets, towels and table napkins, specially printed and quilted bedspreads, and dozens of printed moire cushions for the main saloon and cabins.

She bought a two-storey apartment in Cadogan Square, Knightsbridge, and told the interior designer, Robin Anderson: 'Honey, Ivana needs this guy [her *pied-à-terre*] in ten days. We'll have the celebration champagne.' Anderson said: 'My hit team rewired the whole unit, created an extra bedroom out of a cupboard and redecorated the whole place to my specifications in six days. Antique furniture was delivered and positioned, along with sofas, curtains, beds, bedheads, bed linen, towels, soaps and delicacies from Partridge's. The project was created down to the flowers and, of course, the champagne flutes on a silver tray.'

Explaining the almost manic energy that drove her, Ivana told us: 'I admired Margaret Thatcher, she was just phenomenal but, *per se*, did I have a role model? No, I didn't. I always follow my own instincts. I know what I'm good at and what I'm not good at. I've always worked very hard and I was always, in a sense, very conscious of myself as a leader. I *feel* what's right for me and then I do it and if people follow me with certain trends, that's fine. I have never really said, "Okay, this is how it's going to be and let's see how to do it and achieve it." No – I just do what I feel is right for me.

'I used my instinct in business and I used my instinct with people. In business, you either have the instinct or you don't. I've never been trained in, you know, the business. I only got into business because I married Donald. I watched him, observed him, I saw how he dealt with people, how he dealt with the press. I saw him especially as a promoter.

'Some people can be very talented, but they don't know how to sell their talent. This is why all the designers have business managers because they just don't know how to sell themselves. I have learned how to sell me. I don't dance, I don't sing. Well, I can dance, but I'm not a professional, I'm not a ballet dancer, but I've achieved quite a bit. My name is known around the world – they say "Ivana" and it means a certain personality, whatever that might be. You either have this quality in business or you don't. You can go to the School of Finance for ten years and if you don't have the instinct in you, then what?'

So what gives you the edge?

'I think it must be intelligence, of course. (She laughed.) Education and intelligence and street smarts and, always, a great deal of luck. I don't underestimate the luck. Luck is very important. I heard a saying [from Nancy Reagan], "A woman is like a teabag. You never know how strong she is until she gets into hot water."

'Sure, I had money and I had my health and I had children and many women don't have it as easy, but there is something which is called confidence and a lot of women lack confidence. How did I turn my life around to be a success rather than it being Donald's success? I was always running his hotels, his casinos, his businesses, then I suddenly turned it around into businesses I'd never been in and I made it.'

Are some women jealous of you?

'I have never experienced jealousy from women, at least not to my face, not from ordinary women, but maybe there could be a little of it in the girls who are in our circles, although I've never detected it. Women should not like me. I'm fairly good-looking, I'm young, I have a lot of money and I have all the gadgets. But women somehow adore me. This is why I have such power over this television station. This is why I go on the air and women call me up: she might be a big black momma from Oklahoma, or she might be an 18-year-old girl who looks up to me, or she might be a middle-aged woman, middle-class, wealthy or poor – I love them all.

'Don't get me wrong, I've never had a problem with men, but I really like women, I enjoy women, and it projects. I'm quite genuine and women feel it. This is why I can go on television and sell $3 to $5 million worth of my merchandise over the weekend. The women wait for me. They want to talk to me. I'm also writing the advice column for *The Globe*, one of the magazines in America, and women ask me for advice. I think many of them were, or are, in my position of being divorced and they relate to all that pain, but when they look at what I made out of that mess they say, "If Ivana can do it, I can do it."'

The interior designer Robin Anderson said: 'Ivana is never lacking in understanding and kindness. She is meticulously professional, never fails to see the funny side of the most odious situations and she's never too busy to listen to the smallest problems.'

In addition to running her new life, Ivana had also made a huge effort to repair some of the damage with Donald. She started talking to him again, even though he had married Marla Maples in 1993, two months after the birth of their daughter, Tiffany. 'I'll tell you something: at the beginning, everything is new,' Ivana told us. 'You're just so hurt that you don't want to talk to the person. But eventually, especially when children are involved, you have to talk, you have to be intelligent about it.

'So over the years I never took it out on the children. I told them, "This is the only father you'll ever have," and never said one bad word against him and I never will. And after three or four years, when your life goes on and you have a new lover, then you talk again and you're friends again because all that hurt is past and you get along because you were once married. There had to be a certain chemistry there for the marriage to survive 15 years because we could talk, we could laugh together, we could dance together.'

Ivana's new lover, Riccardo Mazzuccelli, was a plump, middle-aged, divorced, Italian businessman who had spent many years in Africa. They had met in London during Royal Ascot Week in 1991, but did not become engaged until October 1994 when they threw a party for 120 friends, including Shirley Bassey, Britt Ekland, Zandra Rhodes, Valerie Campbell and Adnan Khashoggi, at Syon House, the Duke of Northumberland's Thameside home.

The Ladies Who Lunch, London chapter, were fascinated by Ivana's beauty, high spirits and an apparent ability to laugh at herself while still taking her work very seriously. Kookie Fallah, a Knightsbridge socialite, said: 'I have nothing but admiration for her. I think she's done frightfully well and worked awfully hard getting there. She's not my kind of woman, but that's not the issue. The issue is that she has got up and dusted off and done it over and over again and I think that's absolutely brilliant.'

Anyone as up-front as Ivana, however, was bound to create friction somewhere along the line and that's exactly what happened when she joined some of the Ladies Who Lunch at the Thomas Goode emporium in Mayfair. Ivana turned up wearing the requisite fancy-cut diamonds, but she was unable to take her eyes off the 40-plus-carat sapphire ring that graced one of the other guest's hands.

Recognising the ring, Ivana said: 'My fiancé wanted to buy me that, but I thought it would be too difficult to ski with.'

Riposted the other lady: 'So did I, until I got it.'

Such a putdown, however, was only a minor irritant to Ivana compared with the behaviour of that same fiancé. Ivana and Riccardo had set a wedding date for June 1995, but this was cancelled when they squabbled over Riccardo's reluctance to sign a prenuptial agreement. He also embarrassed Ivana by dropping his trousers for charity in front of the Duchess of York at a Children in Crisis fund-raising dinner. When Ivana expressed her displeasure at the bad publicity, Riccardo described her as 'jealous and hypersensitive'.

These difficulties were eventually smoothed over, the contract was signed and the wedding went ahead in New York in November of that year. Diana Ross, Barbara Walters and Ivana's mother, Marie, were among the 80 guests who saw the bride, draped in diamonds and wearing a pale blue satin Thierry Mugler outfit, given away by her sons, Donald Jr and Eric. But the signs of strain were already evident. After less than two years of married life, Ivana and Riccardo separated and were divorced in September 1997. Asked about Riccardo, Ivana told us bluntly, 'I have no comment,' but she quipped to a friend at the time of the divorce, 'I can't spell anyway, so better to be Trump than Mazzuccelli.'

She was back on the scene as an unattached woman, but not for long. Her new lover was also Italian, Count Roffredo Gaetani d'Aragona, owner of the Ferrari dealership on Long Island. Well over six feet tall and powerfully built, Roffredo had attracted the attention of movie producers as a young man and had made several films, including one with Olivia Hussey. Ivana's own fame had long since spread to Los Angeles and she received Hollywood's ultimate accolade by being invited to play herself in *The First Wives Club*. She had only one line to deliver, but it was *the* line of the times: 'Don't get mad; get it all.'

She was working hard and having fun wherever her travels took her. After dinner at Sir Benjamin Slade's house in Chelsea in the autumn of 1997, Ivana and the eight other female guests retired to the drawing-room while the men remained to partake of port and cigars. It was a traditional British setting until the very un-British Ivana announced: 'We'll play a trick on them. Let's disappear.' While the men were discussing stocks and bonds, or maybe it was bloodstock and bondage, the women traipsed off to the King's Road, where they flagged down a couple of black cabs.

Surprised to see nine glamorous women, all with identical diamond spiders from the House of Ivana pinned to their breasts like the badges of some glittering sisterhood, one of the cabbies said. 'What, are you a coach party or something, luv? Where are all your men?'

'We've left them drinking,' replied Ivana.

'Oh, you mean they're down the pub?'

The women laughed and piled into the taxis.

'Berkeley Square!' ordered Ivana.

One of the group said: 'We went to Annabel's and the men eventually turned up because she'd left behind a little message saying, "Follow us if you want us." They forgave us because Ivana has great humour and it was done with such style. She even paid the £1,000 bill for champagne.'

The day after this escapade Ivana flew to Scotland to stay at Skibo Castle as the guest of the owner, the British millionaire Peter de Savary. And where was Marla Maples, her replacement in Donald's life until she, too, had been ditched? The former Miss Georgia Peach was making a scene in a New York restaurant because Tiffany had been kept waiting for her caviar!

Ivana flew to the former Yugoslavia, where she was invited to become involved in several new projects, including a casino. She said: 'In Eastern countries, I am like a heroine for coming from a Communist country and achieving what I have achieved. Everybody says I'm probably one of the most successful women who ever came out of an Eastern country. In these countries, people know that I'm very good with hotels and designs and that's what they're looking for – they know I'm very good as a promoter with a good product.' The former refugee from a Communist country had returned as a glowing advertisement for capitalism.

IVANA took Concorde from New York to London on Saturday, 6 June 1998, a day of brilliant sunshine in the capital in an otherwise perpetually soggy summer. She always came to London in June for the Season, with Ascot as the highpoint, but she had been delayed in New York and was running 24 hours late. This meant a high-speed dash to her Knightsbridge apartment and an even faster change for the first event on her packed schedule, the Louis Vuitton Concours d'Elegance at the Hurlingham Club. Ivana told us: 'I was late because I bought a hotel in New York City which is going to be called Ivana Suites.' A consortium had approached her and told her they would like to use her name in exchange for a 50 per cent stake in the enterprise. 'Why is my name so powerful?' Ivana asked, then answered her own question: 'Because it has a definitive quality associated with success. Whatever I have done so far in this area (and I'm knocking on wood) has been successful. So people want to capitalise on my good name and the professionalism and hard work which is associated with it.'

At the Hurlingham Club, classic Bugattis, Ferraris, Aston Martins, Bentleys, Mercedes-Benz and a single Stutz Bear Cat were lined up in front of the croquet lawns. The Palladian-style clubhouse was bathed in light and rock music blared over the Veuve Clicquot tent. Dinner for 850 was served in a huge marquee, with black-and-white chequered flags marking the entrance. Ivana's escort was an old friend and former lover, the Swedish banker, Henrik Jonson. She arrived to a broadside of exploding paparazzi flashguns and entered the marquee to find Riccardo Mazzuccelli, accompanied by a young model named Gisele Roman, preparing to tuck into the menu of monkfish, lamb and pavlova at an adjoining table. They did not exchange greetings.

Ivana said philosophically: 'After two divorces, some women say, "I don't need a man," and all that stuff. But I really enjoy men, I love men, I like their company, I want to be with them, I don't want to be without men.' After dinner, Ivana and Henrik adjourned to Annabel's only to find that Riccardo and Gisele had gone there as well for a nightcap. Riccardo was visibly shaken, while Ivana appeared undisturbed and took to the dance floor. She was still there when the lights went out at 3.30 a.m., but was wide awake at 8 a.m. for her morning workout.

Ivana's life of glitz was bound to include the occasional glitch and there was another two nights later when she arrived after the Queen for a royal command performance. Her Majesty was seated beside Prince Philip in the royal box and the house lights had dimmed when Ivana and Henrik slipped into their seats. The show, *Hey, Mr Producer*, was a musical extravaganza celebrating Sir Cameron Mackintosh's 30 years in showbusiness, with songs from the shows of Stephen Sondheim and Andrew Lloyd Webber. The star-studded cast included Jonathan Pryce, Elaine Paige, Dame Judi Dench (singing *Send In The Clowns*), Ruthie Henshall, Millicent Martin and Maria Friedman, but after the show it was Ivana and her friend, Shirley Bassey, who were invited to do a knees-up with a kilted Sir Cameron while the photographers snapped away.

Crowds lining the pavement cried out Ivana's name as she crossed the street to a champagne reception at One Aldwych, where she explained that she had meant no disrespect to the Queen, but had simply been held up in the crush in the foyer. We drove to Annabel's in her chauffeured Mercedes. Ivana liked to plan ahead and someone had to phone the *maître d'* to make sure that the smoked salmon and steak tartare would already be on the table when we arrived.

'First of all, I need a heart, a good person, and I need a brain,' said Ivana, talking about men again. 'I really don't care about looks – they're the icing on the cake. If I could find a man who was short and chubby, whom I could laugh with and have a fabulous conversation with, that would be just fine. I don't look for power; I couldn't care less. Money is good – don't get me wrong – money buys you a better car and a nicer home, but I have been without it. Money is important, but you have to be able to support yourself and the man has to support himself, his wife and his family. But trillions or millions – it doesn't really matter: how many steaks can you eat, or how many cars can you drive a day? At the end of the day what matters is your family and your happiness and how you get along.'

The following morning Ivana worked out with her trainer and breakfasted with Ivanka, who had joined her from Paris. Ivanka was now 16, as blonde as her mother, but slightly taller, and already a star of the Paris fashion shows. She had signed a modelling contract with the Elite agency of New York at the age of 14 and made her catwalk debut for Thierry Mugler the following year, wearing a pout and a daring black PVC dress with fake fur trim. Robin Anderson said: 'Mother and daughter are the greatest of friends. I escorted Ivana and Ivanka to a concert by Shirley Bassey at the Royal Festival Hall and Ivana wore a sequined snakeskin sheath belonging to Ivanka. The incredible love and warmth this woman creates can be seen in the adoration of her three children.'

Ivana said: 'My kids are great. I told them not to cheat, steal and lie, not to take drugs or alcohol, and I taught them that money doesn't fall from trees. You have to earn it, you have to work for it. If they wanted a bike, they had to work for it. My children work all summer long. Donald

Junior is working for his father – he's already at the School of Finance, so he's getting a dose of the business. Eric is working on a golf course and Ivanka studies French in Paris and goes to modelling classes. And I teach them how to manage their money. If I give them some money for Christmas, they invest it on Wall Street. They're learning from their youth because, eventually, they're going to come to the money and so I'm preparing them for it.

'I like to be known, of course, as a mother and I want to be known, hopefully, as a wife – I've been a good wife. My two marriages failed, but it takes two to tango. I want to be known as a business person and, at the end of the day, I want to be known as a woman. This is what is so hard for every woman around the world, the juggling of these four things is very hard. Some people cannot do it, some overdo it in business and have no time for the family. Some women concentrate only on the family and when the kids are out of the nest they're desperate because they have nothing to fall back on.

'The biggest challenge in the nineties for women, and for me, is to be properly balanced, so that you can get the joy and the satisfaction out of the work, but you're still womanly, you're feminine, you're fun and you enjoy your life and still have time for the family and time for yourself. How do I see femininity? I like women who take good care of themselves. They have confidence in themselves. You have to take care of yourself, you have to be confident, you have to like living and you have to be happy because if you're miserable it shows on you and that's sad.

'There is a very fine line for women, especially in business, because during the day if you go around 4,500 employees and you want to be feminine and you want to be soft-spoken it doesn't work all the time because you have to be a leader. Someone has to tell people what to do and you have to be strict. I'm not saying tough, but you have to be strong and strict at times. Some people say that's when you lose your femininity because everybody is supposed to be like a Barbie doll. You're not supposed to say anything and look pretty and blonde, with big boobs and all that stuff. Some people think that's feminine.

'Feminine is also liking people, liking men. All of what I feel contributes to my femininity. I can be strong and I can be a businesswoman, but I believe I'm feminine. I like to dress up nicely, I like to show my assets as a woman. If I have good legs, I show them, if I have a nice bosom, I show it off without being vulgar. But when a woman flirts with men, she shows them the power of the woman. The mind can be very, very sexy. A lot of men are either threatened by it or they love it and you have to find a man who likes it, but a lot of men are definitely threatened if a woman has a brain.'

Ivana broke off the conversation to supervise some building work, then took a telephone call from Princess Michael of Kent to make arrangements for an upcoming gala.

Do you ever get the feeling that people are using you?

'Could be. Could be. I'd love to say no, but you never know what motivates other people. I'm always on my guard and I watch for it. I can smell a phoney five miles away, so I can detect it fairly easily.'

Whom do you admire in international politics?

'Let me think: who do I really look up to? I can't say President Clinton, that's for sure. I don't basically trust politicians, maybe because I was from Communist Czechoslovakia and they were so corrupted. So I definitely don't look up to them.'

Henrik Jonsson bowed out as Ivana's escort when Count Roffredo flew in from New York. At a charity dinner at the Dorchester, she glowed beside him in a simple, sleek, lilac Valentino gown that not only showed her honed body to advantage, but also showed up the over-embroidered *haute couture* outfits of more sophisticated ladies. After another night in Annabel's, Ivana flew back to America to address a symposium of American women in Atlanta on the subject of her success, then returned to London for Ascot Week.

'I have learned from my sport to be confident in myself, but also to have tremendous discipline and competitiveness,' she said. 'If you're not competitive in sport, you don't win the race. And when you finish with sport, competitiveness doesn't go away. You're competitive in life whatever you do and that's good. You have to see what your competitors are up to and beat them to it by being better than them. With discipline, you set yourself a certain goal and try to achieve it. Maybe you're not going to win the Olympics, but let's try to be sixth or seventh. You always have to try your best and I've always had a tremendous discipline.

'I'm also very good at organising my time. I can have a long day of work and then cut it off at night, and I do cut if off and I especially cut it off with a man and my friends. It might be a little bit rough, but in the evening I go with my friends and forget about it. It doesn't involve my friends and I don't want them to see my long face if something goes wrong. If I cut it off, I can have a *leetle* bit of private life and fun.'

With wealthy Americans arriving on every Concorde flight for the racing at Ascot, there was no shortage of partygoers. Members of the Lucky Sperm Club mixed with British aristocrats and self-made moguls to the sound of disco music and popping champagne corks. Annabel's, Harry's Bar and the salons of Chelsea and Belgravia began to swell with rich, blonde women of a certain age, all of whom seemed to have embraced Ivana's axiom of showing off one's assets.

So little cellulite and so much blonde hair, lip gloss and Palm Beach tan were on display that it seemed as though a convention of the Ivana fan club was in session. One party was wall-to-wall with *décolletage* and a number of Viagra suspects could be seen lurking among the potted palms; alas in vain. These women were sharper than the points of their six-inch Gucci stilettos and one of them, Chicago novelist Sugar Rautbord, had been chosen by *Vanity Fair* as one of the most influential women in America.

In a short, strapless, black cocktail dress, Ivana was enjoying the attention of several male admirers when Riccardo emerged through the throng. Their eyes met across a crowded room, but there was not a flicker of recognition. Ivana's smile looked as though it had been painted on and a large man placed a comforting hand around her bare shoulders. For an instant, her vulnerability showed. She departed soon afterwards with her friend, Sugar Rautbord, and Riccardo joined us on the geranium-fringed balcony. One of the other guests, a middle-aged, German-born New Yorker, was delighted to see him and innocently inquired: 'Why don't we see you in New York any more, Riccardo?'

With operatic *élan*, Riccardo pressed a well-manicured hand to the breast pocket of his spotless cream jacket. 'Heartache,' he sighed. 'New York was where I fell in love and where I was divorced. I can't bear to go back.'

'Oh, Riccardo,' chided the lady, 'you're *so* Italian.'

IN THE END, one man was constantly on Ivana's mind and it wasn't Riccardo or Roffredo or Henrik. 'Returning to the question of whom I admire,' she said, 'I definitely admire Donald Trump very much. He started working for his father for $50,000 a year and then he lost a lot because he got a *leetle* cocky, but he just built it all over again.

'The guy's a genius, he's phenomenal. We are now on very, very good terms, but we don't work together any more. Donald always takes the credit for everything and I didn't mind when I was married to him because he was the father of my children, but I don't want him in the business any more saying, "I told her so," or "I did it for her." It's just better like this.'

With three children, a Swedish banker, an Italian count, five homes, a yacht, a ticket to the Royal Enclosure and, now, a hotel, it certainly was better like this.

11

Ladies Who Lynch

CLARISSA DICKSON WRIGHT, daughter of a royal surgeon and a society heiress, was raised in a mansion in St John's Wood and became a *connoisseur* of feminine power among the upper classes. 'The most powerful place I've ever been in was the *Tribune des Dames* at Longchamp racecourse,' said Clarissa. 'You see all these bejewelled, aristocratic, or very rich, well-honed Frenchwomen, very elegant, and they're really sorting things out in a way, perhaps, that we don't do in England any more. It's a real powerhouse and a lot harder to get into than the Royal Enclosure at Ascot. All these silly women who come from nowhere and want to crash in on the male world forget how much power these women have.'

French, English or American, they'd been around longer than Jennifer's Diary, but it took the eighties' obsession with labels to give them a *nom de guerre*. The Ladies Who Lunch made their first appearance as a species in the age of power dressing, JR and Alexis, the mobile phone, Yuppies, bad hair days and the rocket salad. In fact, the rocket salad was invented for Ladies Who Lunch who didn't actually want to eat lunch. 'The food is not in the least important to them,' said Clarissa, one of TV's *Two Fat Ladies*. 'All they want is a well-turned lettuce leaf.'

In common with other totems of conspicuous consumption, the Ladies Who Lunch hit a peak of popularity and, once the Essex girls came in, the genuine article discreetly faded from the scene to regroup. Ira Kettner, a dazzling, green-eyed, German-born socialite to whom the word refinement attached itself like a Dresden glaze, said: 'I always say,

"Better *nouveau riche* than never *riche*"; I have nothing against *nouveau riche*, although they do, of course, like to show off.'

Ladies Who Lunch, *Mark II*, were relaunched in London soon after the last Sharon had returned to Chingford. And where did this favoured few now go? To Daphne's (where the waiters were the fastest in Chelsea), Scalini's (which had survived the Duchess of York and, more recently, the Chelsea football team), Mark's Club (to be seen and not overheard) and, of course, San Lorenzo (to be seen and overheard).

Many of the restaurants at the big hotels were also on the approved list, including the *belle époque* dining-room at the Ritz, Claridge's (where Dame Barbara Cartland was practically a fixture), the Savoy Grill and Cafe Nico at the Grosvenor House. None of these places, however, compared with Harry's Bar in Mayfair. Kookie Fallah, a contributing editor for *Tatler* magazine, said: 'Harry's Bar is definitely *the* premier lunching spot. It's trendy chic rather than the quiet elegance of Mark's Club, and very cleverly done. There are no carpets in the bar, and the tables are very small, with no flowers, but it works.'

It was at Harry's Bar, pre the 1998 Season, that five women, coiffed to the hilt and dressed in impeccable couture with, for reasons not apparent to an outsider, Chopard 'happy watches' in various pastel shades on their wrists, gathered over the one glass of champagne permitted in their diet. Nothing had been left to chance: faces had been beautified by Eve Lom or Janet Filderman, legs hot waxed at the Violet Adair Salon, nails sharpened and painted by Maxine at Michaeljohn, hair tinted by *éminence grise* Joe Hansford and styled at Toni and Guy or Nicky Clarke, and hairpieces fitted into place by Naim of Beauchamp Place. Leaving Versace to the younger generation of Voguettes, they had gone to Dior, Valentino and Chanel to buy their timeless, classical outfits.

These were the wives of men who controlled between them in excess of $5 billion in varying fields of industry and this was not merely a casual lunch to display their finery, but a 'business lunch' played out according to a set of unwritten, but well-understood, rules of engagement. The whispered rumours in the City were that a takeover bid was being considered by one of the women's husbands and the fact that the wife of his intended prey had been included in the group was no accident.

This was feminine power in its most potent form under the guise of a sociable lunch, a fact-finding mission in which every nuance would, in due course, be discussed with their respective spouses. As it happened, Socialite No. 1 gleaned a very useful piece of intelligence from Socialite No. 2. 'She let slip that she would not be attending the Red Cross Ball in Monte Carlo,' she said. 'We later found out that they'd very quietly put their place in Antibes on the market, which meant money was tight.'

So the New Age nineties had developed Borgian overtones and the Ladies Who Lunch were, on occasions like this, the Ladies Who Lynch. Ira Kettner, who is married to the millionaire industrialist Max Kettner, explained the main prerequisite for members of this charmed circle: 'You must have loyalty because there are so many social climbers who may well use you and then drop you at any given time. Loyalty I would define as, if you make a friend, he or she really defends you if need be, and it also means being discreet. If you're loyal to a person, you're automatically discreet.

'I have a zipper where other people have a mouth. I just don't talk. My husband calls me the most secret person he knows. It's something I was born with; it's in my character. I have two very big ears and I listen, but I just don't talk. You're much safer in not making enemies that way – not that having enemies particularly disturbs me at all – I think we all have some enemies.'

The most common enemy for Ladies Who Lunch was the predator. 'I call them sharks, either the barracuda or the shark,' said Ira. 'You can tell them straightaway because their behaviour is aggressive in a super, super feminine way; very flirtatious, very sexy. They pull all the strings and we women all have the same wiles, so we recognise what is going on. Generally, they focus on a powerful man, irrespective of whether he's married or not. Some are cleverer than others, but like the barracuda they go straight for the jugular.

'They come from all different backgrounds. Look, I have seen women who operate this way who come from very good backgrounds, wealthy families, but they were just attracted to that sort of powerplay. And, of course, I've seen women who are extremely hungry; hungry not in the physical sense, but just hungry for fulfilling their ambition. They want this particular person because he's famous, or they have seen his wife who wears the most stunning jewellery with big diamonds, or has racehorses, or a plane – you name it. Most of them would be prepared to become just a girlfriend, but if they can boot out the wife, better still.'

Donatella Flick refused to name names, but it was common knowledge in these rarified circles that a number of barracudas had tried their luck with her ex-husband, the Daimler-Benz heir Muck Flick. One rich, exotic beauty sent a huge tin of golden caviar to his home as a token of esteem. Muck, however, did not appreciate the overture and ordered his housekeeper to throw the contents out of the window. Passers-by were astonished to see a stream of very expensive golden globules raining down into the street from the Flick household.

Marisa Masters, an Italian-born Belgravia socialite, became all too familiar with the predatory woman at the time of her divorce from her husband, Lindsay Masters, who was Michael Heseltine's partner in

Haymarket Publishing. 'When we were separating, there were six or seven women around me and I thought they were like sisters,' said Marisa. 'One of them was Italian like me, but the first time I met her at a party she was very impolite. Then she discovered I had a big country house and announced that she was coming down to stay for the weekend. I said, "Excuse me, but I only invite my friends."

'After that, she started dropping into my London house for coffee. She was soon taking Krug out of the refrigerator and eating the food; I didn't mind that because I always cooked for people to eat. This went on for three or four years and I knew she came to see my husband. Then my husband left home and they all left, too – on the same day. The Italian was the first to go. It was disgusting. I became cynical, really cynical. If there is no loyalty, there is nothing.'

Although she would never admit it, Marisa was one of the godmothers of London's *literati* and *glitterati* and she knew just about everybody. More to the point, they knew her. She had been a force on the London scene ever since her friend, Mary Quant, had sewn her first miniskirt back at the dawn of the swinging sixties. Her Filofax was crammed with the private numbers of people listed in Who's Really Who and her mantelpiece overflowed with invitations to the hottest gigs in the Royal Borough of Kensington and Chelsea.

Marisa was to be found at home in a listed five-storey Georgian house in Walton Place, just behind Harrods. It was here that Joan Collins had got a rare comeuppance after Marisa had turned the house over to charity for a gala evening. House, garden and gazebo were overflowing with contributing guests when Marisa spotted La Collins, all high heels and Hollywood *hauteur*, making a grand entrance in the upstairs living-room. Marisa greeted her with a smile and stopped to exchange pleasantries, but Joan demanded in the stridently imperious tones of *Dynasty's* Alexis: 'Who *are* you?'

Loud enough to be heard over at Harrods, Marisa replied: 'And who are *you*?' Champagne flutes halted in mid-air and all eyes swivelled from one protagonist to the other. The *cognescenti* knew it was Marisa's house and realised that a social gaffe of some magnitude was in progress. As Joan tottered hurriedly past, Marisa added for good measure: 'I never watch *Dallas* anyway.'

The mother of three daughters, Marisa was a smiling, gamine figure in flowing robes, her hair cut Caesar-style long before Tony Blair made it popular. She had kept her place in society despite a regrettable solecism at Lord Porchester's wedding when she refused to curtsey to the Queen. 'I only genuflect to Jesus Christ,' she had told Her Majesty when they met during the wedding reception at Carnarvon Castle.

To Marisa Masters, feminine power meant independence, 'but I'm not thinking about financial independence; I'm thinking about mental independence. In other words, women have to be true to themselves whatever they're doing, whatever they're planning, whatever they're feeling. Their motives must be pure; they must not be thinking, "If I do this, then I can gain that." Nor should women start by thinking, "I'm empowering myself." Power should come automatically and naturally from their actions; otherwise, it's contrived. "Empowering yourself" comes from the inside.'

KOOKIE FALLAH, born in England of Persian parents, had been a big league player among the movers and *sheikas* since the seventies when she owned a house on the Thames at Datchet. The house had a particular significance to American visitors because it was here that Mrs Simpson stayed while her relationship with David, Prince of Wales, later Edward VIII, was still a well-kept secret. 'He used to pop across the river from Fort Belvedere to see her,' said Kookie.

Everybody from Cabinet ministers to Hollywood stars rubbed shoulders at Kookie's summer parties which heralded the opening of the Season. The parties had a different theme every year, long before themed parties became the vogue, and one year she borrowed the entire window display from Harvey Nichols to provide the setting for Cleopatra's Egypt.

Twice divorced and the mother of two daughters, Kookie had her own ideas about empowerment. 'Basically, it means to be in command of yourself,' she said. 'Women most definitely are coming into their own and I don't mean your pushy woman. You can have quiet power; you don't need to shriek and shout and push to get your own way. I've found over the years my voice drops an octave and I speak slowly when I want something and I get it as a result. Women who make the mistake of shrieking and talking fast don't get it. It is quiet power.

'You can't abuse it, either. You can see it in how a woman runs her home if she has staff. I have a lot of lady friends who slightly abuse their staff, which is wrong. They probably don't have the genuine power that they need; it's chequebook power: "You will respect me because I'm paying you." But I think it's much easier, strangely enough, and I think it works better if you do it with love. I can get so much more from my staff with love than with the chequebook – I know because I have that sort of relationship with them. The power of love is important. It works every time in any given situation.

'I'm always very admiring of mothers, but that's not very fashionable. Mothers seem to be very instrumental in making or breaking a child in terms of when they become an adult, more so than the father. They have more influence. Father's daughter is always trying to impress daddy. My daughters live in England and we get on great. This is what I mean about the power of the mother. I think I've probably done everything for the three of us at all times. When they were young, we'd do homework together. We were like three friends, basically, and so now that's why we are very close.'

With a house in Knightsbridge and an apartment on the Croisette in Cannes, Kookie was in a position to pick and choose the men in her life. 'Something I find very easy is to attract men,' she said. 'Flirting is instinctive with me, but I also find it very easy to talk to men and, nine times out of ten, I think they enjoy talking to me. But flirting makes it a more enjoyable evening. Personally, it is not because I'm planning to go any further; it will end at the end of the dinner party, and always does, strangely enough. It's mindplay and, of course, I'm calling the shots. With one exception in the last year, they all know where it stops because I'm sending the message correctly. Some women give out mixed messages which is unfortunate, but I'm in control.

'Powerful men all have a darker side, like Onassis. I had dinner at the Savoy with Ari and Alexander the night before Alexander flew to Athens and he died the next day. Ari was completely and utterly devastated, which was very sad, but then he didn't say, "Well, at least I've got a daughter." He took it out on Christina.

'I prefer a man who is equal to me. What I mean by that is equal in their thought processes rather than their finances. I'm not too bothered if they're not rolling in dough, although I'd like them to be able to hold their own. They must not feel threatened. The really evolved man does not see women as a threat and can take bad jokes about men without feeling threatened.

'It's their personality I go for, not their looks. Looks are a criterion, but it isn't, "Oh, it's because he's not good-looking or he's bald or whatever." But I wouldn't mistrust a man because he's good-looking. I don't mistrust men, but I might prejudge him in terms of, "Oh, he won't be very interesting to talk to." I've often found that when they're drop-dead gorgeous they just stand there and expect things to happen. I've found that after a week of knowing a gorgeous man, you forget how gorgeous looking he is and you need a conversation. And I'm being very generous with a week.'

NEW YORKER Nicole Petschek studied acting in Paris, but became disillusioned with the superficiality of the acting world. She moved to London and married the Marquis Gian-Luca de Francisci, a Sicilian financier. They had a son, Johnny, but later divorced. Nicole had ridden since she was a child and ended up fighting for women's rights in the male-dominated world of high-goal polo, even joining the Guards Polo Club.

'The dirty work was done for me,' she said. 'The suffragists fought for a cause and I'm a beneficiary. I admire women who have fought against the distractions of life to stay on track to achieve their own goals. Along the way, they mastered their own trade so well that they could take it in their stride and, when other opportunities presented themselves, they were able to assimilate and take more on board. They have very clear minds, obviously well channelled, and they put down strong foundations and build on them. Some people fight a losing battle just brushing their teeth and dressing themselves, but these women do 20 other things in the day. In a more developed sense, that's what empowerment is. There's a strength about them.

'We have to know what we want. If you don't know what you want, you're not going to get there. But if you do know what you want and you go after it, everything else seems to get on a moving escalator and comes with you, and it's not that difficult if you're using your own talents. In the Western world, we are in a very lucky period because the universal consciousness is coming back into our lives. Today, it is acceptable to speak about feelings, hopes and fears, and these used to be social taboos. Most fears are unfounded, but it's empowering to talk about them and the empowered woman can help her man and her children to deal with them.

'It's the role of a woman to give what she has and she may not have the same attributes as a man, but she does have gifts. Just using your gifts gives you a power. If you have certain gifts and attributes, you are developing a natural talent. The talent of giving to a man simply comes from sensitivity. I'm not saying that men are not sensitive; I think men are just as senitive as women, and sometimes more so, but they are not allowed in the social context that we live in to show their sensitivity as much or to use it as much.

'Therefore, they grow distant from it and it becomes something unfamiliar to them, whereas women have been encouraged since they were little girls to be attuned to sensitivity. It's a word that girls grow up with; boys grow up with, "Be brave. If he hits you, hit him back. Be aggressive." That sensitivity is what a girl has naturally and she's encouraged to use it instinctively, so when she becomes an adult she then makes a conscious effort to use her talents and that becomes a very powerful attribute if she uses it correctly.

'Women are empowered simply by listening. People who don't talk normally don't talk not because they've got nothing to say. People don't talk because they've been frightened when they were children, or every time they opened their mouths they were told, "That's ridiculous." This man then shuts off and after a while he lives in his own head and when he has a problem it boils around in his head, bouncing from one side of the brain to the other, but it's not going anywhere. It just expands and creates pressure until he can't see where he's going any more, he doesn't have vision any more, his instincts are smothered.

'All he needs is for somebody to sit down and let them talk and they get the gunge out. He trusts the person he's talking to not to laugh at him because he knows she's not going to be judgmental. If the listener can understand and respect that this person has his own reason then that person will finally find the confidence to talk. And we all have our answers within ourselves. It's natural empowerment and it's very powerful.'

CRITERIA for joining the Ladies Who Lunch varies from city to city. 'It's money in New York and it's money in Houston,' said Mary Margaret Valenti, wife of Jack Valenti, president of the Motion Picture Association of America. 'Here in Washington it's power. Money's nice to have and I'm not dismissing it, but it doesn't seem to be quite so important here. Power is important in Washington and the best way to a powerful position is to have a powerful husband.'

Mary Margaret was working for Senator Lyndon B. Johnson on Capitol Hill when she met Jack Valenti, a war hero and rising star in the Democratic Party machine in her home town of Houston. Eighteen months after the couple were married, Jack was in the motorcade when President John F. Kennedy was assassinated in Dallas on 22 November 1963. He was invited by Johnson to serve on his staff in the White House and, three years later, moved into his present powerful position in the movie industry. 'Those were the days of the Washington hostess, but not very many women want to be known as hostesses any more; they want to be taken more seriously than that,' said Mary Margaret. 'It seems to me that entertaining as such has got less important than it was 20 years ago because more women go to work, it's harder to get help and it's more expensive. But Jack likes for me to be involved in entertaining and we occasionally have a fundraiser at home.

'He also likes me to be around if he's entertaining at the office and I go because I like to be with interesting, attractive people. Jack likes me to know people and I'm glad to know them; I like to know the people he does business with and, perhaps, in some undefined way it helps to seal his relationship with these people. I know a number of the wives of chief executives in the movie industry and when I'm in California I have dinner with them. So a woman can carve out a niche for herself if she wants to be helpful to her husband.'

One of Mary Margaret's great friends was Lyn Rothman, English wife of Moses 'Mo' Rothman, former vice-president of Columbia Pictures and owner of the Charlie Chaplin Library. Lyn used her Hollywood contacts to raise vast amounts of cash for the Aids Crisis Trust by holding dinners and film premieres. 'In Los Angeles, it's money *and* power that count and the Ladies Who Lunch are very charity oriented,' she said. 'I'm talking about women whose husbands are very successful in the film industry: the Kirk Douglases, the Marvin Davises, Barbara Sinatra. I used to think of Ladies Who Lunch as ladies who do nothing, but these women do a lot. Out of their lunches come a lot of wonderfully generous fundraising ideas for the foundations they support.

'London ladies are more frivolous. I don't know ladies in New York or Los Angeles who have lunch for the sake of a gossip, whereas people in London say, "Let's catch up. Let's do lunch." So you sit and have lunch and nothing creative comes out of it. There's a certain embarrassment in America about going out to lunch if there's not a reason. What I've learned from the Americans, who are so good at it, is that it's a great way to get people together to exchange ideas, whether it's in the art world or the charity world.

'Life is so quick these days that you don't have time just to sit and have long lunches. In LA, ladies play tennis, they play bridge, they do their hair, they have a massage and then they attend charity committee meetings. I'm talking about women of a certain age because the younger generation don't do any of this. This is a certain Hollywood élite.'

As women like Lyn Rothman, Mary Margaret Valenti *et al* have proved, it would be a mistake to regard Ladies Who Lunch as trophy wives. With great dedication, they have enhanced their husbands' careers and now enjoy displaying the fruits of their success.

'In New York and LA, the smart woman has the same casual chic as Italian women and they certainly wear their jewellery,' said Lyn. 'Mo used to give me wonderful jewels and I never wore them. For a long time I used to put them away in the safe. Then I had a doctor who said to me, "This is a man who started with nothing. He built his life, he built a career, he became one of the most powerful men in Hollywood. He'd love the idea of you wearing the things he's given you." That changed my whole attitude because I suddenly realised it was something to do with my English upbringing that you don't ostentatiously wear jewellery. But it gives him so much joy to see me wearing something he's given me. Now I really don't care what people think if it gives Mo pleasure. He comes first in my life.'

Jewellery has never been an issue in New York, where the only aristocracy is wealth. 'Money, money, money, dahling, is what you need here,' said man-about-Manhattan and *soi-disant* arbiter of social taste, Richard Turley.

High on the New York A-list was Coco Blaffer, a divorcee who, like Mary Margaret Valenti, was originally from Houston. 'My grandparents sold Humble Oil to Standard Oil of New Jersey, which later became Exxon,' said Coco. 'They cleverly set up trust funds for their grandchildren, so we all live well and travel a lot.'

In Coco's case, that meant dividing her time between homes in New York, Newport, London and Monte Carlo. 'There are many social worlds in New York City,' she said. 'It used to be the Gentiles and the Jews, but now it's the Americans and the Euro-stars. Clubs like the Knickerbocker and the Colony are focal points for very elegant lunches. Everybody is beautifully dressed, friendly, the food is superb, the waiters are lovely and the white wine is chilled to the right degree. You have to be attracted to a glamorous lifestyle because expensive lunches mean getting your hair done in the morning, looking fine and wearing just the right dress and jewels.

'It's also important where you go in summer on the seaboard. Newport is the queen of the sea and the horsey set go to Millbrook for the racing at Saratoga. Nantucket is very popular, but it's expensive and you can barely get a reservation. The Hamptons are also popular, but there's a drinking, drugging, fast-driving attitude there that has to be avoided. If you go abroad to London or Monte Carlo, you have to know how to pack and catch a plane and know where to stay when you get there and have some friends to look up. In London, women are much more interested in having a good time than in New York. They're more frivolous and like doing things together. In New York, everybody is very busy with their careers, or their clothes, or their divorce, so they're a little more frantic.'

Divorce, of course, was a vital issue. One of the women on the New York circuit was Joscelyne Wildenstein, who was in the process of ditching her husband, the millionaire art dealer Alec Wildenstein, after catching him in bed with a young Russian blonde. Joscelyne's friends closed ranks to protect her when she was labelled 'the Bride of Wildenstein' by the American press because of her unusual, feline appearance. Coco Blaffer said: 'She told her plastic surgeon that she wanted to look like a cat and he said, "Well, I'll do my best." So she really asked him to make her look strange. She was tired of looking like the average person and wanted to look like Cat Woman in *Batman*. She was also very tired of having been married for 20 years to a very difficult person.'

Ira Kettner said: 'This is not a case where the husband came into money lately and, therefore, had to have a young, statuesque wife; no. I think it's a case where the money has always been there and his wife just turned into a monster. Look at the photographs of her in the papers: she has been to the plastic surgeon and had everything done over and over again, and I think he was fed up. She resembled an alien more than a human being and looking at his paramour, she's delicious and young and beautiful, so I can't really blame him.'

Women in these circles, however, have nothing against cosmetic surgery as such. Kookie Fallah said: 'All the women I know – let's put it this way: the Ladies Who Lunch – talk about it and who one should go to. "Dr So-and-so does noses better than anyone else," or "You should do Diana Ross, but you might get Michael Jackson instead." Julie Christie always said she wouldn't and she has, and she looks wonderful. I don't have a problem with it. I think the day will come when I'll do it. If something needs lifting or pulling or whatever; if it makes *me* feel better, I don't see the problem.'

Lyn Rothman said: 'Many of my British friends look after themselves, but maybe that's because we spend a lot of time in America and all of us are indoctrinated with image. You feel better if you exercise and you feel better about yourself if you look reasonable. I feel rotten if I let myself go so I'm on the treadmill every morning and I have a manicure every week and a facial every month. In America, women don't have facials. They prefer to have the knife, which I find most extraordinary.'

Liz Brewer, public relations *doyenne* and self-described social catalyst, has studied Ladies Who Lunch in many different settings. 'Femininity has a certain gentleness; it's not abrasive,' she said. 'Some women who are very powerful are not powerful by being loud and aggressive. It's strange that, behind closed doors, some of the more powerful and what you might consider aggressive women absolutely go to pieces. They're very vulnerable and they desperately need to be reassured.

'Liz Taylor is vulnerable – desperately so! I was a guest at the Khashoggis staying at La Baraque in Spain and Liz Taylor was staying there; George Hamilton was there – there was quite a gang of us – and it was the first time that Liz Taylor had met Soraya Khashoggi or maybe it was the first time for a long long time. Anyway, I remember Soraya was there with all the children around and she was going to meet Liz at tea. Well, Liz Taylor had one of Soraya's dressers helping her to unpack and, afterwards, she said, "You know, she changed eight times before she finally came out to meet Soraya for tea." She changed *eight* times!'

Kookie Fallah had also had an opportunity to observe Liz Taylor's vulnerability. 'Perhaps she's not as empowered as one would like to think she is,' she said. 'I saw her in Acapulco when we both went to lunch at a friend's house and she walked in with her hairdresser, her personal maid, a white fluffy dog and some sort of make-up man or scriptwriter. They were all clucking around her and they were all superfluous to the occasion. There was no need for them to be there, but she *needed* them there. It was a perfectly nice, little – strangely enough for Acapulco it *was* little – lunch party; there were only about eight or ten of us and there was no one there who was going to interview her or misquote her or take a picture of her – none of that – yet she still needed these three handmaidens. She's a sad case.'

Least vulnerable among the Ladies Who Lunch was the redoubtable Raine, Countess Spencer. Who else had the panache to walk through Mayfair on a sunny Sunday dressed in a Laura Ashley sailor-style dress in the requisite shades of the season, lilac and white, and shielding her delicate complexion with a dainty white parasol? Princess Diana's stepmother was lunching that day at Scott's restaurant on Mount Street and her entrance caused something of a sensation.

When she sat down at a table with a male companion, an awestruck American socialite insisted on changing places with her husband to get a better view, even though a waiter was in the middle of serving vegetables on to her plate. Astute as ever, Raine spotted the manoeuvre and quietly asked to be moved to a more secluded part of the restaurant. There she took a compact from her Chanel handbag and nonchalantly powdered her face. As Princess Diana knew only too well, nothing fazed Raine.

Diana herself had gained enormous support from American women who understood the problems that liberated women faced in male-dominated societies. 'I admired Princess Diana's vulnerability and I admired her continuance at trying to develop herself under duress,' said the London-based American model Christina Estrada. 'She taught us something of love and love is the only thing that really matters – loving yourself, loving your neighbour, loving your country, loving your work.

'The last time I met Diana was just after she had done the *Panorama* interview on television. The Duchess of York was giving a Children in Crisis fundraiser at Kensington Palace. This was a time when Sarah and Diana were coming back together. There had been some problems between them and they'd just re-established their friendship after a period of separation. There was that old sense of fun again; they were there to support each other and it was just a very happy, friendly feeling.

'Sarah introduced me to Diana and I said, "I just want to say something to you. I saw your interview and I think it was a really courageous thing you did." She looked very nervous because she'd had a lot of comments about it. People were saying, "Oh God, how could she do it? How could she air her dirty laundry?" But it's the truth, isn't it? Why are we so afraid of facing the truth? Why should she deny it or hide it?

'So I said to Diana, "Well done." If it wasn't for that interview, the press would continue to blow up every aspect of her life. Now that she's passed on, I'm kind of happy that she did what she did because we have these tapes to look back on. She had a chance to absolve herself, however manipulative people thought she was. This is a royal soap opera, yet this is the story of our lives. We're all living it, we're all growing up with each other, and it's important, especially before the Millennium when a lot is going to happen, that we have the courage to be honest with ourselves. That is what Diana taught us.'

In death, Diana still wielded the power of influence and nowhere was that power more visible than in a glittering tableau that took place under the Dome of the Victoria & Albert Museum on the evening of St Valentine's Day, 1998. Here, in the vast chamber beneath the crowning cupola of a monument dedicated to a young English Queen and her German-born Consort, 250 or so rich and powerful women gathered with their partners to honour one of Princess Diana's favourite charities, the Great Ormond Street Children's Hospital.

Many of these women had known Diana personally through their charitable work for the hospital and one of the organisers, Mrs Chrisanthy Lemos, had been shaken to receive a letter from Diana about tonight's function some months after her death. In remembrance of the Princess and her devotion to sick children, the evening had been titled The Greatest Love and, as a further reminder, Diana's photograph was printed in the gold-embossed souvenir programme which was handed to guests as they entered the museum.

One of the guests was Raine Spencer, who worked for Mohammed Al Fayed as a director of Harrods International. Only a few of Raine's closest friends knew that she had encouraged Diana's friendship with Mohammed's eldest son, Dodi Al Fayed, and that she had suffered a double blow when they were killed in Paris. While Raine bore her grief with dignity, Mohammed moved mountains to convert Diana's fleeting appearance in his midst into something far more substantial. Several of Dodi's friends knew that this was not the first time Mohammed had meddled in his romantic life. In accordance with Arab custom, he had previously tried to marry Dodi off to Nabila Khashoggi, the actress daughter of his former brother-in-law, Adnan Khashoggi. 'Mohammed saw an arranged marriage as a means of consolidating two family fortunes,' said a friend, 'but Nabila turned down the proposal. As first cousins, she and Dodi already knew each other too well to be anything more than friends.'

At the V&A, Raine was accompanied by the ubiquitous Riccardo Mazzuccelli when she joined other guests for champagne in the Gamble Room. In the absence of a Beardsley, it was left to a photographer from *Hello!* magazine to record the images that would provide a permanent record of this event in the terminal years of the Millennium: Raine in a stunning gold-and-pink patterned Elizabethan ballgown crowned by a strawberry blonde bouffant; Riccardo in his dinner suit, his black hair so brilliantined he appeared to have just stepped out of the shower, puffing furiously on a cigarette in defiance of a no-smoking ordinance from the museum authorities.

But it was not so much the eye-catching glamour of Raine and Riccardo as the rich assortment of different nationalities among the assembled guests that showed how Diana's influence had recrafted English society. One thing the English had learned during their long tenure of Empire was how quickly wealth could be redistributed and, with Arab sheiks, South African entrepreneurs, Chinese tycoons and the new breed of Russian capitalist buying up large chunks of London and the Home Counties, the lines of social demarcation had been hastily redrawn to accommodate the new dynasties and their millions.

There were Greeks, Americans and Gulf Arabs, Italians, Lebanese and Australians at the V&A that night and the names of committee members read like an International Who's Who. These were all Diana's people because, more than any other member of the Royal Family, she had succeeded in becoming a truly global royal, Princess of the World.

Just before 9 p.m., the guests adjourned to the Raphael Gallery, where they took their seats for a little pre-dinner entertainment. The acting fraternity was represented by Jeremy Irons and his sister-in-law, Niamh Cusack. Raffishly attired in a velvet Regency jacket, Jeremy played the love-struck Roman emperor Titus in a rendition of Racine's play *Berenice*, with Niamh in the role of the beautiful eastern queen.

The tragic story of how Titus was forced to send his loved one away because she was unacceptably foreign to his Roman countrymen fitted in perfectly with the evening's Greatest Love theme. Few could ignore the unspoken reference to Diana and Dodi and several ladies dabbed their eyes with scented handkerchiefs. When the guests sat down under the Dome to dine on fillet of salmon, rack of lamb and *feuillantine* of raspberries, there were red roses and red hearts everywhere and Diana's legacy was impossible to miss.

They were still nibbling on pink-and-white chocolate truffles when Lord Archer bounded into the spotlight to conduct the fundraising auction and the spell was broken. Jeffrey Archer was such a dab hand at squeezing money out of people that his presence at such a dinner was almost obligatory. Few people here could forget that it was Lord Archer who had introduced Diana when she made her 'time and space' speech at the Hilton Hotel before bowing out of public life. But they also knew that she had made a spirited comeback to fight for the causes dearest to her heart. 'I'm not a political figure, nor do I want to be one,' she had said during a visit to Angola to campaign against anti-personnel landmines. 'But I do come here with my heart and I want to help people.'

Diana had owed it to Prince Charles to make her the most famous woman in the world, but she owed it to no one but herself in becoming a free woman. And, in the last year of her life, that hard-won freedom had been vastly more important to her than the HRH title which had defined her bondage.

THE DUCHESS OF YORK, however, was a royal divorcee of an entirely different hue. The Ladies Who Lunch were far from puritanical in their attitudes and often breached well-established social taboos, but they drew a line at outright vulgarity. 'I had tea at Santini with Fergie and Allen Grubman, the most successful entertainment lawyer in the United States,' said a Belgravia socialite. 'He acts for Michael Jackson, Madonna, Sting and Elton John, but he didn't think Fergie was marketable. He didn't take her on and I had to agree with him on that. She was a very charming young woman, very likeable, easy-going, but it was plainly obvious that she was just not cut out to join the Royal Family. I mean *really* not. She has the common touch a little bit too much.

'I found her extremely charming and immediately likeable. She has this great sense of camaraderie: she comes along, she slaps you on the thigh, on your back, she's like one of the boys almost. She's this exhuberant redhead who comes in and bubbles over. I hate to say this because it sounds cruel, but she's not refined. She really doesn't have class. Class is not something you can learn. You may pick up hints here and there, but then you make a mistake again.

'She ordered a canarino – hot water with lemon peel – and this friend of mine said, "What are you drinking?" and she said, "This is canarino. Would you like one?" He said, "I'd rather have a cup of tea." And when she saw that he didn't like the look of it, she proceeded to say, "It looks like pee, doesn't it?"'

When the Ladies Who Lunch want to misbehave, they take the precaution of entertaining in the privacy of their own homes. Ira Kettner said: 'I give this luncheon maybe twice a year just for girlfriends and it can be a little raucous because whenever you get girls together we crack a joke and it can be very girlish and gigglish. There are no boys around, so we don't have to blush.

'I gave one luncheon for 12 girls and somebody in America had faxed me this sheet all about cucumbers. It was called A Girl's Best Friend and it was very naughty. I had this photocopied and then I bought these little green cucumbers and in every sheet I rolled a cucumber and then, with a nice green satin bow, I made it look very pretty and placed one at every place. All the girls undid the bow and out fell a little cucumber and everybody proceeded to read. We had such giggles.'

But even the best-intentioned jokes sometimes backfired, as Marisa Masters once found out to her embarrassment. 'I had a lunch party for a group of women, some of them young and attractive,' she said. 'It was a sunny day and lunch was served on the balcony. I didn't know some of the girls very well, so I told a joke to lighten things up. I said, "What is the best animal for a woman to have?" No one knew the answer, so I said, "A mink in the cupboard, a Jaguar on the street, a tiger in bed and an ass to pay for it all." No one laughed. Then I realised that three of these young ladies were the mistresses of rich men.'

12

Women in Love

ONE of the young women on Marisa Masters' balcony that sunny day was Christina Estrada, the beautiful American fiancée of Sol Kerzner, the self-styled, self-made Sun King himself. Anyone who took Christina for a kept woman, however, would have been making a serious mistake because Christina was a highly paid international model. She had been engaged to Sol ever since he popped the question in a Swiss ski resort on St Valentine's Day, 1994, and presented her with a pear-shaped, diamond engagement ring. She was then 32 and he was 59.

Although the couple remained extremely close (he phoned twice from the Bahamas during our interview with Christina), he had never actually found the time to pencil a wedding date in his overloaded diary. Word quickly spread around the Royal Borough that Sol had been married three times before and was already the father of five children. He was also on record as saying: 'The price I've paid for my success is in my personal life: three failed marriages don't amount to a very good track record. It isn't easy for any woman to hang on to me.'

All of this meant that Christina had to dig deep inside herself not only to contend with Sol's daunting track record, but also to deal with the gossip-mongers. She learned to move through the London social scene with such consummate skill that the *doyennes* had been won over, while she had made many friends among the vastly intrigued members of the younger set. 'I found that people were fascinated by me,' she told us. 'I could tell they were thinking, "What *is* she? She's with this older guy. Is it the money?"

'Then I started getting a lot of bombardments of looks and judgments and I knew what was going on: "Oh hello, darling, how are you? Everything fine? You must come to lunch. *Blah, blah, blah.*" Which is great because everywhere you go people like you, but it's the really close friendships when you can expose your heart and your vulnerability that actually make you feel you have something in life.'

Christina sought professional counselling from Pia Melody, the American therapist, to deal with the demons from her past which had bedevilled her relationships with men all her adult life. 'I met Pia in Arizona, then again in London,' she said. 'She was doing some workshops which I took. I found her incredibly fascinating and I understood a lot of what she was trying to teach. I absorbed it very quickly, but expressing it took time because it was heavy and it could, like, change my whole life. It's a healing job and I went through a lot.

'I always thought I had this great childhood; that it was idyllic; that even though my parents divorced, I could handle it. I wasn't angry at anybody, but I wasn't connected with how it affected my own self until I had enough of the same experiences that produced a lack of confidence. I thought I was acting confidently, but the side-effect was insecurity and I didn't know where it came from.'

The frantically complicated life of Christina's fiancé would have been sufficient to induce insecurity in most women. A shortish, stocky, barrel-chested man with curly black hair and the broad, battered face of the pugilist he once was, Solomon Kerzner was born to Russian Jewish *emigré* parents in Johannesburg on 23 August 1935. At the age of 29, he raised £150,000 to build his first luxury hotel on a beachfront site on the outskirts of Durban. With shameless bravado, he called it the Beverly Hills Hotel.

He liked the feel of the hotel business from the beginning and decided that the guys in Las Vegas had the right idea by surrounding their hotel bedrooms with thousands of slot machines and money-hungry games of chance. As gambling was illegal in South Africa, he founded Sun City in the tribal homeland of Bophuthatswana in 1979 and went on to open the Lost City there a few years later, as well as building luxurious hotels in Mauritius.

In 1987, he bought the Buckinghamshire manor house that had once belonged to Dame Rebecca West and put down some roots among the English gentry. He hung his collection of Picassos, Matisses and Chagalls on the walls, converted the squash court into a palatial dining-room, added an indoor swimming-pool and bought 450 acres of adjoining countryside to prevent anyone spoiling his view of the Chilterns.

The following year Sol met Christina in Morocco when she was on a modelling assignment. They didn't get together, however, until they bumped into each other at a party in Cape Town a year later. The relationship developed into a deep love that had survived one long, painful separation. The main problem seemed to be that Sol, quite apart from being old enough to be Christina's father, was incapable of controlling his entrepreneurial spirits. In 1994, he paid $85 million for Paradise Island, an unfinished holiday resort adjacent to Nassau in the Bahamas. Miraculously, the Atlantis casino-hotel, surrounded by lagoons and the world's biggest aquarium, rose like something out of Jules Verne Goes To Las Vegas beside the aquamarine waters of the Atlantic within six months. Sol had been putting the finishing touches to this masterpiece of kitsch and glitz ever since. With a private jet at his disposal, however, he was constantly airborne on trips to other leisure developments. Christina also clocked up her fair share of air miles to keep up the long-distance relationship.

When we met for this interview, she had just completed a fairly average two weeks: after spending a few days with her *fiancé* at the Atlantis, she had flown to New York to catch Concorde back to London, stayed there long enough to attend the Krug party at the Ritz, dashed down to Monte Carlo for the Monaco Grand Prix, then returned to London. She would barely have time to unpack her bags before she was off again to the Bahamas.

Home between flights was a top-floor apartment in a redbrick mansion block in Cadogan Gardens, just behind Peter Jones. She had acquired the flat a year earlier and, of course, the gossips claimed that Sol had bought it for her, even though she was quite capable of paying for it from her own earnings. The flat was cosily small and decorated in shades of beige and pale gold. The living-room lacked a bookcase and she planned to build one to accommodate the numerous volumes which were piling up on the oatmeal carpet. 'One of my favourite things in life is spirituality and if I see a book that grabs me, I study it and I evolve,' she said. Such titles as *A Guide for the Advanced Soul* by Susan Hayward, and *The Vision* by Kahlil Gibran testified to her interest in metaphysics, but there were also more terrestrial works like *Too Damn Famous* by Joan Collins, Toynbee's *A Study of History*, and a Dick Francis novel.

Christina served freshly brewed coffee in plain white china cups and placed a plateful of digestive biscuits on the coffee table before sitting down on a gilded *faux* Louis Quinze chair with leopardskin upholstery. With big brown eyes, long brunette hair with chestnut highlights and a slender figure, she glowed with good health, unlike the emaciated 'heroin chic' appearances of some of her pasty-faced, younger rivals. The smile suggested Julia Roberts and the various accents brought to mind the young Shirley Maclaine.

'It's funny you should ask me about feminine power,' said Christina, 'because there's a meditation that I do with a man named Ali Wasil. He said, "I want you to find your own mantra. Find three things that are important in your life now." And I said, "Power, beauty and strength." I like threes, I like thinking in concepts of threes, which is somehow a balance. I picked power and I picked beauty because power without beauty to me is corrupt, and I picked strength because even though you can be powerful you have to have the strength of your convictions to follow through. I needed to be strong. I was feeling very tender for a while and unconfident. I don't know why. Maybe it's my past or maybe it's because I gave my power away to somebody stronger than myself and the only one you should give it to is God.

'When you have that emotional anchor you suddenly feel absolved of those weaknesses. A lot of people I see in society are depressed. They've got everything in the world, yet they're unhealthy, or they're insecure. It gets really boring after a while, seeing all these insecure people running around. They're insecure of your beauty, or they're insecure because men are attracted to you. Why? They don't really love themselves. When you really love yourself and can love another human being, it's like a beacon in the world of some sort of goodness.

'There is a point at which you recognise and attain your own power by recognising your own uniquenesses, by recognising how you can effect change, and by recognising that you are influential to people at some level. The power that a woman exudes – her influence – is it a power to effect good, is it a power to manipulate, is it a power to heal? What's her power being used for? So in every aspect of my life I tend to try to be of the higher good.

'Femininity is half of a whole and the other half is maleness. When a woman has feminine power in the highest good, she is wholly woman. She is beautiful, she is tender, she has graciousness, she understands her own femininity – what it's like to be a woman – but I also find that being feminine is about understanding masculinity; it's like nature: you have to relate to the seasons of it.

'Different men expect different things from a woman's femininity: maybe it's big breasts, maybe it's the fact that she's caring, loving and understanding, maybe it's the fact that she just wears a dress. Men have a feminine side and women have a masculine side and I find that what's happening in our culture is that more women are exerting their masculine selves. In their jobs, they're getting used to handling it like a new tool and it's not something that my grandmother had to deal with. She was just told what to do and she did it. And men maybe never had the same understanding of what it's like to do housework or raise kids.

If a woman is going to assume a feminine role in life, it has to be coupled with a husband's respect, but it's also about her own self-worth. When a woman is truly feminine, she owns the right to be herself; it is not something that the man has a right to tell her.

'My mother went through her divorce with the women's liberation movement and a lot of those things affected us kids and by the time we'd grown up we'd be saying, "Never am I going to be in that position. I'm going to make sure I'm independent."'

CHRISTINA was born in Santa Monica, California, but moved to Washington State with her mother when her parents divorced. After graduating from high school, she started work as a model and was scouted by the Karin agency in Paris. She also worked in New York, Italy and Japan and, when she was 25, moved to London. In every city, she'd left a boyfriend or two wondering where they'd gone wrong.

'I've broken a few hearts, very terribly so,' she said. 'Then I met Sol in 1988-89. Since that time, we broke up for two and a half years and we've been back together for five years. I had two different boyfriends during our separation. I was living in Monte Carlo and I learned a whole other lesson. It was an interesting time of restraint, a time of dealing with Italians, with French, on a different level, finding a way of life that was very special, yet feeling like I'd just retired from life. So I moved back to London. All these guys were after me, including Sol. For one or two weeks I was out having a good time, loving my new-found freedom, not having to make decisions, just being me for the moment and not knowing where I'm going next and loving it.

'Then Sol proposed to me and I said, "This time, if you mean it, then do it, but don't screw me around." Four days later I met somebody else at a dinner party and we went to Italy and fell in love. At the end of the month, Sol said, "Okay, I want you to move back in." I said, "Oh, that's a bit difficult. I've met somebody and he's wonderfully in love with me and we're going to get married." He said, "What! Already? What's happening?"

'I got engaged to the new guy. It lasted a year and a half, but I never went through with it. Sometimes, I wonder why and I wonder how, but it was just an intuitive thing at the end of the day. This guy was just really wonderful and he's still wonderful and he's still my friend today, but I think I kind of broke his heart, too.

'You're probably getting all this bad karma, but I do know what I'm doing. Sol is a workaholic, a big workaholic, and I was having to balance not being married but wanting to be married, and wondering, "Am I going to have kids? Am I not going to have kids? What about my career?"

I worked very hard and I travelled a lot with him and I felt amazingly insecure for as long as I believed in what I didn't have.

'My relationship is my priority because I'm very feminine, I'm very Piscean and part of the way I love and feel most comfortable is when my man has power over me. If he's beneath me, then I don't give that respect to him; I retain my independent mind. But if I'm competitive and he's competitive, or I want to be too powerful, then it doesn't work. And it shouldn't be that hard.

'My career is very important to me and it's going through a change right now because I'd like to do something else besides modelling. I don't quite know what yet. My *fiancé* has a place in the Bahamas and a place in New York, and between New York, the Bahamas and London and the country house, I no sooner get off a plane than I'm repacking for the next trip. If I go to school, I need to be committed for at least a year. He's now in the Bahamas, so I've got to go back and forth to be with him.

'I'm a bit of a late bloomer, obviously, because of all the different transitions I've been through. The last thing I wanted to do at 22 was go have a bunch of kids, sit home and try to cope, but now I'm ready to settle down. In terms of being a woman, we find power within ourselves. Women should always be looking to the highest of themselves because there's a real goodness in being a woman, a real purity. I've let myself down before and I know what it feels like and I don't want to be there.

'I spoke to Sylvester Stallone last year and I said to him, "I gotta tell you that one of the most important lines in *Rocky* was when he's in the meat locker and he's banging away at the meat and he's working out and he's with Pauli, and Pauli is giving him his meat for his training, and Pauli says, "Hey Rocky, do you love my sister?" He says, "Yeah, I love your sister." He says, "I don't believe you. Why do you love my sister?" He says, "Well, she's got gaps and I got gaps and together we fill in the gaps." Sly laughed when I told him and he said, "Wow! How did you remember that?"

'It was so important to me because I was doing some psychological work on myself with Pia Melody, who was talking about love addiction and facing up to co-dependency. I used to think, "We've got this incredible relationship and we're hooked on to each other", not realising that the hook was the problem. If I really want to change this, I have to let go of my fears. But as long as I hang on to my fears then I have to find another person who can latch on to those same fears – maybe they're abandonment issues or intimacy issues – same as in the film. She was insecure and he needed to protect and love someone. They complemented each other's insecurities, as well as their ideas of what they needed from a woman or a man. So the line that Sly wrote 20 years ago was an amazing truth because it really showed how relationships are formed.'

BRIGITTE NIELSEN, the former Mrs Sylvester Stallone, was on her own spiritual journey inside the Great Room at the Russian Embassy in Kensington Palace Gardens. The kudos of being married to Rocky *and* Rambo had given her a certain reputation and it was one that she was anxious to dispel. 'I've changed,' she told us over the savoury blinis. 'Change can be learned: it's about really knowing yourself, understanding yourself, accepting yourself and making yourself a better person.

'I've been hurt many times and I've made many mistakes, but I've learned that we can be strong if we want to be. And then I think the message is to teach other people how good life can be to you. I know about life because I can read between the lines. I was sort of pushed into the fast life and I never really enjoyed it. They *made* me a role model, but it's never really been me; in fact, I was never really happy, was I?

'I never really liked LA, but if you want to do movies it's *the* place: all the production companies and the castings are there, but I'm a Dane and I missed Europe and I wanted to go back there. When I saw this house beside Lake Lugano in Switzerland, I fell in love with it because it's so beautiful and peaceful and calm. I can have a private life there and raise my children.'

At 6ft 6in tall in heels, Brigitte towered over the Russian ambassador's other guests. These were mainly members of London's *haute bourgeoisie* who would normally be found at the cocktail hour with a drink in one hand and a chequebook in the other at a fundraiser at Claridge's. And, indeed, the *lietmotiv* here turned out to be exactly the same as at Claridge's: money. The purpose of this reception was to announce that a committee had been set up under the patronage of His Royal Highness Prince Michael of Kent with the object of commemorating a visit by Peter the Great to London in 1698 by building a monument in his honour beside the Thames. With not an *apparatchik* or revolutionary banner in sight, the Great Room was more Romanov than Molotov. The walls were hung with paintings by Russian masters and the furniture looked venerably antique, with sheaves of spring flowers sprouting from every bureau, shelf and table. With a burst of spring sunshine providing the back-lighting from Kensington Gardens, the double doors of the Great Room had swung open and, as though entering a movie set, Brigitte, star of *Beverly Hills Cop 2* and other less celebrated Hollywood epics, had breezed in wearing a white minidress with sufficient *décolletage* to defrost a tundra.

'I may not look very spiritual in this dress – it's an old Thierry Mugler – but I *am* a spiritual person,' she told us. 'I became aware of a spiritual connection at the age of 14 and it got stronger two years ago when I read Pushkin and made a connection between the mind and the heart. No one lives from the heart any more. It's the bicentenary of his birth in 1999 and I want to set up a charity for him and dedicate the money to the children of Russia – they need help.

'I first read Pushkin two years ago and found his work very powerful. He was a romantic figure and such an amazing man; he had so much unconditional love to give and so much respect for others. He loved his wife, Natalya, unconditionally even though she did not love him, and he died fighting a duel to protect her honour. Unconditional love is love that comes from the heart and doesn't expect anything in return. It can be learned, and it involves a spiritual change from the inside. I learned to change my personality and I learned to love myself. It's difficult to give out love if you don't love yourself.

'If you don't understand yourself or take care of yourself, you can't accept life as it is – and that's what happens to so many people. It's a very spiritual thing to accept and respect, and I really feel that if all of us just made a small effort, we could change the world. I've got four sons aged from 14 to three – Julian, Killian, Douglas and Raoulino – and I know about kids. It's all about respect, and many parents forget to teach their children that.'

Brigitte was just 20 when she married Julian's father, Kasper Winding, but he was left behind when she sought fame and fortune in the United States. In Hollywood, she met and married Sylvester Stallone despite the opposition of his possessive mother, but the relationship changed soon after the wedding and the couple grew apart, separated and divorced without having any children.

She left Killian's father, American footballer Mark Gastineau, soon after their son was born, but in her third husband, former Swiss ski champion Raoul Ortolani Meyer, she found a man who fulfilled the roles of father, husband, friend and business manager. 'I believe that the man will dominate, but woman is the clever one,' she said. 'I was brought up like that; I'm a Danish viking who grew up the old-fashioned way.'

Late that night, Brigitte dined with friends at the Ritz and then, even later, indulged in a little moving-and-shaking on the dance floor at Annabel's. She was staying in Belgravia and, when she rose around 11 a.m. the following morning, we asked her if she was in the mood for a little Pushkin.

'I am so in the mood for Pushkin it's scary,' she said. 'I'm always in the mood for Pushkin; I dream about him. I've read all of his work, but it's not what you read but how you read it that matters. Pushkin taught me unconditional love and the respect and the courage never to give up and to be a good person and to be good to others. It became so close to me that it really became part of my life. It's totally spiritual. I believe I can talk to this man. If I was to tell someone else that they would say you've gone mad, but I'm not – I know he's there. I know he's there and I think he's also really appreciative of me speaking about him and understanding him. I'm going to teach myself Russian so one day I can read my Pushkin stories again, but in Russian.

'I feel like I'm married to him. I think I'm the love he didn't find in his life – I really do. I have the deepest respect for the man. It's very powerful to me. I really want the world to know about this man and out of knowing him and loving him at least close to the way I do I want to help kids. I think it's the nicest thing you can do and spend your time on. I would call it the Lost Kids of Russia because nobody thinks about them; no one really cares. They live on the streets, they die; there's prostitution and drugs. I saw it for myself when I was there five months ago.

'I took a car and went everywhere – Moscow and St Petersburg, of course, but I also went to visit really sad areas of deprivation. I just wanted to see it and feel it, and you do feel it immediately. Most people don't do that, they don't want to deal with it, so they just go to Moscow and hang out in the right places.

'There's so much change in Moscow, but it's desperate and it's going to explode. It's not right; it happened too quickly and not correctly. There are too many people who are miserable – too many poor and too few rich. Politics to me is such a game and I do believe when people say they stand and speak of their country often, unfortunately, they don't really think about their people at all, they just say what is convenient. I'm sorry to say that politics doesn't really look into the hearts of people.

'When I left Russia, I cried; I was so upset about leaving because I felt I had more things to do. And that's when I said to myself, "Get with the programme," because there's so little time for everything.

'Last night I sat at the Ritz and I looked at this crowd of people and they were all out of their minds: no one was really thinking about what they're doing; they were just there, pretending. No one was there because they had come to see a friend they really cared about. It was, "Go to the Ritz and be cool." I'm not into that at all and I will never be again. It's over. I guess I've come to a stage where I just say, "No, I don't want it," and that's it.'

13

Bonded Women

SOMEWHERE along Shaftesbury Avenue there should be a plaque to Sam and Jude: Ms Samantha Bond and Dame Judi Dench, two bonded women. The bonding process began when they met at rehearsals of *Much Ado About Nothing*, with Judi directing Samantha in the role of Beatrice, a role upon which the Dame had stamped her imprimatur of greatness. Sam and Jude were on stage together ten years later, playing mother and daughter in Sir David Hare's *tour de force*, *Amy's View*, to thunderous critical acclaim. But, in the interval, it was the unlikely combination of Sam's Miss Moneypenny to Jude's M in the James Bond movies *GoldenEye* and *Tomorrow Never Dies* that gave a memorably comedic *frisson* to the relationship.

The Bond people always had a sense of humour and, after the death of the legendary Bond producer, Albert 'Cubby' Broccoli, his daughter, Barbara, carried on the tradition. Sam believes she was cast as a gimmick simply because of her surname, but it would be nice to think that the pairing of Sam and Jude as two Bond girls was down to the fact that they were seen as two actresses who could cut Pierce Brosnan's Bond down to size without causing a riot among his male fans. So there was Dame Judi upbraiding 007 for being 'a sexist, misogynist dinosaur', while Samantha was a sparkier Moneypenny who no longer swooned over every one of his chat-up lines. Pierce Brosnan cheerfully acquiesced to feminine power and, as the box office records show, the fans lapped it up.

'It was one of the most fleeting experiences of my entire professional career and it constantly amuses me that the smallest part I've ever played should be the one that people hang the hook on,' Samantha Bond told us. 'Judi Dench and I were both Bond virgins in *GoldenEye*. We shot our scenes in a disused Rolls-Royce factory in Watford. I went on set first thing in the morning and I was finished at half past eleven' – and forever a Bond girl, convinced that she only ever got offered the job because of her surname, of course, but the publicity worked well. 'I now feel much more relaxed about it. I'm very fond of Barbara Broccoli and Michael Wilson, the producers, and I now rather enjoy the whole thing.

'The second one was *Tomorrow Never Dies*. We made this in a disused factory somewhere else. It was ten days' work this time and I got to go out on location. I did a speeding car chase through London, which is the first time Moneypenny has been out of the office. Judi Dench was M again and it was quite bizzare. Barbara Broccoli said it brilliantly over supper one night, "The great thing about you and Jude is that you've only got 30 seconds to make an impact and the pair of you can do that."

'And it *is* like that. These terribly small parts that mean *the world* to the rest of the world and are so insignificant in your life, yet you do have this responsibility to 30 years of film history. It was a very strange situation. Jude and I were there doing our tiny little bits on the Bond set in April 1997 and two weeks later we were at the National Theatre playing the two leading ladies in *Amy's View*.'

Samantha Bond was born in Hammersmith, West London, and grew up in the sixties. Her father, Philip Bond, played a lead role in the BBC costume drama *The Onedin Line*, and her mother, Pat Sandys, was a former actor turned script-reader and, later, a television producer of programmes including *The Bill*.

'If your parents were living through the sixties, it wasn't the easiest time to be a child,' said Samantha. 'There were a lot of confusing signals going on about what women were supposed to be doing and what they were actually doing. With all the falling of boundaries that happened in that period, it was quite an unsettling time to be a child. You were well aware of a sexual liberation. My mum was not a part of that, but a lot of her friends were separated women who had different boyfriends constantly around the children.

'I'm a great believer that the Pill was one of the most important things that ever happened to the female sex and I think they should all be thrown in the dustbin, not because we now know that we can be sexually equal, we now know that that is our right, but to go on poisoning our bodies is a disgrace.'

Samantha was educated at Godolphin Latimer Grammar School and her ambition was to be a ballerina, 'but by the time I was 16 I was far too large'. She was 5ft 7in tall with red hair, a *retroussé* nose and a voice as distinctively husky as Judi Dench's. Her mother insisted she learn typing as a practical, money-earning skill and then she went off to drama school. 'As the child of two actors, it was just like going into the family firm,' said Samantha. 'It wasn't an exceptional thing to do, it was very boring, really. I went to the Bristol Old Vic Theatre School between 1980 and 1982 and I got to play all the old bags, the character parts, Lady Macbeth and Lady Markby [in Wilde's *An Ideal Husband*], so much so that I didn't think I'd work until I was about 35 because it never occurred to me that I might look like a young person. It very much surprised me when people asked me to play 21-year-olds.

'I spent four or five years doing a thing that young actors don't really do nowadays. When you left drama school, you went out and did your training in the repertory system, which was then vast in England. I did 35 plays in the first three years all over the country, as well as bits of television, until I was 25 and then I did *Romeo and Juliet* with Kenneth Branagh at the Lyric, Hammersmith, and that's when everything changed. We found that we worked very well together because our attitude towards the Blessed Bard is very much the same, so it was a very young, spirited, clear, passionate and fast production. We all got paid £100 a week and we packed out. He went on to do *Fortunes of War*, where he met Emma Thompson, and I went into *Les Liaisons Dangereuses* as a stage play, playing what is now known as the Michelle Pfeiffer role.

'I went back to Ken's company 18 months after *Romeo and Juliet* in 1988 and we did *Much Ado About Nothing*, which was directed by Judi Dench. She was very, very frightening for me. I'd always been a huge admirer of her work and the shape of her career, but I was playing her part, Beatrice, which, in everyone's memory, she had had a huge success with. But Jude had played Beatrice when she was in her mid-forties and she played it as a woman who was at the last chance of love, a woman at the end of her sexual life, a woman who, if it wasn't going to work this time, that was it.

'I was 26 and my Beatrice was telling a very different story. In fairness, I can say now that Jude found it quite hard to direct me because she didn't want to be seen to be telling me what she'd done and, anyway, that wouldn't have made sense because of the age difference. It was quite a daunting time, really. We started in Birmingham, then we toured all around England and Ireland, and then we came into the Phoenix in the West End. We had queues around the block.

'I met my husband, Alex Hanson, when I went to see a girlfriend of mine, Kelly Hunter, in *Brel* at the Donmar Warehouse. It was a musical celebrating the work of Jacques Brel and I met him after the first night. I would go and meet Kelly for supper after the show and Alex would be there and that's how we got to know each other. We got engaged, very old-fashioned, in September 1988. Then I made a four-part series called *The Ginger Tree* for the BBC which made me a household name for about six months. This is what happens with my career: I become a household name for about six months at a time and then it goes away again, which suits me very well. It's Miss Moneypenny now. The press think, "That's her identity, that's who she is and we'll put her in that box."

'*The Ginger Tree* was ten weeks in Japan and Taiwan, then we came back to England and shot scenes in Liverpool and the Isle of Man. The rest was in BBC studios. The character I played was in every scene that was written, so I was never not on the set. The English crew and myself became terribly close, added to which we'd lost one director and we'd then had a Japanese director who couldn't speak our language. By the time we got to our third director, we were very, very close knit. Faced with adversity, actors get an incredible family feeling and we were all supportive.

'The director tried to put me in a box. He'd say, "You are an actress. You will behave like an actress. You will not ask questions." You get to a shorthand with the cameraman and you know if you take two steps to the right you're making his life a great deal easier. So I'd say, "Does it help if I do this?" at which point the director would say, "Can you just let him do his job?" and it all got very, very nasty. Every time we finished at each location, this man and I would end up having some kind of row. This was the time when you had unions in television and I was told not to talk to a particular man because he was the union representative on the shoot.

'It was just absurd. We would have these huge arguments. It was the first time in my career when I'd been in a confrontational situation with anyone, but also the first time I had any professional weight at all because of the sequence of unforeseeable events I ended up being the one person on the floor who knew most 1) about my character, 2) about the script and 3) about the continuity of the story. I had a clearer overview than he did.

'I'm not in my professional life a confrontational person and it was the only time that it's ever happened to me that unless I spoke out volubly the end product would not be nearly as good. It was a tremendous growing-up point. My mum was incredibly supportive through the whole thing and kept giving me advice. She was an actress, she is a producer, she's a highly intelligent woman, and I was young – 26 is very young to be dealing with that kind of thing – and I'd ring her in England and say, "Am I allowed to say such and such?" and she would say, "Absolutely!" or "No, that's pushing it" and just guide me through. It was the first time in my career I'd ever had to fight that corner: professional assertiveness.

'The whole process gave me the confidence to be able to fight my corner in the way that I then had to. I don't read critics, so I don't know what they said, but we got very good figures. It always makes me laugh. They celebrated the fact that *Pride and Prejudice* got nine million and we got 11 million on BBC1 ten years ago.

'Alex and I got married in Camberwell Register Office on 20 September 1989, just after I had finished *The Ginger Tree*. We were both working and they had to change the schedule at Chichester Festival Theatre so that Alex could get to his wedding. I then went into a really horrible Alan Ayckbourn play in the West End called *Man of the Moment* with Peter Bowles and Michael Gambon.

'Alan, who is a wonderful and very inventive writer, writes the kind of character I have no interest in. The characters and the situations are almost formulaic and there aren't any layers. You're there to fulfil a function and that can be a funny function. I was largely the engine of the play, which means you're the stooge and that's very hard work and quite unrewarding, being set up for all the pay-offs. It doesn't make it any less valid a piece of theatre or any less enjoyable for the audience to watch, but it isn't something I would choose to do again.

'My daughter, Molly, was born in 1991 and the next year I and Molly and my nanny went up and lived in Stratford. I was playing Rosalind in *As You Like It* and I was also asked to play Hermoine in *A Winter's Tale*. She's heavily pregnant for most of the play and by the time we'd been in rehearsal for two weeks, I had to tell Adrian Noble, who was the artistic director at Stratford, that I was indeed pregnant again. So I played Rosalind until I was 27 weeks pregnant which, I think, has been matched by Vanessa Redgrave. She played it until she was six months pregnant as well. I went on playing Hermoine until six weeks before my son, Tom, was born.

'In 1993, I went back into the Royal Shakespeare Company and we went on a European tour with a six-month-old and a 19-month-old. I travelled everywhere with a nanny and nine pieces of luggage, including two travel cots and a box of instant-formula goat's milk because my son was allergic to cow's milk. It was hilarous. Everyone in the company would pick up things, saying, "I've got a cot," "I've got the goat's milk." We did *A Winter's Tale* in Geneva, Paris, Budapest, Dublin. We'd be in an aeroplane and Molly would get impatient and I'd pass her behind and she'd just get passed around the whole company – 25 actors. They took on a collective responsibility for Tom because I'd got pregnant at Stratford and they felt Tom was theirs. Alex was on tour in England [with

Aspects of Love] and, when we got back in November 1993, we moved back to London, near Richmond.

'Then a big thing happened in my private life. Alex and I separated. That's a huge thing that happens in life and shifts how you feel about yourself and how you feel about your family. We separated for the whole of 1994 and we were apart almost to the day for a year. I did a television series called *Tears Before Bedtime*, ironically about couples in their mid-thirties and their nannies, which was very much what my life was like at that point. It was very much growing up and understanding this extraordinary phrase "to live in the moment" which only ever seems to become a reality when one is thrown into a period of crisis, either through illness, or, in my case, through separation.

'You have to come to terms with who you are, what you are, and that, and the arrival of the children, gave me a very different outlook on my work. I'm not nearly as ambitious now as I see other people being, or certainly as I used to be when I was younger, and I'm beginning to look on my career as a business that's going well or it's not going so well, in which case what do you do about it and how do you earn enough money to live the lifestyle that you wish to live?

'So it was a very clarifying time. It was an exceptionally painful time and a very, very sad time, but both of us, individually, worked incredibly hard through that year on ourselves and what it was we both wanted and by the end of that year we were able to come back together and be reunited far more successfully, far more equally and evenly, than we had been previously in our marriage or our relationship. It would be stupid to say, "I'm glad it happened." I'm not glad it happened at all. It made me very, very sad. But I think our relationship is much stronger now for it having happened and I also feel terribly proud of both of us that in this modern world we live in, where people throw marriages away like dirty tissues, it makes me incredibly proud that we managed to work through that period and sort out that, as two adult people, we were each with the person we wanted to be with.

'I was forced to live in the moment. I had never understood the phrase and people had used it to me in acting: "Act in the moment. Be in the here-and-now." It's living for exactly where you are now: not dreaming, not hoping too much. One of the hardest things to deal with in life is expectation because expectation will nearly always let you down. And appreciating. Another big thing that happened that year is that I went to South Africa to do a workshop. I walked around the shanty towns that are a part of Soweto and saw mothers who were living in shacks made of corrugated iron. They had absolutely nothing, but had produced these wonderful kids.

'This was coming towards the end of the year of separation when I truly believed that Alexander and I would be divorced fairly soon. I came back to my house and realised just how much I had. I had my two magnificent kids, I had a lovely home, there was one part of my life that hadn't worked as my plan had been but that was okay. I would be okay. We got back together just after New Year in 1995. It was those sort of experiences that change you and make you not necessarily stronger – almost the reverse – they make you more open, more vulnerable, but more understanding of human frailty. I got enormous support from my girlfriends. My girlfriends are a constant source of strength to me. They've always been relationships that I've valued and treasured. I believe you have to work quite hard to maintain a proper friendship and relationships with my girlfriends is something that I put enormous energy and commitment into.

'Am I a feminist? Yes. I never know what the p.c. expressions are, but I'm part of an immensely privileged generation who had the battle fought for them. I was educated in a magnificent school at that time to believe that everything was possible for me. I'm lucky enough to believe that all those things are my right. I believe that I have the right to expect my husband to do as much in the house as I do, I have the right to believe that he can be as involved with the children, I have the right to believe that my career is as important as his. So, yes, I am a feminist and a huge beneficiary and I thank them all very, very much because it can't always have been easy.

'I'm aware of my power as an individual. I am confident of my own "voice". I am confident of my intellect and that side that empowers me. A coquette is a dull thing. I don't think it's very attractive to watch women trying to persuade with fluttering eyelashes. I don't believe that's a very useful thing to do. However, I do believe that we have character traits as women that are different from men. We can look at things in a different way. There were businesswomen in the sixties who felt they had to fight their corner almost as a man and I feel that that has gone and our qualities as women, our compassion, humility, gentleness, understanding – all of those attributes, those *feminine* attributes as opposed to masculine bits of us – are now allowed to come to the fore. I have a friend who is a television executive who has fantastic legs and she in recent years has been in a position of immense power and has worn incredibly short skirts. We no longer have to hide the fact that we're women. We don't have to walk around in suits and appear to look serious to be taken seriously.

'After Bond, I did plays at the National and I did lots of telly. I did a series called *Family Money*, playing Claire Bloom's daughter. I think

Claire is a tricky woman. We got on fine. I don't think she is very at ease with herself and I think she could probably forgive herself much more than she does. And because she's not easy on herself, she's not easy on other people. She was lovely to me, but she could be quite hard with people, quite abrupt with the unit, and I think that's because she's not very comfortable with herself.

'I did *Three Tall Women* with Maggie Smith in the West End. She's fantastic. I'd been warned so much about her because she can be ferocious – I'm sure she can – and eats young actresses for breakfast, but I fell totally in love with her and she was wonderful to me and amazingly supportive and I love her passionately. You can't be on stage with people like Maggie and Judi and *not* learn. You'd have to be an idiot. It was thrilling to watch Maggie. She has a magnificent technique, yet she spins on a sixpence. She absolutely lives in the moment and it changes nightly. She can get a laugh with an eyebrow and break your heart as well.

'Then I did *Amy's View*, which was written by David Hare and it's the story of a mother, played by Jude, and her daughter, Amy, played by me. It's an incredible, insightful play about a mother-daughter relationship spanning 17 years, all the more amazing because it was written by a man. He writes with devastating accuracy about a relationship that I thought no man would ever fully understand.

'There is the remaining inequality which is the whole ageing process; that men are allowed to age and remain attractive and women are not. When a man realises that he doesn't have to be procreating madly with 25 year olds at the age of 60, then he might grow up a bit. I can't imagine ever having a facelift mainly because I'm frightened of knives and needles, so the process is too distressing. I also find it distressing that a woman would want to look 20 years younger. I'm sure some women do it for themselves and I'm sure, sadly, there are some women who do it for their man. We didn't used to be able to do that. We used to be able to have different haircuts and dye our hair and have perms. It's part of this whole ageing-and-accepting thing and, in a sense, almost being proud of who you are and where you are, of not wanting to go back.

'My mother is always saying, "When I grow up, I'm going to be . . . " and it's a joke and here I am in my midish thirties thinking, "Hang on a minute, I *am* a grown-up" and I'm quite proud of the things I've achieved. I'm desperately proud of my children, I am, at moments, quite proud of what I've professionally managed to do. I don't want to go back and I'd rather get to 50 and actually be proud of who I am and what I look like. I'm finding the ageing process as terrifying as anyone else, but I would hope emotionally to want to be where I am, to emotionally accept that physically that's where I am.

'Maggie and Judi are both comfortable with themselves and that's a huge thing, particularly in our industry as opposed to business, because we have the humiliation of being recorded on celluloid. When you go to a cinema and see yourself 20 feet high, it's not an easy thing for anyone to sit through, even if you're Helena Bonham-Carter and absolutely stunning. It's a huge thing to have to look at and deal with.

'Maggie and Judi were both very beautiful young women and I think they're both very beautiful older women. When Judi was nominated for the Oscar for Queen Victoria in *Mrs Brown*, I asked her if she was looking forward to the bash in Los Angeles. She said, "Oh, it isn't my cup of tea." Then she said, "You realise I'll be the only unlifted face there?" You look at that face and those eyes and you realise age doesn't matter.'

14

Tigress from Tiger Bay

ARMS outstretched to embrace the faithful, Shirley Bassey seemed anything but vulnerable. Enveloped in a diaphanous, silver *lamé* coat trimmed with ostrich feathers, she was the embodiment of a superstar dripping in jewels and self-confidence and sexual allure. Her fabulous voice had brought her a long way from a terraced cottage at No. 182 Bute Street, Tiger Bay, to the high point of her Diamond Tour on the silk-draped stage of the Festival Hall, London, and there wasn't the slightest whiff of insecurity about her. Not on the outside, anyway.

The spotlight picked out the familiar, smiling face and the familiar, statuesque curves and a hundred Canons flashed to capture the moment. But you had to be there to *feel* the intensity of Shirley Bassey giving of herself to young men and elderly women, to sophisticates and suburbanites alike. Her performance had electrified the packed house and the applause had brought her back for three encores, but still they demanded more. All Shirley had left to give, however, was herself and hundreds of fans rushed towards those outstretched arms to claim her. They laid gifts of chocolates, flowers and champagne at her feet and reached out to touch her dress, her shoes, her beringed fingers, any part of her within reach. Caught up in this outpouring of emotion, one middle-aged mother gasped: 'I can't believe I'm doing this, but I just had to get close to her.'

As the hall emptied, the lucky few with passes made their way backstage to meet the star. Ordinary fans, a clutch of friends, a prince, a renowned jeweller and a Parisian socialite all gathered in the small hospitality suite, each group staying firmly with its own class. Fifteen minutes later Shirley emerged, changed into a simple trouser suit and silk shirt. For an instant, she paused at the entrance as though slightly hesitant about entering the mêlée, and then, almost as if taking a deep breath, she walked in, greeting the great and the ordinary with equal warmth, insisting on a glass of champagne for a pensioner and joking with another fan who wanted to be photographed with her, a request she readily agreed to.

Remarked one Chelsea socialite who had attended Shirley's concerts since the sixties: 'Some stars go on the stage and they *perform*. But they perform for themselves. She's performing for her audience. She gives it everything. She's at one with the audience.' It was the same off-stage: not a single person in that room was ignored. She spoke to everyone, unhurried, as if she had all the time in the world. As one one by one the guests started to leave, friends entreated her to join them for dinner, but she declined. And then she was alone.

'It is lonely, but sometimes you have to be lonely in order to do what you're doing,' she told us. 'When I'm on a tour, I don't want anybody else around me. I wrap myself up in cotton-wool. I go from the hotel to the theatre and from the theatre on to the bus to the next town and the next hotel. It's complete dedication and it has to be that way. It's 100 per cent – you could give a little less, but I like to give 100 per cent, if not 110, and to do that I have to be on my own and to be focused.'

Ivana Trump, a long-time friend, said: 'One of Shirley's best qualities is her professionalism. She will not party, she will not go out, she'll have her sleep because she takes her profession very, very seriously. At the same time, when that is over, she has the ability to seriously enjoy herself.'

Shirley explained: 'I don't feel the need to be going out all the time. I enjoy it occasionally and then I'm busy looking at other people. I don't take that star thing with me everywhere. I enjoy it on stage and I leave it there when I'm through, which doesn't help me in the men department because men are afraid of powerful women. They're attracted to me, but that's about it. They're really quite nervous being around me until they get to know me and then they find that I'm really down to earth. They like that aspect of me as well, but eventually it comes to loggerheads because a man can't take a successful woman out anywhere.

'People are constantly coming up to her and it puts him in a terribly uncomfortable position unless it's a man who totally believes in his own strength and knows all about himself and I've not met many men in my life who have that. So all these successful women are on their own. The powerful man who's attracted to a powerful woman can't take that constant interruption because he gets jealous. Ordinary men can't bear it, either, when men come up and talk to me. It's very difficult being a successful woman.'

That Shirley Bassey was successful and had immense talent as a singer had never been in doubt, but many other talented performers had overdosed on fame and self-destructed in the four decades since she became an established star. Nobody survived in showbusiness that long without making a complete commitment to their work or without attracting criticism.

Although those who know her well and those who've worked with her, even briefly, testified to the contrary, she had been accused of throwing tantrums and behaving selfishly. Hairdresser Derek Morris at Joe Hansford who did her hair for a Sainsbury TV commercial said: 'There was so much bad publicity about her at that time and, knowing I was working with her the next day, I was filled with trepidation, but she couldn't have been nicer or funnier. She said, "Do exactly what you want to do. I don't mind." She trusted a complete stranger and I was very impressed with her. She's a very bright lady, warm and friendly. Her humour and my humour were on the same wavelength – we're both piss-takers, if you like. Nobody's at their best first thing in the morning, but she was the complete professional. It was as if we'd worked together for years.'

Even though Shirley hid her pain behind an unfailing sense of humour, the gossip-mongers had wounded her deeply and it was that hurt which finally prompted her to speak out about the human frailty behind the star-glazed image in the frankest interview she's ever given: 'The woman is vulnerable and, even on stage, the vulnerability is there,' she said. 'Yet everybody says, "She must be very difficult to work with. All those tantrums." There *are* no tantrums, I haven't got time for tantrums and I would like that character to come over rather than the one that people hear about. Everybody wants to hear that stars are difficult. They prefer to hear that, but I've heard it long enough and it's about time somebody said, "She's vulnerable." There has to be vulnerability. It has to be there or I would not be making that contact with an audience. Of course it hurts when the press exaggerate my private life or they take words out of context. I don't know why they do it.'

One reason for the hostile press was that Shirley's exacting professionalism had alienated some of those who worked with her, while professional jealousy certainly played a part. 'I don't get on with people in the business, which is very strange – not that I don't want to, it's just that I find *they* don't want to mix,' she said. 'Not like the old days when we had variety and we all got on very well. We'd meet after each other's shows at the Stork Club or the Café de Paris and we'd have a great time. Today, that doesn't exist. The kids in the business today are mainly pop groups and they just don't want to know, and I also find that other singers are not very interested in me. Judy Garland was. We were great soulmates. She's the one I admired, Judy and Frank Sinatra. They had such incredible talent that you wondered where it came from. It encompassed you and made you part of *them*. They had that wonderful ability to make eye contact, whereas a lot of singers don't do that today. But I adore Michael Bolton. He impressed me with that unique voice. I don't know how men can get up so high – I can't do that. And I love the Spice Girls. I thought they were a breath of fresh air as opposed to all the male groups that came along. It was about time we had a girl group and they were fun, they were modern, they were hip and they wore clothes that I wore when I was their age and I loved it all.'

SHIRLEY was speaking at her Monte Carlo apartment, where she had gone to rest during a break in her exhausting Diamond Tour. Overlooking the sea, the apartment was a mixture of antique and modern, 'furniture that I can look at and not get fed up with,' she said. 'My favourite room is my bedroom: it's huge, with a huge mirror and a huge television and a huge bed that would sleep about four.' There were chandeliers and antique mirrors and pictures of her daughters, her son and her grandchildren.

'God gave me children for a reason,' she said. 'I have an adopted son and I have had two daughters of my own. My son is my great-nephew and he was only 18 months old and he was going to end up in a children's home and I couldn't bear that. Children have to have a home and mothers should be at home looking after them. I wasn't working so much then, but my destiny was to sing and I found it very difficult and heartbreaking to leave them, it really was.'

She was born Shirley Veronica Bassey on 8 January 1937, to Eliza Jane Bassey whose husband, Henry, was a West Indian seaman. 'I was the last of my mother's seven children,' she said. 'I left Tiger Bay at the age of three. I was a happy kid, oh yes, I was a tomboy. It was wartime, but my mother made sure we didn't go without anything. I had so much freedom and it helped me to leave home at 16 and go into showbusiness without being terrified. I enjoyed all that. When I made it, my mother was overjoyed. She said, "At least one of my children made something of themselves." She loved it, she really did.'

After performing at working men's clubs in Wales, Shirley came to London to sing in the Astor Club, where she was spotted by bandleader Jack Hylton who gave her her big break in the revue *Such Is Life* at the

Adelphi Theatre. The audience were unanimous about her star quality and 'the press came on my first night and the next day they printed the Tigress from Tiger Bay hits London and I thought that was absolutely incredible. I thought, "They're talking about me! The Tigress from Tiger Bay!" I was always excited and I hope that never leaves me.'

After *Such Is Life*, the impresario Major Donald Neville-Willing booked her for the Café de Paris. Her youth, beauty and show-stopping style led to invitations to work in the States. 'The first time Judy Garland came to see me, she said she wanted to speak to me. I thought she'd be very grand, but not at all. She sent a waiter to ask me to join her table, which I did and I couldn't believe it. There I was sitting in front of my idol. She was saying how great I was and I was saying how great she was and it was like a mutual admiration society. Then I told her I was going to America soon and should I change my act and have new songs? She said, "Do the songs I heard tonight and it will go well, but don't do what I did. I had lights coming on here and lights going off there and costumes and I ended up looking like a clown." And that was a great piece of advice.'

Shirley was a big hit in cabaret in Las Vegas and Hollywood but, for the first time, she encountered racism. 'I had a white mother and I'd been brought up in an all-white area, so colour wasn't a big issue for me until I went to America and found out what black Americans were going through,' she said. American audiences were already enamoured with her when it emerged she had a fan in the White House.

'I met President Kennedy and when I shook hands with him it was the weirdest experience in the world,' she said. 'Something shot right up my arm like an electric shock. I realised that I was shaking hands with the man who had the most power in the whole world. I'd never met a President of America and I was a great admirer of Kennedy. I was in America watching all that going on – the race between him and Nixon to get in. He came across so strongly on television that he glowed and that personality! I never thought I'd ever get to meet him, let alone sing for him, and I did in Washington at his inauguration. It was so exciting, one of the most exciting moments of my career.

'Somebody who had seen me in cabaret was arranging the show and they wanted somebody to represent each country around the world. When he called me, I said, "If this is your idea of a joke it's not very funny." And he said, "No, it isn't a joke. We really want you to sing for the President." Kennedy looked at me and said in *that* voice, "Thank you very much for being part of the show. Your opening song [*Everything's Coming Up Roses*] was Vice-President Johnson's campaign song." I remembered I couldn't understand why everybody was laughing when I sang it. I thought one of my boobs had come out.

President Kennedy had picked up on it. With that he was gone and I was left thunderstruck.

'We sang at the Armoury and after the show there was a party at Vice President Johnson's house and we were all ushered there in a motorcade with police everywhere. It was terribly exciting. When we got there, I realised everybody was in a group ready to sing again and I just disappeared. I hid under a table, so much for feminine power! I mean, I just couldn't face it. Everybody else was doing another turn privately for the President and I was terrified.'

The Presidential seal of approval gave Shirley a huge boost in America and she sold a million copies of *Goldfinger* in 1964, the first of 25 gold albums. The diversity of her fans ensured that she never had to worry too much about changing trends in the music world and her universal appeal transcended apartheid in South Africa and crossed social and sexual barriers everywhere. Loved by housewives and feminists, she also succeeded Judy Garland as a gay icon. 'I can see them in the audience which gives me the power to give more,' she said. 'I can actually see them – that's why I have lights on the audience, so I can see them. There's no point in being a singer if you can't see audience reaction. They identify with the songs I sing. They're about love lost, love won, *I Am What I Am*, which they call the gay anthem, and *This Is My Life*. They identify with that: even if I'm gay and everybody is against me it doesn't matter. This is my life and I am what I am. But I'm an entertainer myself and I don't believe in promoting political or social causes.'

Shirley admitted, however, she had not escaped unscathed from criticism of her work. 'It used to be terrible, but it gets less and less,' she said. 'But I learn from criticism and now the notices are getting better and better. I had a manager who said, "Don't only read the good notices, read the bad ones as well and learn." And he was right. Some that were really bad I actually kept and framed.

'I don't have strong views about myself. I've had an impact but I don't understand the impact. It's just something I have. I certainly didn't acquire it. I was born with it and I worked on it and honed it into the skill that it is today. It took years of practice. My power is in my voice, I suppose, and I work hard to keep it. If that's feminine power, so be it. You just have to get on stage because if you don't go on you get sued unless you can show a good reason, like you're dying, and even then you have to show a doctor's certificate. I find I can pull myself out of a down situation, which I've had to do in order to go on stage. I've been in pain and gone on stage and the adrenaline acts like a painkiller and it goes away while you're on stage.

'My happiest time was when I first started because it was all great fun.

I wasn't known, it was thrust upon me and I went along with it and I said, "I've got to do the best I can." At the beginning I loved it and I still do to a certain extent, but it's harder because success makes things hard because life is never the same again. Now you're on top of the world everybody adores you. You're a big success, thousands of people come to see you and you're making *lots* of money so things can never be like they were in the beginning. Now more concentration goes into it, you have to think more than ever what you're doing. It isn't all fun, it now becomes work, serious work, at which you can't fail, whereas when you're starting out you have nothing to lose and everything to gain. Once you're at the top, there's always somebody who wants to bring you down and you have so much to lose so you have to keep on top of it all the time. That's why it's so important to take a break and walk away from it. I come home here, I sit in the sun, I go out occasionally for dinner with friends, I go to the gym, I swim and that's how I get away from it.'

LIZ Brewer recalled one occasion when Shirley's fame was a distinct advantage. 'We had been overdoing it on champagne all evening,' said Liz. 'It was about 2 a.m. and we were driving down Park Lane when suddenly I saw a police car and, at the same time, I saw a red light. We were probably singing at the top of our voices. I can't remember, but the police car and the red light, combined with the fact that we'd had a pretty good evening, put me in such a state of shock that I went through the red light. We were the only car on the road and the police car's lights started flashing, the siren went off and I said to Shirley, "You'd better think of something. I've just crashed a red light and the police are after us." We stopped and four burly policemen got out of their car and marched over. I wound the window down and said, "I know why you stopped me, officer, but how can anybody expect me to drive with this woman singing at the top of her voice?" Whereupon Shirley got out of the car, climbed on to the bonnet and started singing *Hey, Big Spender*. The police officer said, "Well, I hope you're not as high spirited as she is." Shirley replied, "Lizzie, drive on. This is a waste of time. He's wearing a wedding ring." I said, "This is not a drive-on situation. We are being arrested." The police officer said, "Where are you going?" I said, "I'm taking her home, which is about 500 yards further on," and he said, "Take her home and go straight home yourself." Which I did. Shirley is a very loyal friend. For a person of her calibre and status, she surprises me with her loyalty because she doesn't need to. There are other people in her position who are too self-centred to worry about others.'

Another close female friend said: 'Shirley is very much a woman who has fun with her girlfriends. Once we were in Paris and all the men in our group had dropped out one by one pleading fatigue, but Shirley was still full of life, even though she had been on the go all day. There we were at about three in the morning in the bar of the Ritz, laughing, joking and having woman's talk. But, unlike some other stars, she could not have been sweeter when a group of Canadian men asked for a photo and autograph. We were guests of Sheik Mubarak Al Sabah, Chief of Protocol in Kuwait, and while all the other guests perhaps took liberties with the host's generosity Shirley never did.' Sheik Mubarak told us: 'Shirley never expects or demands the star treatment. She does not travel with an entourage or the trappings of a star, but she is a star and it's amazing how people are drawn to her. She's a wonderful, thoughtful guest.'

Shirley said: ' I get on well with women and I get on well with men. In fact, I get on equally well with both sexes. I met a man in a bar in Lebanon once who said, "I'll bet you $1,000 you won't sing *I Who Have Nothing*." So I got up and sang it and he had to pay up $1,000. I found that very romantic because it was his favourite song. I don't have a favourite song myself, I love them all, but I do have a favourite fun song, *Big Spender*, because I'm a big spender. Money doesn't impress me, but it allows me to buy what I want and to help my family and friends.'

Shirley's generosity, however, sometimes exposed her to hurt and criticism, such as one published report that she had demanded £30,000 to sing at a charity gala. 'When I do a charity concert, all they pay for is the hotel room and travel, and it's a load of nonsense that I asked for £30,000,' she said. 'We in showbusiness who have a name have had a lot out of it so we feel we should put something back.

'Some people invite me to parties because they're hoping I will sing for my supper and sometimes I will oblige them because I'm having a great time, but if I know they've just invited me for that, then I won't sing. I feel that the business makes you like a man. If you're the head of the company, you have to give orders and that makes you like a man and I really don't enjoy that part of it. But in order to get on the stage and do *my* thing I have to go through that. This is the tough part, the man part, and that is not me. The real me is what you see on stage and what you see off-stage. That is me. Sometimes I dislike that sort of power and I want to say, "I don't want to do this," but I'm terrified to say it because if I say it I won't do it and that's what the loneliness is about. You have to keep it all to yourself. If you tell anybody that you're feeling down and a little unhappy, the people around you will not understand. They don't want to, actually, because you are Woman and without you they don't have a job. You can't tell them that you're not up to it because they don't want to hear that. You have to keep everything to yourself and sometimes you just want to scream.

'I came from a poor background and I made it in a man's world, but it was terribly difficult. I started off as a very cheerful, young, bright thing and I ended up as a hard, cold businesswoman in a man's world, which success brings. The business side makes you rather tough.

'Does an empowered woman need a powerful man? No, not at all, she's strong, but she needs a man to love and understand her and know what she's all about. Yes, I'd like to have a man in my life. It's nice to share, it's nice to go on a cruise with somebody you're romantically involved with. I've yet to meet the greatest love in my life. The men I'm attracted to don't have to be good looking, but they have to have that animal sex appeal, and they have to have a sense of humour and not put me down because of who I am. It's unconditional love and wanting to be with me and I don't think that man exists. I've had most of the men I wanted, but I've not had the man I *really* want. Men and women are very, very different and we'll never understand each other, so I don't know why God made us for each other, maybe just to have babies because we really don't get along on a one-on-one basis.

'Men are comfortable with me because I make them feel comfortable, but in the long run it doesn't work. I'm a late-night person. I work late and even if I'm not working late I like to go out and I like to party and I'm out late. Even when I get home I cannot go to bed and I have to put on television and come down. I have to think about the evening and get things out of my system and if I'm with a man I can't do that. He doesn't want the television on, he wants to sleep right away and he's up early in the morning and I'm still asleep so it really doesn't work for me and it's better that I stay on my own. If I can have the occasional fling, then that's all right.'

In the meantime, Shirley Bassey, the Tigress from Tiger Bay, superstar, mother and good friend, could always fall back on one of her greatest pleasures in life. And what was that? With her playful humour, she giggled: 'Shopping, shopping, shopping.'

15

Design and Rule

EVERYTHING about Amanda Wakeley, one of Princess Diana's favourite designers, testifies to a very proper English pedigree: tall, blonde, beautiful, country home in Cheshire, father a surgeon, public-school educated. But like her deceptively simple clothes, Amanda has a layer of rebellion beneath her apparently orthodox demeanour. 'I wanted to get away from the whole English system and change my life,' she said.

At the age of 19 she moved to New York because 'I didn't want to do the whole university bit here. I was just in a hurry to get on with life and be independent. I was lucky I had a good education, but I didn't have loads of money thrown at me. My privilege was my education rather than anything else and, ironically, that sort of encouraged me to become a dressmaker because I suppose I was quite social as a teenager and I did a lot of dressmaking for myself and my friends.'

At only 35, Amanda appears to have it all: three Glamour Awards in the British Fashion Awards, her own successful business and a clientele that includes royalty and celebrities such as Natasha and Joely Richardson and Yasmin Le Bon, as well as designing a collection for the high street chain, Principles. The chairman of her company is also her husband, Australian Neil Gillon. 'It's wonderful to have someone you're married to as your business partner because who better to completely trust than your husband?' she said.

'It's going to be a very interesting and difficult couple of decades for men adjusting to feminine power because it's intimidating. It throws out all they've been brought up to believe is their right, so it destabilises their position. It's going to take some very special men to cope with this new breed of powerful women who are coming through because there's much more equality in modern marriages now. I know that's the case in ours and I feel very blessed to be with a man who's big enough to say, "Okay, let's share this." He doesn't feel emasculated by it.'

When Amanda started designing clothes ten years ago, she faced some scepticism from the industry because of her youth and Grace Kelly looks. 'But I didn't waste time worrying about it,' she said. 'I just got on with my job because at the end of the day appearances don't matter and the proof of the pudding is in the eating. In retrospect it's not the easiest thing to do, but you blindly start and get into it and I didn't start in a big way, I grew it in a very small way. My first collection was tiny and it was just for private clients, but it just takes time and persistence. Friends of friends, that's how it started, then word travelled and it was more than friends of friends, quite quickly, actually.

'I know that the predominance of international designers are men, but I think women designers understand women more because you know what bits you want to hide and what bits you want to show off and I think as a woman I'm more in tune with what women really want. Women weren't expected to have a career and it's still tougher being a woman because it's a man's world, but it's changing. What happens now is that we have a company philosophy not to work with pigs whether they're male or female. We work with people we like and there are still some extremely chauvinistic men out there.'

Even as a child, Amanda had a natural flair and passion for dressmaking, but she had no formal training. After modelling for a brief period in New York, she worked in the retail and wholesale ends of the fashion business. 'I was impressed by most American designers from Calvin Klein and Donna Karan to Ralph Lauren because they all have stable, steady businesses, but there is no one in particular, to be honest, whom I'd put on a pedestal

'When I came back from America after four years, I couldn't find the clothes here that I'd learned to love in America, that understated, clean dressing that I think American women do so well and American designers provide them with so well and I just felt there was a gap in the market here for that type of dressing and I've been proved right ever since. There has been an apathy among British women to spend money on their wardrobe that it has been a dirty word about spending money on clothes. It's far more correct to spend money on your antiques, your house, your garden, your this and that. It's a rather sort of *nouveau*, bourgeois thing to do to spend money on your appearance.

'But London is becoming far more cosmopolitan with the American influx over the last 15 years. British women have had to slightly pull their socks up. It's not good enough. The world is a much smaller place and you can't hide in Britain in your Barbour and green wellies. So I think you have that crowd of English women who think it's still a dirty word and they'll still buy their clothes in sales all the time even if they've got more money than whatever. I find it disappointing personally because it doesn't have to be conspicuous consumption. You don't have to be spending a lot of money on it. It's more an approach to how you lead your life.

'Women who four years ago were wearing quiet, classical clothes now want more fashion. They're prepared to experiment more because I think the whole thing of Britain being put back on the fashion map is that people are really taking a pride in that. That doesn't mean they have to be loud, big, brash clothes. Glamour is an approach to dressing where it encompasses you, making yourself feel special and I think you make yourself feel special by being in clothes that are cut to flatter you and give you confidence and that's my real design philosophy. I want women to feel good about themselves, which I know sounds too corny for words, but the worst feeling in the world is going out and feeling you're in the wrong clothes. It can wreck your evening, it can wreck your day and I want my collection to help women not feel like that.

'Feeling special is important and if what you're wearing makes you feel comfortable and special then you're going to look as pretty as you can; you're going to feel good about yourself. It gives you confidence in what you're trying to say. I find the Henley thing *passé* personally although I know some people think it's a lovely charming English tradition, but I find it all a bit ridiculous to be perfectly honest, but that's a designer's point of view. As long as you're dressed respectfully for the occasion then that should be enough. But they shouldn't say to you you have to cover your knees or you have to cover your shoulders but if you're half naked then that's not good enough either.

'After a certain age you definitely look better in expensive clothes. You can't get away with a little flimsy slip dress any more, it looks really cheap. But you can dress well on a budget and I think with what the high street are doing now and with what Marks and Spencer and others are doing, you don't have to spend a fortune to look good. But if you want that extra designer edge then you have to pay the money to get it.'

Expanding their business has meant that Amanda and Neil have delayed starting a family. 'I would find it difficult to have children at the moment,' she said. 'We haven't made any final decision on whether to have them, but we certainly don't want them at the moment. It's a difficult one, that. I have untold respect for women who can play the juggling act. I just don't know how I can squeeze it into my life right now, but maybe in the future I will want to and so will make the effort to make it work. But I really do have enormous respect because I think they must do it at a huge personal cost.

'I have an absolute burning belief that women are just as good as men. They have strengths that we don't have and we have strengths that men don't have. But our strength over theirs, or theirs over ours, doesn't make women any lesser people, so it's not a feminist point of view – it's just stop beating about the bush and get on with it.'

This is very much the message of Amanada's superbly cut clothes, subtle, elegant, yet wickedly sexy. 'Some of my glamour clothes are for the already confident woman but I think there are quite a few that are designed for the woman who doesn't want to go into a room and scream, "Look at me!"' Nevertheless, her evening dresses are much coveted by actresses attending premieres. 'It's a barter system,' Amanda admitted. 'You know who is going to get photographed in the dress. They get to borrow a dress that they don't have to spend £1,000 on, so they've got a dress for the night and you know that you'll get photographs of that person in that dress. It's really a straightforward, old-fashioned barter system.

'Feminine power is having the confidence to be yourself. That is the most important thing for me. Confidence is power; it's huge power and if you're just calmly confident it's one of the most powerful things you can be. I'm excited to see a whole breed of women designers with individual styles coming through and getting international recognition. I think it's wonderful.'

Stella McCartney, for example?

'Her name creates a lot of hype and good on her. She was very lucky to be born with a famous daddy. But it takes longevity. Time will tell and I don't doubt that she has the talent.'

WHEN Stella succeeded Karl Lagerfeld at the House of Chloe in Rue Faubourg St Honore, Sir Paul warned her about the dangers of being her father's daughter. 'The name is terrific for getting the job,' he told her. 'But, if you fail, that name becomes a weapon with which you will be beaten.'

Stella took her father's words to heart. She had been appointed as Chloe's new designer on 15 April 1997, after designing only three commercial collections of her own and just 18 months after leaving Central Saint Martins College of Art and Design. 'Sure, the name opens doors,' she said, 'but it doesn't design the collection for you.'

Sir Paul and Lady McCartney were in the front row at Les Jardins du

Trocadero when Stella's *prêt-à-porter* collection for autumn and winter 1998-99 was shown. Described as 'clothes for Millennium Women', the fashion writers praised her 'saucy lingerie-dressing in satin and lace; frilled, flamenco slinks; and curvaceous, eighties-inspired trouser-suits in worsteds, checks and flannels'.

'Stella hasn't had much time to show what she can do,' the Parisian designer, Sonia Fares, told us.'She's very new and her first collection was not the most creative or the most amazing, but one has to give her time. She's young and the French are very difficult to deal with, but it was a brilliant idea to bring in English talent.

'Every decade or so there is a trend to give fresh blood to French couture. The French have the exposure and the know-how for *haute couture*, but they were going on and on in a very classical way and people were bored. England is the best country for designing and British designers have more ideas and greater creativity. Trends all start there because of the social structure – it's a much more democratic society than France. I'm not biased, but I do believe that fashion starts in London; that's for sure.'

Sonia was born in Lebanon and studied at the Chelsea Art College before moving to Paris in 1979 and training in *haute couture* at the House of Dior. She started selling her own clothes in 1981 after opening a boutique in a small street off Avenue Montaigne. 'My styles are contemporary and avant-garde,' she said. 'I believe very much in the sexy look. I don't believe in the idea that character should overcome the dress because, for me, character is only a starting point. What I like is a dress that is sexy and attractive and provocative, not in a vulgar way but in a very subtle and exotic way, with an element of surprise.

'Alexander McQueen and John Galliano have been doing wonderful things – unwearable, but it doesn't matter now because *haute couture* clothes are for fantasy. Society has changed and it's publicity for the house of fashion that sells so many other items: perfume, make-up, accessories, handbags, household products, underwear, with outlets licensed all over the world. They count on the name to sell these things to make money. In high fashion, the window is only for publicity. I saw Galliano's last show and it was amazing, like a dreamland. But the only women who will wear his clothes are a few actresses who are given them free of charge.

'Fashion has become so international it's very difficult to tell who is who, although French women are much more classical than anyone else. They always go for a blazer, two pairs of trousers, two shirts, a very classical pair of shoes and a scarf from Hermes. That is the typical French look. American women with money, like Sharon Stone and Ivana Trump, dress very elegantly, but everyone else in the big cities has become so international that you cannot tell them apart.'

ONE of the big names in American chic was Diane Von Furstenberg. Not only was it the longest name in the style pantheon, it was also one of the most enduring. She had been compared with Coco Chanel and, like the *petite* French couturier, she had made a comeback. 'Coco stopped for 25 years then, in her 70s, she did it again,' said Diane. 'I went from Wunderkind to tycoon woman to recluse to a has-been and now I've been turned back into an icon.'

Diane's new studio was a big, sky-lit loft in a pink-brick carriage house in the West Village. In the open reception area, a huge chandelier illuminated lots of ethnic pieces and original rugs, but it did not appear cluttered. The main staircase was carpeted in bright purple and there were different shades of orange on each wall. For meetings, exotic little alcoves were provided, but there was nothing remotely approaching the formality of a traditional boardroom. Several Andy Warhol paintings of Diane adorned her office and, even higher up, was her yoga room, complete with Arabian tent.

'I meditate every morning and I do yoga,' Diane told us. 'I try to be in touch with myself and my soul and whatever else I have. I'm a pragmatic person with a soul, hopefully.'

It was 9.10 a.m. and Diane was speaking on the phone from the bathroom of her atelier. 'I'm dressing up while I talk to you,' she said. 'I actually slept in my office last night. I sometimes sleep here, and I sometimes sleep elsewhere. I'm like Fidel Castro – no one knows where I sleep.'

Unlike Fidel Castro, however, Diane Von Furstenberg had homes in New York, Connecticut, Paris and the Bahamas. She was born Diane Simone Michelle Halfin in Brussels on New Year's Eve, 1946. 'My mother, Liliane, was a prisoner of war and she survived,' she said. 'She was very brave and courageous, but doesn't make a big thing about it. She worked for the resistance in Belgium and she was arrested and she went to the camps for 14 months, then she came back. I was born after that.'

Diane was studying economics at the University of Geneva when she met Egon Von Furstenberg, an Austro-Italian prince whose mother was an Agnelli of Fiat fame. They were married on 16 July 1969, which made Diane a princess, and, soon after the wedding, the couple moved to New York, where their two children, Alexandre and Tatiana, were born. In 1970, Diane founded her first women's clothing company, Diane Von Furstenberg Ltd, selling easy-knit dresses.

Adopting the slogan, *Honest in all ways – honest product, honest and straight approach to needs*, she expanded the company into Diane Von Furstenberg Inc, which marketed a full range of DVF-licensed products from eyewear to luggage. There was also the Diane Von Furstenberg Cosmetics and Fragrance Division, one of whose first products was a scent named Tatiana after her daughter.

In 1976, at the height of the sex war, Diane created 'a little bourgeois dress' in cotton jersey which crossed at the front and tied around the waist. She called it 'the wrap dress' and it was an instant sensation. Betty Ford and Aretha Franklin were among millions of American women who paid $89 to buy one. The wrap dress did for Diane Von Furstenberg what 'the little black dress' had done for Coco Chanel a generation earlier: it made her famous. Her darkly beautiful face was on the covers of *Newsweek* and the *Wall Street Journal*, Andy Warhol painted her portrait, and she was labelled 'the most marketable female in fashion since Coco Chanel'.

One writer rhapsodised that the wrap dress 'captured the spirit of women's liberation. With its plunging neckline, knee-grazing skirt, and sashed waist, it celebrated in-your-face femininity and sexual freedom.'

So where did the inspiration for the wrap dress come from?

'I don't know – whatever!' said Diane, probably too busy with the eyeliner to think deeply. 'The point is you look back and think, "Oh my God, how did all this happen?" and I don't know. I just threw myself into it, and I did it, and it was very influential in people's lives and, therefore, it's not just about huge sales promotion, but it's also about having made people feel good and that *is* nice.'

In 1983, she and Egon were divorced after a 14-year marriage and she moved to Bali, then to Paris in 1985. 'I sold my company at the time and, at the same time, Europe felt more exciting again and I decided to move,' she said. 'It was also personal, because I fell in love with a writer and I went back to my original love and passion, which has been books and publishing. I wanted to have a literary salon, which I did for five years [she started the French language publishing house, Salvy, which was still trading], and then I came back here again.'

While she was away, she had been awarded the New York Mayor's Liberty Medal, which recognised citizens of the world who'd achieved the judges' idea of the American Dream. Sales of products stamped with the DVF name had passed the $1 billion mark, but the company no longer belonged to her.

'I said, "Okay, how do I relaunch my company?" and it has been a long process ever since,' she said. 'That's what I'm doing now. How's the progress? It's good, I don't know – it's okay, it's fine, no, it's better than okay – by anybody's standards, it would be better than okay. By my standards it's . . . it takes a long time to make it what . . . it takes me a lifetime to put visions together. But, then again, I operate in a very unusual way, I guess.'

In 1991, she published *Beds*, her first coffee-table book in a Random House series about stylish homes, and similar books followed on baths and tables. She pioneered TV shopping with the live, on-air selling of her Silk Assets collection and became a contributing editor to *Vanity Fair*. In 1997, she opened the Diane Von Furstenberg Studio at 389 West 12th Street and celebrated with the launch of the new 'Diane' line of signature dresses, including a revamped version of the wrap, at Saks Fifth Avenue, Neiman Marcus and Bloomingdale's stores across the nation.

The new wrap, in bamboo, snakeskin and diamond prints priced at $190, made its comeback to rapturous applause from fashion writers. *Tatler* raved about her 'boldly printed wrap dresses synonymous with Studio 54 style', while *Vogue* commented that the wrap was 'back with a vengeance'.

From the bathroom, Diane told us: 'It turned out the dress I created was more than just a dress. I made five million of them and it meant a lot for a lot of women at that time. I'm realising it now, because it's coming back again. Those women were either my age, or a generation above, and now I'm starting again and dressing the generation under, so I'm on my third generation and I'm only – well, I'm *only* – I'm 50. So I guess I have played a role in people's personal lives and I hadn't realised it. I'm writing a book, [*Signature Life*, for Simon & Schuster] and, when I look back, I realise I've dressed *millions* and *millions* of women.'

Diane gave credit for the wrap's revival to her 25-year-old daughter-in-law, Alexandra Von Furstenberg, the third daughter of duty-free tycoon Robert W. Miller and his wife Chantal. Alexandra wed Alexandre Von Furstenberg, a 28-year-old investment fund manager, in 1995 in New York's society wedding of the year: a three-day extravaganza that culminated in a black-tie ball. Alexandra's sisters were Pia, who was married to J. Paul Getty's grandson, Christopher Getty, and Marie-Chantal, wife of Crown Prince Pavlos of Greece. Alexandra grew up in the Carlyle Hotel, two floors above the Von Furstenbergs' apartment, and met her husband-to-be in the lift.

Still on the phone, Diane said: 'Alexandra works for me as a designer; she's part of the design team. I'm very, very close to my children and now to my daughter-in-law. I've known her since she was 14.' Apparently Alexandre had suggested to his mother that his wife might work for her, and Diane had agreed to take her on. After spending a few months familiarising herself with her mother-in-law's designs, Alexandra said to her, 'Why don't you do these dresses again?' and the wrap was reborn. Alexandra reworked the design to make it shorter, slinkier and omitted the dominant seventies cuffs and collars.

Diane said: 'I'm very close to my family. None of this is unusual for us. We're people; I treat my children as people. What is most important for me, other than health, is freedom. I have never compromised on freedom. Freedom has definitely been the one thing that has been most significant to me. What I try to do, therefore, with the clothes and whatever I do, is to give people a choice and a certain freedom about themselves. All the clothes, and anything I do, very much adapt to your personality: you wear it the way you want, so it's a tool in order to be more you, and if I've made any contribution I hope it is that one: to help women to get always a little bit more themselves.

'What I accentuate, hopefully, is a way to flatter them and a way for them to like themselves better and to be more themselves. I think that is the most important thing: to be yourself and to be true to you. Of course, there is no guarantee to happiness but, certainly, honesty towards yourself is a major way to get there.

'What's always remarkable and always kind of fascinating about women is their courage. Women very often pretend to be weak because it's part of an inherited quality; something we're supposed to do. But women, when they need to, really are very, very strong and very brave and very courageous. I personally think it's a privilege to be a woman for the mere reason that we have the secret of life: we give life. So women have the first power, so to speak, but then, of course, there's all the other things women aren't supposed to be and they often play down their strengths. I don't know why; it's just what we do.

'When I deal with women, whether it's in a sitting-room or when I make them up – I used to do make-up – you have an intimate and very personal connection with them. I think all women are the same; it doesn't matter whether they're European or American, or whatever social background they are, once you deal with them in intimacy all women are the same. They're all insecure and strong at the same time, fearful and courageous.

'I don't know if I've had a very influential woman in my life. My mother, for survival and daring and all of that, but, no, not particularly any woman. There are a lot of women for different things you like. There's a lot of women I think are great. I don't think friends are something that one chooses carefully; I think that friends are things that happen; encounters that become somewhat more meaningful than others. But I do pay an enormous amount of attention to friendship.

Loyalty is extremely important – I know no other way. Loyalty is important, but the most important thing is honesty. Women aren't stupid. I love men, but I like women. I think they're strong and capable.

'The most influential man? I don't know. I can't think of anyone in particular. I do like men a lot; I have a lot of men friends. What I like about men is that they're nice, they're sweet: what I like about men, usually, is their vulnerable side . . . yeah, the side of them they don't know they have. Maybe I help them find it.'

On that note, Diane Von Furstenberg ended the interview and emerged from the bathroom in a black-and-white snakeskin wrap dress to meet the challenges of the new day.

THE word on Seventh Avenue was that Mary McFadden was something else. 'She's attractive and sensual – extremely sensual,' said one admiring male. 'A very powerful personality,' said another man, 'but playful.' Within minutes of opening the front door of her *bjiou* apartment on the Upper East Side, Ms McFadden had verified both descriptions.

'Sex is a fantastic tool,' she said as nonchalantly as though discussing some dependable DIY product, 'and I think it's very good to be a fantastically sexually oriented person. I'm attracted to two different types of men: one who is very brilliant and, generally speaking, usually ugly; and the other one is a super model who's, generally speaking, not as brilliant, although street smart.'

Are you intuitive about men?

'Within a few instants of meeting anyone, I have already decided whether they'll be in my life or not. If I'm attracted to someone, I'd immediately say that to them.'

You don't have any coyness?

'Not the slightest.'

And it works?

'It hasn't failed yet. I've been married a lot. Eleven times. Three were killed and two died and one I married twice. If you're a cold woman, your success with men would obviously be less. Maybe they should go to Madam Claude to be properly educated; I think that's a really good training school.'

Are you sensual?

'Sensuality is an important aspect in a woman. The geisha maybe gets kissed once and it's really clinical. The life of a whore, however, is a little bit more sexual and sensual. They have to play a lot of different games that a geisha would not be privileged to play because of the way they're disciplined and schooled in their art. The geisha system is totally restrictive.'

How do you interact with men in business?

'I have a great deal of power in my personal life that attracts men in any way I want to use it. I've always had it.'

Do you ever advise other women about relationships?

'The other night a friend said to me that she has a roommate who's from Israel and what should she do. So I said to her, "Well, darling, this weekend, in the kitchen, when the iron is hot, seduce him." He's 20 years old and she's probably 60. If an 80-year-old man can go out with a 15-year-old girl, why shouldn't she?'

Pause for a moment to take in the scene of these exchanges: Mary McFadden, president of the New York clothing-and-jewellery corporation that bore her name, was drinking champagne in her living-room. The living-room, like its owner, was a one-off: big, purple, gold and turquoise silk cushions scattered over a hessian carpet; a parrot in a huge, gilded cage; numerous phallic-shaped knick-knacks in odd places. The colour combination should have rendered it kitsch, but Mary McFadden had all the unnerving self-assurance of a Yellow Cab driver.

In a neighbourhood of incredibly beautiful, stylish women, she was one of the most beautiful and stylish, with a stunning face framed by short, slicked, black hair and a pair of long, thick, gold earrings. She was tall and slim, her eyes the languid green of a South Seas lagoon, her outfit a cultural collision that few women would have survived. 'The jacket is from central Java,' she said. 'I did a collection based on Javanese textiles six years ago, then I did a Russian collection two years ago, so the jacket is Javanese and the skirt is Russian. I just mix and match, really.'

Mary's interest in different cultures extended to her spiritual life: she was a member of an esoteric Islamic sect. Even sitting perfectly still, Mary McFadden was dynamic, with an elegant posture that merely accentuated her sexuality. 'She has many young lovers,' one of the admiring males had added, somewhat gratuitously. A very dry sense of humour, however, saved her from vanity and friends also testified to her intelligence, loyalty and determination.

As president of Mary McFadden Inc since 1976, she had remained a big player in the garment game while many other designers had folded their tents and moved on, or simply folded. 'Being a woman is a great advantage,' she said. 'We're more attractive than men to sell products all across the board. When I started, there were very few women in the field, so it was an extremely great advantage. I was very lucky; first of all, I was elected to the

Hall of Fame within two years of starting my business, not only for clothes, but also for my designs. Once you get elected to the Hall of Fame, the whole world writes about you, so I didn't have any problem. I was lucky.'

Mary Josephine McFadden was born in New York City on 1 October 1938, the daughter of Alexander and Mary McFadden. She was educated at the Sorbonne, the Traphagen School of Design and Columbia University. Despite 11 marriages, she had only one child, a daughter named Justine, who was 33.

'She's like my best friend,' said Mary. 'We talk about sex to each other. She knows everything about my friends and I know a great deal about her friends. It's like two girlfriends who talk about their companions or husbands or lovers. We look very much alike, we have the same kind of figures and we party together. Even though I'm her mother, we still have other levels of our relationship which have to do with sister relationships and mother-daughter relationships: it's broken in half.

'My daughter is a filmmaker and a journalist. Her first talent is writing and that was my first talent – I started off as a writer too. No, I started off as public relations director for Christian Dior when I was 18 years old. I knew it would be very difficult to get into the fashion industry, so I went to South Africa and I became an editor of *Vogue* South Africa and then a journalist, particularly a political journalist for the *Rand Daily Mail*. This was an anti-government newspaper and I found myself in a very difficult position. I went up to Zimbabwe, where I did these sculptures for Frank McEwen at the National Gallery in Zimbabwe. That was also a politically dangerous area, so I had to come back to America.

'I became an editor of American *Vogue* and was photographed in clothes that I had made in Africa. From there, I went over to someone and asked them if they would buy these products because I had these pages in *Vogue* and they agreed. And then I asked them to give me a merchandising credit and also to give me a technician to make the clothes.

'That was in 1972. When the clothes were made I was given a national press show and out of that I sold a million dollars worth of product. So at that time I made a career change and I've been making clothes ever since. I never had to go to a bank; my vision was correct and I've sold millions and millions of product. I was always very successful and I have always run responsible businesses.'

What stops a woman getting what she wants?

'She's going to get what she wants if she has some intelligence; it's automatic. If she hasn't got the looks, she can make herself look good – there are enough plastic surgeons around who can turn you into Elizabeth Taylor.'

Can they really help?

'I know so.'

How do you know?

'I have enough knowledge of what can be done today in plastic surgery.'

Can a person acquire a new personality as well?

'Of course. You just have to look at television. Look at Billy Crystal and copy Billy Crystal. Billy Crystal's quite clever and so's Jack Nicholson – I mean, you can copy anyone.'

What makes one person more successful than another?

'The most important thing is that if you don't find a specific, individualistic product whereby you get into the market place, then don't bother. The main thing is that you have to do enough searching in the world to find what is unique, something that can give you a stamp in the marketplace. If you just go with the flow of other products, you will never make it. If you have a really individual product in the marketplace you stand a really good chance of staying for a long time. There are three important traits: you have to be a great saleswoman, you have to be a great administrator and you have to have a great sense of business. In my case, you also have to be a great designer. So you need four ingredients in order to survive in the market place.'

Which women do you consider attractive?

'I thought there were certain great beauties this century. I thought Greta Garbo was very well dressed by Adrian. I think Madonna, dressed as a pre-Raphaelite, is very creative and imaginative, I thought Grace Kelly was able to achieve a great American look and Audrey Hepburn, as a non-American, was also able to achieve something very unique this century. I suppose in Mexico Delores del Rio was able to achieve something extraordinary. They all had some incredible state of beauty: it was magnetic. It was like looking at a really extraordinary diamond. They were born with unique physical properties and took advantage of them and film studios that worked with them picked that advantage and made them more extraordinary.'

16

Chelsea's Champion

RUTH HARDING was discussing the finer points of the Season over afternoon tea at the Ritz. The Palm Court was packed with well-heeled refugees from rainy Ascot, but Ruth Harding was not talking about that season. Her speciality is the football season and, as a major shareholder in Chelsea Football Club, she is the most powerful woman connected with Britain's biggest winter sport.

Ruth's husband, the boyish-faced, tousle-haired tycoon Matthew Harding, was vice-chairman of Chelsea and when he was killed in a helicopter crash at the age of 44, she inherited much of his £400 million estate. 'I was there when he had nothing,' said Ruth. 'I remember what it was like and I hope the money hasn't changed me. And, if it has, I just tell my friends, "Sort me out."'

A slim, stylish woman with short-cropped blonde hair, Ruth was slinkily dressed in a leopardskin minidress from her favourite shop, Harvey Nichols. She was also wearing a new diamond engagement ring. Her fiancé, Richard Gist, was an NSPCC manager in Coventry and they met after Matthew bequeathed £50,000 to the charity and they discovered that they shared a mutual love of football, although for rival teams. Nine years younger than Ruth, Richard was as tall and reserved as Matthew had been short and boisterous. He was as totally dedicated to Arsenal as Ruth was to Chelsea and the couple weren't planning to wed until the end of the next football season. Referring to her leopardskin print, Ruth said: 'Richard calls this a dead animal dress. He doesn't like it at all, although it's really silk so it doesn't matter. I have a lovely coat that has a nice dead animal collar and I've not been allowed to wear it. It stays in the cupboard.'

As a pianist tinkled away at Gershwin and Cole Porter in the background, Ruth remembered the days when she and Matthew had first gone to watch Chelsea in action. 'We were both 16 and we'd come up to Chelsea on a Saturday and we had this little pact that if I could look at the shops in the King's Road in the morning, I'd put up with watching football in the afternoon. I have to say I didn't enjoy it. It was all right when it was warm and you could stand there in the sunshine, but I've stood there and been freezing cold in pouring rain. In those days, if you got there early enough, you had an iron railing in front of you for support and that was so cold that it would burn your hands if you touched it.

'Chelsea were brilliant in those days. They were a well-respected club with good players like Peter Osgood, Alan Hudson and Peter Bonetti. It was when they won the FA Cup in 1970. They were a smart club, the club to follow.'

Matthew Harding started his career as a bank clerk and went on to lead a management buyout of the Benfield Insurance Group, which specialised in high-risk re-insurance. After watching Chelsea lose to Bolton on a blustery Tuesday night in October 1996, he and two other fans had boarded a helicopter to fly back to London. The helicopter crashed soon after take-off and Matthew was killed, along with the two other fans and the pilot.

'When Matt died, Chelsea very kindly asked me to be patron of the club,' said Ruth. 'I was totally overwhelmed and I was delighted to accept. It meant the Harding name would hopefully always be in the club. Matt's name was put on the North Stand and I want the Harding name to be with that club forever if possible.

'For my duties as patron, I make sure I represent the club in the best way I can and that's generally gaining respect from other clubs. When they visit I make a point of welcoming them and treating them well and I also have a brilliant rapport with the fans. When we play in Europe I always go out there and talk to them. They always come up and say, "'Ello, Mrs 'Arding." They never say Mrs Harding. It's Mrs 'Arding and I like that; it's important to me. The morning after we won the FA Cup in 1997 Dennis Wise very kindly let me take the cup outside the Waldorf and all the fans were lined up there to see it and I let all the kids touch the cup, which must have been a dream for them. We hadn't won it for 25 years and I really enjoyed that.

'I was born and brought up in Oxford and I went to school in Abingdon and that's where I met Matt. Dad was a probation officer and my mum stayed at home and brought me and my sister up full time. I love ballet and I'd always wanted to be a ballet dancer. I used to dance in the house to ballet music, but I never had proper lessons. Instead, I ended up watching football. I went to teacher training college and lived on a grant of £5 a week. I worked every holiday in factories or in Boots. I've never had an overdraft in my life. Buying nice clothes was a dream to me, really. That's why it's so nice now I can afford that stuff.

'We got married in Woking because that's where my parents lived at the time. It wasn't a very big wedding, just the family, because we didn't have any money. We just had a little afternoon reception and then went on holiday for five days in the Lake district. We bought a small house at Burgess Hill, just north of Brighton. I paid the mortgage and Matt paid the bills. He worked in Lloyds Bank then as a clerk and we just about scraped through. I was still working as a teacher and I taught for three years before I had my daughter, Hannah. We had four children, a girl and three boys, including twins, and I stayed at home and brought them up.

'If you've got a husband who's in business and works long hours, children need the security of a mother at home and I felt that was more important than my career, so I gave up teaching and I started a playgroup and I did voluntary work in schools. We moved several times, but we've lived in that area for 25 years.'

The Hardings' last home was a £1 million mansion in a quiet East Sussex village. Matthew joined the Chelsea board in 1993 which enabled Ruth to meet other directors' wives in the boardroom on match day. She formed some enduring friendships, notably one with Linda Hutchinson, the managing director's wife. 'I went to the boardroom lunches and became part of the boardroom community,' she said. 'I didn't have a say in how the club was run, but I became much more involved and found I really, really liked it. I liked the women I was mixing with and I liked the life.

'The travelling could be quite daunting to some women, but it became part of my life to get on a train and travel wherever. If I was travelling to Newcastle or Everton they'd invite me to lunch and entertain me. I've come back from a Man United game at 3 a.m. and wondered what am I doing, but you do it: that's part of your dedication. There's this very strange feeling that if you're not there supporting the team then they'll miss you, which is absolutely crazy. But if you talk to any football fan they have this feeling that it's so important to you that you're there for them.

'Boardrooms used to be male-dominated and the women were in a different room, but whenever a club now builds a new boardroom the partners of the chairman and the directors have been invited in, so we don't have this separation any more. At Chelsea, we have lunch in the boardroom and then we're requested to move into another room afterwards. This is quite an antiquated system, in fact, and something I can't change, even though I own a lot of shares in Chelsea. I'm the patron, not the chairman. But generally in football clubs now women are invited into boardrooms and are treated equally with the men. If there are things we women are not happy about then we will discuss them with the directors and if changes can be made they will make them for us.

'I'd like to see more families attending Chelsea matches. I'll stick my neck out here and say you reduce the price of the tickets because I feel very sad that the ticket prices are now the equivalent of getting the best seat in a West End theatre and I think that's ludicrous. You can book to go to *Les Miserables* and you know you're going to see a good show and you can pay that amount to see Chelsea play in an afternoon and they can be hopeless. You can come away thinking why did I spend the afternoon doing that? If you're a dedicated fan you accept it. In the directors' box, it's £250 per ticket. I've paid that to take Tom Watt to an Arsenal game.

'The ticket prices vary and it depends who you're playing – say £20 in the North Stand. It's a lot of money. If you're going with your wife and two children you're talking about a very expensive day out. The problem is that fans want their club to be the best, they want the best footballers and to get the best footballers you pay them phenomenal rates, whatever they're asking a week, which is astronomical money. Therefore you need to charge that for the fans to watch. It's just a spiral really and I don't know what the answer is. I feel very sad about it because it's a shame that dad goes off on his own on a Saturday afternoon and I would like to see a situation where the whole family goes.

'I would like to see a chairwoman of a Premier League club running it well and everybody saying, "Good on you, girl, you've made a success of it." But it's a hell of a risk because if you made a mess of it you'd have the tabloids and every man in the country saying, "Ha, ha!" It's a very male-dominated sport and I'm still not 100 per cent sure that men really like an awful lot of women to be there. It's an escape for a man and he's thinking, "This is my afternoon away from it all." Some men love it when their girlfriends come along and I think a lot of men would be happy if their families came along, but there's still that male gene that says, "This is nice. I'm out with the lads on my own. I'm young again." I think for a woman to run a club she'd have to be a pretty strong woman.

'As the patron of the club it's not right for me to comment on the price of the tickets, but it does sadden me that, whether we like it or not, football clubs are run as a business. Therefore you have corporate entertaining and you have sponsors, which you've got to have because they raise the bulk of the money. But I have in front of me a row of sponsors at the moment – and they won't like me for saying this – but they turn up late for the game, they've had a good lunch so they're pretty high, they're on their mobiles, they go off five minutes before half-time, they come back five minutes after half-time so you miss what's happening on the pitch. It's a good day out for them, probably free actually because the company is paying for it, and I think that's sad because in those ten seats in front of me should be real fans who want to watch the game. But that's the way it's probably going to go. I'm very much for the fan in the street. Although I'm on boardroom level, my heart is very much with them. I sympathise with them. It irritates me seeing people watching a game who are only there because of corporate entertainment.

'There are always changes in one's life that you'd like to make, that you can't make now but I'd like to make in the future. I've got great aspirations for Chelsea one day, but I'm not prepared to discuss that. It's not the right time.'

Matthew had also pledged £1 million to Tony Blair's New Labour Party and Ruth had ensured that the money was paid after his death. She became friendly with Tony and Cherie Blair and their family. 'As patron, I have two tickets in the directors' box and that enables me to take another person and I make a point of taking young children if I can, but I also take fans from the opposing team. I take Cherie Blair's mum, who's a Liverpool supporter, to the Liverpool game and I really enjoy it. You have this affinity with them.

'When Matt died, some Everton supporters gave me a lovely poem. It was not neatly written, it wasn't nicely presented, it wasn't anything other than written from the heart and it made me cry. It wasn't slushy, just beautifully written. I had it framed and it's beside the fireplace in my living-room. Matt died in October and when we played Everton in May I'd spoken to the Everton directors' wives and they arranged for me to meet the couple. Their little boy, aged about seven, gave me his Everton scarf which I promised him I would take to the FA Cup final in two weeks' time, which I did. After Chelsea won, I was interviewed by Des Lynam on television and I was holding his scarf and I wrote and told him. They might be Everton, but we're all in this together.

'My own children have had a lot of pressure on them. They've had the media eye on them right from the start. They've had a lot to cope with. The press have been quite kind to us, but they do struggle with it. All of the children are being brought up to go to work and have a job and fulfil themselves. Hannah is training to be a nurse and the poor girl turned up on the ward to find her mother on the front page of *The Sun* on the bedside tables. She wasn't very happy about it. The children knew about the engagement, but they didn't expect it to be front page of *The Sun* that morning and nor did I. But I try to protect them as much as I can. I try to make their lives as normal as I can. I hope they'll grow up to be as normal and as happy as they can be. They've not had a normal start in life, but I'm very proud of them most of the time and I'm sure they're proud of me most of the time.

'I don't regard myself as a feminist and yet I'm constantly being told that I am. The fact that I support Refuge, which is for women who are desperate, and the fact that I'm totally involved with a man's sport says something. I wouldn't march for women's rights or anything like that. I don't fully believe that women are equal to men. I think our genes are just so different that you can't possibly say that we are equal. I'll probably be shot for saying that, but when I got married I knew it was my job to stay at home and look after the children and for Matt to go out to work and that was fine. That's not feminist, that's traditional and old-fashioned, but it worked.

'Women and men have different brains – they are slightly different; they've proved it now. My philosophy is that women can think of ten things at once and men can only think of one and that sums up the difference. I'm always thinking of the next hour, the next day, the next week – juggling ten things at the same time. Men can only deal with what they're doing half an hour ahead. If women are good enough and they can do a job as well as a man then brilliant, they should have the opportunity. Equality of opportunity is a different thing from saying they are equal.

'The prospect is that the children [Hannah, Luke and twins Patrick and Joel] will come into a lot of money. There's no way I'd give it to them. I want them to work for it and to appreciate it. I would give them a down-payment on a house but I would like them to work towards achieving it. My son Luke has just finished his GCSEs and he's working in a garage in Surrey which involves getting up at a quarter to seven in the morning and making a long train journey and I'm pleased he's doing it. He's earning nothing but he's doing something for himself. I think it's so important.

'It's so difficult when you're the child of rich parents to be given everything and go wrong. I don't want any of that. I want them to value people, value money and to fulfil themselves, to get some self-satisfaction. That's really important. It's so easy for privileged children –

if you call money privilege – to go totally off the rails. The children have not been privately educated. They went to the local playgroup and three local three schools. They've been with their friends in the village from day one. So they've had the support of the village and the friends around them and it's been very important for them. They're treated like anyone else in the village. They're not special, although everybody knows them wherever they go and they're recognised. But they're just children in the village. They play football in the park with them. I just hope I've got it right. You never know, do you?

'The most important thing for children is to know they're loved and to be secure. They all get along with Richard, except that he's an Arsenal supporter. There doesn't seem to have been a problem at all. I think I've been very lucky. I think it's impossible for someone to come in and take over four teenagers. It's brilliant that Richard managed to deal with that and they in turn seem to like the fact that he's come in and made me happy, which is lovely.

'I'm a happy person. I've been to hell and back, but I've always said look forward, hold your head up, there's always some good that comes out of bad and there is, always, always. Maybe I've just been lucky, but I've got some brilliant friends and they've got me through the last few years. I love opera and ballet and I'm lucky I've now found someone who'll take me. I'd never want Richard to change and I know he'd never want me to change.'

Outside the Ritz, a chauffeur-driven car was waiting to take Ruth and Richard to the Albert Hall. They were going to see *Romeo and Juliet*.

17

First Among Equals

MARY ARCHER sat on a cream sofa with the River Thames framed behind her like a vast Canaletto. The panoramic view through the wraparound glass walls of the fifth-floor penthouse on the Albert Embankment served as a perfect backdrop to her life with Baron Archer of Weston-super-Mare, better known as Jeffrey Archer, bestselling novelist, controversial politician, charity auctioneer and, in this phase of his helter-skelter career, wannabe Mayor of London.

In the foreground was Lambeth Bridge and the redbrick fortress of Lambeth Palace, with Westminster Bridge and the Palace of Westminster further downstream. So much water had flowed under various bridges during Lord and Lady Archer's 33 years of married life that the symbolism was ideal. A short, brusque, bullet-headed figure, Jeffrey Archer had fought more campaigns than Napoleon, so it was also apt to note that Waterloo Bridge was just visible in the far distance.

The Thames was almost at high tide, with glowering clouds piled high in dense banks above it. Shafts of sunlight broke through in places and danced on the water until the surface was blanketed again in shadow. As a scientist, Dr Mary Archer was one of the world's leading experts in the study of light, while living with Jeffrey had given her ample opportunity to examine the nature of shadows.

Her husband, now 58, had entered the House of Commons at the impressionable age of 29 and had been at the cut-and-thrust end of politics ever since, making many enemies along the way. He'd been forced to resign his seat after losing all his money in a crippling financial disaster; he'd fought, and won, a headline-making libel case involving a girl called Monica; and he'd created high drama at the Stock Exchange after being accused of insider trading. There was also a whole string of allegations that he had falsified his academic record to get into Oxford University and had even made exaggerated claims about his father's war record. But despite every single scandal that had threatened to engulf them, the Archers had noticeably prospered. The totems of worldly wealth and material success were everywhere to be seen in their *pied-à-terre* on the south bank of the Thames.

The apartment was actually a duplex, with steps leading from the living, dining and kitchen areas to bedrooms and an office upstairs. On the first level, the lift doors opened on to a lobby which was decorated with two of Warhol's Marilyn Monroes and a gallery lined with Jeffrey's highly prized collection of political cartoons led into an L-shaped living room with outer walls of sheer glass. Here, among the beige marble and blond pine, were several Lowrys, as well as Vuillards, Pissaros, Dufys, the Renoir nude and Monet's painting of the Houses of Parliament. In bookshelves placed at either end of an oriental divan were numerous works on art and literature: F. Scott Fitzgerald's *Ledger*, the paintings of Dante Gabriel Rossetti, a volume on *The Queen's Pictures* and another entitled *Oriental Erotic Art*. There were sculptures and family photographs and an engraving of one of Jeffrey's most famous books, *Kane and Abel*.

The butler, Joseph, served fresh orange juice and we waited for Mary Archer, Baroness Archer of Weston-super-Mare, to arrive. According to the hands on the black grandfather clock, she showed up 15 minutes late for our appointment. As a self-confessed workaholic, she simply tried to cram too much into each day and punctuality, she admitted, was not one of her virtues. The visiting professor of biochemistry at Imperial College, London, was wearing a plum-coloured woollen suit, with a black beaded necklace, black tights and black high-heeled shoes. She was 5ft 5in tall, with shortish, black hair and ultra-slim legs, and looked a decade or so younger than her 53 years. 'She is feminine without being sexy,' one male admirer whose idea of sexiness was clearly rooted in Page Three had opined. She, too, drank orange juice, smiled constantly and giggled easily, not at all the staid, professorial type from academia. It became abundantly clear that Mary Archer really enjoyed the power of being her own woman. 'I dress for myself,' she said. 'It's got to be comfortable, it's got to be smart, it's got to be something I don't need to fuss about. I'm not a dedicated shopper, still less a dedicated follower of fashion. I just want to put something on and forget about it. But I do look in the Italian shops in Sloane Street, for example, Armani and Dolce e Gabbana. The one I'm wearing is an Irish design, I think.'

She whipped off her jacket and handed it over for inspection: the label was Paul Costelloe, Ireland. This one little action revealed the more extroverted side of Mary Archer which only her family and closest friends normally ever saw, such as the time she performed a cabaret (including a rendition of *Who Wants to be a Millionaire?*) at a party to mark her 30th wedding anniversary.

Her image in political circles, however, was of an aloof, self-sufficient woman who kept her feelings and her thoughts to herself. 'You can't really tell what goes on behind those eyes,' said one Tory Party stalwart. Mary appeared to confirm this view when she said: 'I think I am reserved and don't find it at all difficult to disguise what I think. In fact, I would find it a great deal more difficult to express what I feel, but I'm not introspective.'

She was, nevertheless, something of an enigma. The one thing that everybody was agreed upon was that Mary Archer was a very attractive and highly intelligent woman and quite a few people marvelled over the fact that she had chosen Jeffrey Archer as her life partner. In 1994, the *Sunday Times* boldly asked: WHAT ON EARTH DOES SHE SEE IN HIM? The following year, it answered its own question: AN ENDURING ATTRACTION OF OPPOSITES. One of Lord Archer's former colleagues said: 'Opposites? Definitely. But I don't think that is what makes her stay. I suspect he leans on Mary. She is a stabilising factor in his life. That is not to say Jeffrey would not have made it on his own because he is a natural survivor, but it would have been more traumatic for him and those around him.'

But what does *she* see in him? 'I was intrigued – I don't mean in the sense of amorous intrigue,' Mary said, describing their first meeting. 'I was intrigued by him: different odour, non-academic, tremendous fun. He thought I was terrific, which was all very good.'

More forcefully, she added: 'I've always been glad that I haven't been married to somebody in my own field. I like my independence, my intellectual independence, a lot and it's also great fun that he's in all these other worlds which I'm very interested in. I don't resent it at all – I am very supportive of his bid to be Mayor of London.'

Mary spent much of her time at the Old Vicarage – the family home at Grantchester, near Cambridge – while Jeffrey often ventured on to the London scene alone. Numerous women spoke of his flirtatious manner: a *risqué* joke here, a raised eyebrow there, the impish Archer smirk, but none could take it further than that, even though Mary was on record as saying that sexual fidelity 'doesn't rank very high on my scale of the importance of things'.

Observing Lord and Lady Archer *á deux* at a party at the Roy Miles Gallery in Mayfair a few weeks earlier had added a vastly more human element to the equation. They were a well-matched couple, Jeffrey and Mary, both small but perfectly formed, and smartly attired without being brash or flashy; he smiling and courteous, as befitted a man who was seeking the Conservative candidacy in the election for Mayor of London; she, as a High Court judge had once phrased it, 'fragrant and lovely' (her favourite perfume was Calèche by Hèrmés). Like a couple of entrants in a *Come Dancing* contest, they moved as one through the gabbling throng, a neat turn here to greet someone, a sudden twist there to avoid someone else; then, having met everyone who was anyone, they waltzed off into the night.

The intriguing thing was that Mary's presence at Jeffrey's side seemed to have the effect of making him whole, a complete man, thus removing the need for him to seek other female attention. As he had once explained: 'I've lived with a woman who is my superior for 30 years.'

Dr Archer was quite sanguine about the hostility shown towards her husband by certain sections of the media, the most recent attack coming from Paul Foot in the *Evening Standard*. Jeffrey's face, scowling over his reading glasses, was printed beside the headline: WHY THIS MAN IS UNFIT TO BE MAYOR. The article included a none-too-fragrant pot-pourri of every allegation ever made against him, but it did not upset his wife. 'I don't seek out things that are written about me or Jeffrey,' she said. 'I read them if they happen to come under my nose. I think I've been pretty fairly treated myself.'

A number of exciting things have happened during your married life.

'Yes indeed. Amazing things.'

How did you deal with these amazing things?

'I hope by standing my ground. But I have been pushed off position at times.'

Who was doing the pushing?

'Oh, the forces of mischief; sometimes Jeffrey's own imprudence. Fortunately, I have a fairly – what's the word I want – not calm, exactly; what's the adjective from equanimity? Is it equanimous? I think it probably is – anyway, one of those temperaments.'

Are you non-judgmental?

'No, I'm quite judgmental, but I usually keep my own judgments to myself. I have difficulty in coming to decisions about what I think about people.'

You must have seen the slings and arrows coming.

'I didn't see all of them coming, no. If somebody acts impetuously as Jeffrey has done . . . he didn't see them coming and I see them coming even less.'

You're not shaken by them, or are you?

'No, I don't think so. I'm not somebody who really dwells on or thinks about the past and, anyway, if I do, some of the problems we've encountered have turned into tremendous opportunities. The hardest thing was undoubtedly getting into debt – the Aquablast thing. That was much, much the worst thing, and that was the first thing.'

Aquablast was a Canadian company in which Jeffrey invested £500,000, most of it borrowed. When Aquablast went belly-up, he was financially ruined. He informed Mary that they were broke during their son William's second birthday party in 1974. Mary was pregnant with their second son, James, and the years of hardship that followed prevented them from having a third child, a hoped-for daughter.

Instead of going bankrupt, Jeffrey opted to write his way out of trouble like Sir Walter Scott and repay his creditors from the royalties on his books. The family moved to Cambridge, where they rented a house from Trinity College and, while Mary took up a teaching fellowship at Newnham, Jeffrey started burning the midnight oil over character, plot and motivation. Success was not instantaneous. His first novel, *Not a Penny More, Not a Penny Less*, published in 1975, sold a modest 3,000 copies in hardback, but *Kane and Abel* was auctioned in America four years later for $2.7 million and that bonanza cleared the debt.

'Nothing since has been as hard or really gone on as long,' said Mary. 'Perhaps you might say I've been weakened by that and I couldn't stand another such blow. But it turned out magically well. It was good to move out of London, good to take the boys to Cambridge, good to teach in Cambridge for ten years, certainly good that Jeffrey turned his hand to writing. At the time we had no concept that that would be the case. I really thought we'd be in debt for the rest of our lives.

'But I had a skill and I had an income. When you've been through some of these things and you know what it's like you're not exactly tolerant of other people, but you're certainly more understanding. I learned a tremendous lot. One learns through painful experiences, not through pleasurable ones on the whole. I've learned a lot about keeping it together and keeping on, which is the best way – it's the only way.'

Do people believe you're unemotional?

'I believe so. Jeffrey's always saying I come over as very cold. [She giggled at this; in fact, she giggled several times at the mention of Jeffrey's name.] I guess I am. Certainly no one could accuse me of being demonstrative, that I do know.'

Some people start throwing plates around.

'I wouldn't do that. I'd hate to lose control. There's a great deal of self-indulgence in the maverick and the rebel and I don't have a lot of sympathy for them.' Realising that Jeffrey was both maverick and rebel, she hastily added: 'Sometimes, of course, the maverick and the rebel are absolutely right, so one can't absolutely generalise, but I am rather intolerant of people who go through systems, and feed off them, and benefit by them, and then turn round and stand apart and say, "I'm different and I reserve the right to criticise this whole life-support system." I don't admire dropping out, chilling out and all the rest of it. I don't admire that.'

Do you have anyone in particular in mind?

'There might be a few aged flower children still toddling around Longleat.'

MARY Doreen Weedon was one of those self-possessed young women who had followed a more conventional path than many of her contemporaries in the love generation. She was born in a nursing home in Ewell, Surrey, on 22 December 1944, the middle child of an accountant, Harold Weedon, and his wife, Doreen. A thin little girl with spindly legs, Mary had been nicknamed Weedlet at school.

'I went to Cheltenham Ladies' College and and then I went to Oxford,' she said. 'In the sixties, we did feel we were throwing off some tremendously stuffy post-war consensus about life and priorities, although I think I was less revolting than most students. 1968, of course, was *the* great year of student unrest and nobody passed through that unmarked. We had the Prague Spring, Red Danny and all the rest of it. I wasn't involved in student demonstrations – as I say I wasn't as revolting as some students. I kept my nose stuck into a book. I was a hard worker.' Her most *outré* gesture was a Mary Quant haircut, which she had 'for probably longer than it was fashionable, but it suited me very well'.

When she met Jeffrey Howard Archer, she was a 20-year-old chemistry undergraduate at St Anne's College and her cool, alluring beauty was in full bloom. 'He'd come up to Oxford to do a DipEd – a Diploma of Education

– well, that was the *ostensible* reason; he'd really come up to run, which he did with great success. I met him at a party of Nick Lloyd's* and that was it, really. We got married in 1966 just at the end of my undergraduate career. I was 21, very young by current standards; too young, really. You're a child when you're 21, I think. I didn't think so then, of course.

'I wouldn't say he was more sophisticated than me, but he was slightly older and certainly more worldly wise – and still is. I've never been very deferential and nor do I think he would have wanted that. My father was concerned when I married so young, most particularly that I would somehow mess up what clearly was going to be a reasonably good academic career. He said to Jeffrey, "Don't stand in her way." Not that he wanted to, and he said, "No, I won't," and he never has.'

Jeffrey kept his promise when, in 1969, he was elected MP for the safe Tory seat of Louth and Mary, instead of becoming an orthodox constituency wife, returned to Oxford to work on a post-doctoral thesis after taking her PhD at Imperial College, London. She returned to London to the Royal Institution for her second post-doc, then took 'a serious academic posting', a fellowship at Newnham College, Cambridge, in which she stayed for ten years.

'He's always been extremely supportive,' Mary said, 'and I've always been very grateful for that because it means there isn't always food on the table, there isn't always a wife at home, there isn't always somebody fussing about the children. It can have its difficulties.'

Hugh Colver, former director of communication at Conservative Central Office, said: 'Mary is very much her own person. She'd have made it on her own. She'd have made it *anywhere*. In fact, he might have been an impediment. A lot of women married to someone like Jeffrey Archer would have reacted emotionally and publicly to his various indiscretions. That she didn't and remained cool and pleasant, yet detached, is a testament to her strong character.'

A glint of Mary's strength came through when she said: 'One of the questions you haven't yet asked me is, "What does a career woman need? Does she need a successful man?" and I'd say, "No, she needs a good wife, like everybody else."

---

* Sir Nicholas Lloyd was editor of *Cherwell*, the Oxford student newspaper, and went on to edit the *Sunday People*, the *News of the World* and the *Daily Express*.

'There are some women who don't need men, or some women who have had men and been widowed, or separated, or divorced, and they do very well without them. People sometimes just lose interest and then others need them very much. I don't think you can generalise about it. On the whole, a conventional arrangement seems to work better than any other, but I've seen a whole range of things work perfectly well, so I hesitate to lay down the law. Going to Oxford broadens your horizons a hell of a lot.'

Do you recall any vivid awakenings?

'Life with Jeffrey has really been punctuated by that sort of thing and it would be quite hard to surprise me now.'

Do you want to be Lady Mayoress?

'It's not that kind of job. I wouldn't be Lady Mayoress any more than he'd be Lord Mayor. It is a political and executive appointment and inevitably there are a lot of social things, but I don't think you would have a chain hung around your neck.'

It's said that you don't like the title Lady Archer. Is that so?

'I don't dislike it, but I don't use it professionally because I well remember in my young days if I met somebody called Lady X I'd assume she had no O-levels and that's still the working assumption.'

Mary held very positive views about the rewards that her chosen field had to offer women. 'Science is a great career, both for men and for women,' she said, 'and in fact particularly for women because it's something which has very few frontiers and boundaries, whether it be class, or nationality, or indeed sex. It is a very co-operative venture. The nature of science is that you research something, you establish something and you publish it, so it's as though you were putting another brick into this great temple of knowledge of the natural world. Pretty well everybody is a contributor – people don't stand on the sidelines and criticise, they *do*, some more successfully than others.

'A lot of the qualities that are typically found in women – and I don't believe men and women are alike; I believe they're different – such as patience and persistence and intuition are actually very valuable in science. They will also need the male characteristics of boldness and making wild leaps and skating successfully on thin ice. You do need a good dash of that, too.

'Science in general makes a set of wonderful careers for women, although the physical sciences are sometimes regarded as unfeminine. I've simply never been able to understand that; in fact, one of the attractive things about science is that you're experimenting on things, you don't deal with people very much and, while you might regard yourself as a feminist historian or a feminist theologian, I don't really think you can be a feminist chemist or physicist. I quite like that. You don't need to be self-absorbed to be a good scientist, you need to be involved in things outside yourself.

'Of course there are issues about employment and career opportunities and all that, but the subject in itself, intellectually, is just great. I still do quite a bit of science, but I'm not at the coalface in the laboratory. I have a visiting chair at Imperial College in the Department of Bio-chemistry and I do a bit of lecturing for them and I'm editing a series of books for Imperial College Press. I suppose that's the most directly academic thing I do, but, equally, some of the committees I sit on really draw quite heavily on a scientific background. For example, my research interest was and is in – a rather long and boring-sounding title – photo-conversion of solar energy, which is turning solar energy into electric power or chemical fuels by things like solar cells.

'Arising from that, I've developed quite a broad interest and, I hope, expertise in energy, renewable energy and energy policy. I sit on a couple of committees that relate to that: for example, the Energy Advisory Panel of the DTI. They require, as it were, broad scientific literacy rather than a specific chemical qualification. Actually the one doesn't embrace the other; one of the things about science, like most other professional specialisms, is how incredibly specialised it is. You do emerge with a very specialised training and pretty widespread ignorance about the rest of the sciences. One of the nice things that's happened since I stopped teaching chemistry is that I've been able to draw back a bit and start reading around other bits of science which I find fascinating. I'm reading *Fermat's Last Theorem* at the moment – absolutely wonderful, terrific.'

Dr Archer then went into a discourse about the uses of solar energy and photo-voltaic cells with an enthusiasm that would have put the Ladies Who Lunch to shame when discussing their latest designer acquisition.

'Margaret Thatcher started life as a chemist and published one paper,' said Mary. 'Interestingly enough, we established that we were taught by the same teacher. She was staying with us one time and we were talking about chemistry. In volume one of her autobiography, she mentioned her chemistry teacher and the name was M.P. Keay. I never knew what the M was for, but it's Margaret. I said to Margaret, "That's interesting because when I went to Cheltenham there was brought in one year when our regular chemistry teacher was on sabbatical a fairly elderly lady called Miss M.P. Keay to teach us. Could it be the same lady?" And it certainly was.

'I remember her to this day: she was short, she was slightly on the

Widdecombe frame, she had a lovely brogue, I think Scottish but it could have been Irish – I wasn't very good at accents in those days. Margaret Thatcher said to me, "I modelled the way I write Margaret in my signature on Margaret Keay." So that's how I know it's Margaret. She was influenced by her and I was influenced by her, too.'

How did you get involved with the policy-making side of renewable energy?

'The first body of that nature was the Renewable Energy Advisory Group I sat on in 1992 when Colin Moynihan was Minister for Energy and he convened a working party to update Britain's renewable energy policy. He was a very good, very energetic minister and he invited me to sit on that because we'd met a couple of times in the context of photo-voltaic technology. He's very interested in renewable technologies. He's president of the British Wind Energy Association and, in fact, he now has a very successful start-up company which is involved in cleaning up energy technology in the former Soviet Union and other parts of the world and I sit on the board of that company. We don't do it in Russia but in the -stans: Kurdistan, Uzbekistan and other places. There is some old junk hanging around the -stans.

'Usually the plant is technically okay, though old-fashioned, but it normally needs replacement of things and proper maintenance and that requires money spent on it. There's been such problems with funding in these places that the workers haven't been paid, so things just haven't happened, but technically they're very competent. We're not talking nuclear stations – I don't think much of Soviet nuclear technology.

'There are some very good young women in research now. I don't think there's any problem with the quality of the women who come into science and stay in it, but there are certainly issues about the usual pyramid, where there are fewer women as you go higher up the ladder.

'I went to the Royal Institution because I wanted to work with George Porter who was the greatest male influence on my career – he was director of the Royal Institution then; he went on to become Professor the Lord Porter, OM, President of the Royal Society and the rest of it. He's now retired, but when I went to the Royal Institution to join his research group, in addition to having a research laboratory there, they had a famous amphitheatre, where every Friday evening there was a discourse and lecture demonstration on a scientific subject.

'And it was listening to those that first kindled my interest in science more broadly. As I was saying, you really don't have time as a modern undergraduate to think beyond what they're force-feeding you in the way of knowledge about your own subject. There's a lot of showbusiness in it. I like doing lecture demonstrations myself. William Bragg, who was a very great director of the Royal Institution, rightly called it "the repertory theatre of science" and that's exactly what it is – the audience does love flashes and bangs; we all do. They took a very catholic view of what was science. We had a wonderful discourse on the physiology of a ballet dancer and we had a charming young ballerina on the bench showing the amazing things she could do with her limbs.'

What are the traits that distinguish men and women apart from the obvious biological ones?

'The distributions are very broad, so for every woman with one set of characteristics you could find me a man with exactly the same. I'm not saying that they're totally different. I do think, and I've had this view reinforced by teaching both girls and boys for some years, sometimes together, sometimes separately, that the common view that women are patient, persistent, intuitive, hard-working, cautious, careful, sometimes wrongly lacking confidence in their own ability, particularly young women, is true, whereas on the whole men are more aggressive, creative, slapdash, brilliant in flashes, sometimes idle, stupid and thick.

'I think those differences are genetic, probably. I'm no social anthropologist, but they seem to me to be pretty widely spread. It may be that our English culture reinforces these differences a little. When I was a young woman there were still the echoes of Charles Kingsley's aphorism "Be good, sweet maiden, lest you can be clever" – there were just echoes of that. It was prefectly okay to be innumerate as a daughter, but I don't know if it would have been very good to be illiterate. I think that's changing and rightly so. There just are these differences in attitude and they both have their role to play. Men and women can complement each other very well.'

Do you think there's too much emphasis on competing with men rather than working with them?

'Yes I do. Women who get angry about things should remember that their position has really been advanced by goodwill on the whole. For a disadvantaged group to gain ground it is necessary that the advantaged group displays goodwill. John Stuart Mill? Now he was a remarkable early champion and I can think of a couple in science: Lawrence Bragg and, before him, his father, Willie Bragg, and J.D. Bernard, a very good scientist. The reason there were so many early women crystallographers was that those individuals encouraged women into their lives and trained them up. That's what I mean by goodwill.'

What does femininity mean to you?

'Femininity is the quality, obviously, of women in general. I don't think in terms of frilly negligées and, still less, simpering attitudes, but it's something gentler than masculinity. It means not being butch, not consciously striving to behave other than one would normally wish to behave. I have doubts sometimes about all this assertiveness training. It's perfectly true that women do adopt a range of styles: some do dress up in frills and some do dress down in T-shirts and brush haircuts – I find that quite an attractive look, actually, in young women. They look much more unisex than they used to, young men and young women.'

What would a normal week entail?

Mary Archer opened her diary at the current week and read out her list of engagements. It covered an astonishing array of interests and commitments: a TV interview with Jeffrey, a meeting with a local sculptor, Christopher Marvell, a fortieth wedding anniversary party in one of the Cambridge colleges, making plans to landscape the garden, a council meeting at the Royal Institution, a session with her dressmaker, an Energy Advisory Panel meeting, a choral event in Ely Cathedral, a meeting about security measures at home, our interview, a lecture at the Isaac Newton Institute by the Astronomer Royal, coffee in the village with a friend 'who's writing a book about a previous owner of our house', a lecture about Rosie Franklin, 'the girl who *didn't* get the Nobel Prize with Crick, Watson and Wilkins', dinner at Magdalen College, a reception at Hughes Hall, Cambridge, and dinner and jazz at a friend's house, 'which sounds rather nice'.

'I don't know if that's typical, but that's my week. I like reading, usually about science. I also like singing. Until very recently I managed the church choir at home, but I've had to step down because I'm not always there at weekends. I don't get a lot of free time.'

Literary influences?

'Proust, first and foremost. Flaubert, yes, *Sentimental Education*, Macaulay, George Eliot.'

Rupert Brooke?

'A very interesting character, very engaging and immediate one, leaps off the page of his letters and his prose writing, and, indeed, I think some of his poems are very fine, some of them are very derivative. I'm asked about Grantchester all the time. He lived in the house, the Old Vicarage, but he never owned it. He lodged there on and off in the period 1910-1912 and wrote the eponymous poem in Berlin. It became associated with him because he died, of course, of blood poisoning in the Great War.

'When he was in training with his platoon in Kent, he heard a rumour that the Old Vicarage was about to be demolished and dashed off a letter to his mother and various friends saying, "You mustn't allow this. It's a complete act of vandalism. If I survive the war, I'm going to buy the Old Vicarage."

'He didn't survive the war, but his mother bought the house and gave it in trust to his very great undergraduate friend, Dudley Ward, for whose marriage he'd been in Berlin, and it was at that time he wrote the poem. Dudley Ward lived in the house with his wife and family and when he died in 1954, it passed to his son, Peter, and Peter sold it to us in 1979. We moved in after some renovations in 1980.'

Which women do you admire?

'I admire Margaret Thatcher. She was a tremendous political figure and her great legacy, I have to say, was the curbing of the power of the unions, the sale of council houses and the privatisation of so much of nationalised industry, although I know that sophists argue that central control remained. The poll tax was clearly her undoing, but I admire her tremendously.'

Who else do you admire?

'As an actress, I enormously admire Vanessa Redgrave – wonderful, wonderful. I've seen her many times. I think nothing of her political opinions. Daffy. And it's a very cheap posture for any actor or actress. A cheap way of buying popularity. I'm not saying that's why she did it; I think she's deeply convinced by what she does and maybe has suffered because of the extremism of her opinions . . . '

At this point one of the blond timbered doors opened and Baron Archer of Weston-super-Mare entered the living-room. He reminded Mary about the guests who were arriving imminently to support his bid for the mayoralty and, without breaking stride, marched towards the kitchen to check the catering arrangements with Joseph. The unflappable Mary showed us to the lift.

Jeffrey the charity auctioneer was back in action at a fundraising dinner at the Dorchester a few nights later. Warming up the audience, he quipped: 'I've just completed a tour of Scotland for the Conservative Party and I must say how nice it is to see a crowd.' This was greeted with laughter, but such cracks only infuriated his enemies at Conservative Central Office.

As we left the Dorchester, we bumped into Mary Archer, late as usual, as she hurried along Park Lane. 'Is Jeffrey still on?' she asked, breathlessly. Assured that he was, she said, 'Oh good, I thought I might have missed him.' Then she dived through the entrance like a starstruck teenager on her way to see her idol. Jeffrey Archer admits he's made mistakes in his life, but marrying Mary Weedon, aka Baroness Archer of Weston-super-Mare, a clever, assertive, entertaining woman, wasn't one of them.

Epilogue

WOMEN have made tremendous advances since Simone de Beauvoir defined them as the Second Sex and Germaine Greer deplored the plight of the Female Eunuch. Times, and attitudes, have changed dramatically. None of the women interviewed for *Feminine Power* saw their position as 'secondary' to men, nor did they consider themselves helpless victims of male domination. This is, indisputably, progress.

Our sampling was, admittedly, selective, but the women in this book have nevertheless made many significant comments on the state of gender politics at the close of the Millennium. Their contributions are all the more valuable because none of their comments is inflammatory or intended to wound. For long enough, the various campaigns for women's rights have been fought in the context of a 'sex war', with the language of belligerence more prevalent than that of a conciliatory or healing process. Yet, as Mary Archer indicated, all of the legislative gains that have been made in the name of equal opportunity have had the goodwill of male collaborators, or 'the advantaged group', as she put it, behind them.

That female emancipation is still work-in-progress is incontestable and only the most chauvinist of men, or the most reactionary of women, would argue that the clock should be put back to the days of female suppression. In the words of one male writer, A.N. Wilson, 'the feminist revolution of the past 20 or 30 years has been one of the great steps forward in the history of civilisation, comparable to the ending of the slave trade'.

In the Western world, women now have greater freedom of choice in their lives and their careers, irrespective of whether they are single, married or divorced, and there is easier access to power for those who desire it. Empowered women are playing vital roles from Westminster and the City of London to Wall Street, Capitol Hill and Hollywood; from the Elysée Palace to the desert kingdoms of the Middle East.

Feminine power, of course, is not a substitute for feminism, but it is a term that covers a hitherto unmined source of female liberation. As a concept, it provides a means through which women can express their confidence, their independence and their influence without sacrificing their uniquely feminine qualities. Women who exercise feminine power to achieve their ambitions are not seeking revenge against men for the wrongs of the past and they would find the idea of subservience to their partners abhorrent. Many of our subjects are divorced, which shows that, unlike Hillary Clinton, they refused to stay in marriages that patently weren't working. They have new lives to lead and a bad marriage is too heavy a burden to carry.

To repeat the words of the world's most famous divorcée, Ivana Trump: 'The biggest challenge in the nineties for women, and for me, is to be properly balanced, so that you can get the joy and the satisfaction out of the work, but you're still womanly, you're feminine, you're fun and you can enjoy your life and still have time for the family and time for yourself . . . Feminine is also liking people, liking men.'

Some commentators, however, raised the question of whether, in the process of establishing a fairer and more equal society, men were in danger of being 'feminised' and 'destabilised' to such an extent that they no longer valued their inherent manly qualities as partners, providers and protectors. Have they, as some suggest, been forced into a choice between being either wimp or woman-hater? Deborah Hutton, writing in *Vogue*, claimed that the emphasis was now on what social anthropologists called Hyperwoman, 'a model of *bourgeois* feminist triumphalism, tirelessly – even maniacally – industrious'. The menfolk in the lives of these self-sufficient, super-efficient women had been turned into 'disempowered males' who were incapable of looking after themselves.

The theme of male capitulation conjured up pictures of husbands burying themselves in mindless pursuits on the Internet, or boyfriends escaping to the refuge of the pub, while women made the decisions and more or less ran their lives for them. As a consequence, women were exhausted and the male libido acutely deflated. Camille Paglia warned in a lecture in London for the Festival Hall's 'Sounding the Century' series: 'The sexual weather is cloudy and stormy. There's an atmosphere of suspicion and mutual recrimination. The sizzle has gone out of sexual relationships.'

There was no more visible symptom of this malaise than the 'new laddism' of the nineties, with its defensively sexist agenda and implicit rejection of women. When the feminist novelist Fay Weldon drew attention to the fact that men had indeed become the new underclass, she was accused by hardline feminists of betraying women. Replying, Ms Weldon said: 'I want women to stop the hate speak. I never want to hear again a feminist joke like, "How many men does it take to wallpaper a room?" – "It depends on how thinly you slice them." Reverse the gender roles and you can see it's unforgivable. More importantly, I want the feminist movement to extend its remit to include the welfare of men, if only because we need them as partners and fathers, and life without them isn't all that much fun for most women.'

Despite such pleas for female tolerance, there was substantial evidence to show that there had been a malevolent male backlash against women, the most blatant sign being the avalanche of pornographic videos, magazines and web sites designed to denigrate women in male eyes. There were also subtler, though still highly pernicious, forms of male subversion which stemmed from a strong sense of insecurity and inferiority.

In 1997, a MORI poll on British women in the workplace found that 53 per cent believed that men found ways to undermine them at work and 45 per cent thought that most of their male colleagues and bosses were sexist. More than a third believed that there were inadequate laws on equal pay, harassment and discrimination, and almost as many believed that one of the most pressing problems women faced was the attitudes of the men they worked with.

A superficial feminisation took place in Westminster after Tony Blair came to power, but there was no sign of anything remotely representing a revolution. On the contrary, Blair installed himself as chairman of Cool Britannia Inc., cronyism became the new patronage and, in theory, we became a nation of caring, sharing stakeholders. Despite record numbers in the House of Commons, many female Labour MPs were so docile and 'on message' that they were ridiculed as 'Stepford Wives'. At Prime Minister's Question Time, there was standing room only and, whenever Tony moved to the Dispatch Box, they swooned and cheered his every riposte like groupies. Even Baroness Thatcher was a fan. 'She thinks she created him by decimating the Left and that enabled him to come through as her successor,' said one of her *confidantes*.

Fay Weldon returned to the fray in a lecture on gender politics entitled *Adam and Eve and Tony Blair* at the Edinburgh Book Festival in August 1998. Under New Labour, she said, Britain had changed from a patriarchal society to a matriarchal one with 'the traditional female language of caring and feeling, apology and sentiment, consensus and feel-good. Even God has become female. God is no longer the bearded patriarch in the sky, He has had a sex change and turned into Mother Nature.' This caused some men 'furiously to run in the wrong direction, lost to all responsibility and decent feeling, vandalising and tearing everything to bits as they go'. Today's alienated men required help and encouragement to be good fathers, she said, not to have feminism rammed down their throats.

So the objective of achieving a harmonious balance between women's legitimate demands and masculine self-esteem had still to be attained. But if women were expected to modify their behaviour, then men also had to meet the challenge with a positive new attitude. Amanda Wakeley made a very salient point when she said that it would take 'some very special men' to cope with the new breed of powerful women emerging in Western societies. 'It's going to be a very interesting and difficult couple of decades for men adjusting to feminine power because it's intimidating,' she said.

EQUALITY, however, has brought a new set of problems for women in the you-can-have-it-all philosophy so beloved of Helen Gurley Brown, high priestess of *Cosmopolitan*, and the other girlie glossies. According to a national survey reported in the *Daily Mail*, no fewer than 78 per cent of British women wanted to quit their jobs because of the combined pressures of home and work, and only financial obligations prevented them from doing so.

The *Mail* commented: 'The consequences of increased female empowerment has, it seems, culminated in modern woman feeling overworked and underpaid, depressed about the way she looks and too shattered to even contemplate home life.' 'Downshifting' had entered the language.

But when *Newsweek* asked Ms Gurley Brown to choose 'the quintessential *Cosmo* girl', she stuck to her guns and selected the most radical example of all: Madonna. 'That woman did everything you could do to be better than she was,' she said. 'Madonna has taken what she's got, which is okay but not great, and look what she has done with it.'

'Reinvention' was the term most commonly applied to the many phases of Madonna's mercurial career, yet the real reason she had stayed at the top of her profession was that she was brighter and tougher than anyone else and vitally aware of her feminine power. As the 'Material Girl' said herself: 'I have paid a high price for fame, but I'm the last person to complain about it now, since it was the thing I sought for so long.'

The 'reinvention' tag was also attached to another Hollywood icon,

Jane Fonda, whose dramatic makeover from Ho Chi Minh cheerleader to aerobics goddess to politically correct wife of a liberal politician to surgically enhanced corporate wife of media mogul Ted Turner infuriated feminists. Jane, though, was delighted with her own progress. 'One of the most fascinating things I have learned,' she said, 'is how utterly *possible* it is to change.'

Women with the essential qualities of feminine power are unafraid of change; in fact, they desire it. They generate an aura of respect, they communicate and socialise well and they're attractive people, not only because of their feminine physiques, but because of their personalities. No one described this better than Samantha Bond when she said: 'I'm aware of my power as an individual. I am confident of my own "voice". I am confident of my intellect and that side that empowers me.'

Jonathan Toomey, managing director of the Fitness Management Group, who acts as personal trainer to many successful women, noted: 'Women with feminine power have an intrinsic aim to achieve their true potential. They have high levels of self-esteem, self-confidence and self-responsibility. Looking good and keeping fit are high on their agenda, but they do not work out simply through vanity. It's more an intelligent reaction to an awareness of the benefits derived from exercise and a healthy diet and lifestyle. They are attractive people and you feel you want to get to know them more and more.'

IN THE GLOW of the dying embers of the 20th Century, the opportunities for women to seize the initiative have never been greater. Consider the political scene: in the corridors of power on both sides of the Atlantic, the spin doctor has replaced the *éminence grise* and the think tank has acquired the trappings of a couturier salon. Style, not ideology, sets the agenda and the best haircut and most telegenic smile win the argument.

Sexual indiscretion abounds from Westminster to Washington, where the love bite outnumbers the soundbite. As one scandal after another tumbles into the headlines, *peccadillo* has become the spiciest dish at every power lunch and, after Bill Clinton's confession that he had lied about his sexual escapades with Monica Lewinsky, shame is finally dead.

Yet this *fin-de-siècle* Age of Sleaze, with Babylon and psychobabble as its motifs, the crony as its chief beneficiary and the paid liar as its protector, has also seen the emergence of a new female élite. Oprah Winfrey does not consider herself politically motivated and scorns suggestions that she should run for the presidency. But her vertiginous rise from absolute nobody to media superstar shows how it is possible for a woman of humble origins to transcend the obstacles of race, sexual abuse and ignorance and become a power in the world.

Referring to her audience of 20 million viewers in the United States, she told an interviewer: 'I have what all the politicians want – that's why they all want to do my show. If you really want to change people's lives, have an hour platform every day to go into their homes and say what you want to say. I've purposefully stayed away from politics. I'm only interested in presenting issues, so that I can allow people to see the truth for themselves.

'My goal is to do what I can to change the way people think, so they can hold the highest, grandest vision of themselves. I believe the way to do that is through education, and not just memorisation skills, but teaching people *how* to think. I don't know of anything more powerful than to influence people to bring themselves closer to themselves. I want to use television not only to entertain, but to help people lead better lives. I have survived because of my faith in a power that is greater than me. In your moment of darkest pain, you know that you will be all right.'

Our search for feminine power ranged across the political and social extremes of the Middle East to the salons of New York, Paris and London. It crossed the barriers of wealth and class that divide the peoples of the world and found unexpected similarities among women from conflicting cultures. As Diane Von Furstenberg said: 'They're all insecure and strong at the same time, fearful and courageous.' And if there was a common denominator, it was that the spirit of womanhood was a pure and beautiful thing and quite, quite inviolate.